A HISTORY OF EXPERIMENTAL FILM AND VIDEO

From the Canonical Avant-Garde to Contemporary British Practice

A. L. Rees

A BFI book published by Palgrave Macmillan

First published in 1999 by the
British Film Institute
21 Stephen Street, London W1P 2LN

Reprinted 2000, 2002, 2003, 2005, 2007, 2008, 2010

The British Film Institute is the UK national agency with responsibility for encouraging
the arts of film and television and conserving them in the national interest.

British Library Cataloguing-in-Publication Data
A catalogue record for this book is available from the British Library

ISBN 978–0–85170–681–8

Cover designed by Toby Cornish

Typeset by Fakenham Photosetting Limited, Fakenham, Norfolk
Printed in China

Contents

Acknowledgments

I thank my teachers and mentors, formal and informal, who have given invaluable advice and criticism (most of them over a long period of time) to support my interest in the avant-garde and related matters: Professor Christopher Frayling and Professor Dan Fern of the Royal College of Art, Geoffrey Nowell-Smith, David Curtis, Laura Mulvey and David Hall. I also thank, in similar vein, Nicky Hamlyn, Peter Kennard, Claire Lofting, Jill McGreal and Michael O'Pray. Many other friends, artists, colleagues and students have generously given time to debate and explore the issues raised in this book, as have the excellent editorial teams, past and present, at the British Film Institute.

List of Illustrations

(Plates between pages 88 and 89)

Preface

LUCIE-SMITH: Can you give a definition of 'avant-garde'?
GREENBERG: You don't define it, you recognize it as a historical phenomenon.
(Interview with Clement Greenberg conducted by Edward Lucie-Smith, 1968)

The aim of this book is to give a brief, historical account of experimental film and video. It puts the film avant-garde into two contexts – the cinema and moving image culture on the one hand, and modern art with its post-modern coda or extension on the other. But it also sees the experimental or artists' movement in film and video as an independent, living and vital force which has its own internal development and aesthetics.

To emphasise art rather than cinema in a book about film and video, which this book does, needs to be explained and even defended. Cinema as a whole, together with all those media arts which are not more simply and better understood as 'information technologies', is certainly an art form – the latest and most powerful audio-visual art in Western and world history. Many influential books stress this, from Arnheim's *Film As Art* and its distinguished predecessors,[1] to the widely used course text *Film Art* by Bordwell and Thompson. The BFI itself enshrines the word in its charter, 'to encourage the art of the film'. So the claim made for the experimental film and video work discussed here is not an exclusive one, as if only the avant-gardes make art in cinema. The view taken here is simply that one way to understand the avant-garde (as specified here, because there are also film avant-gardes beyond the experimental circuit) is to see it more firmly in the context of modern and post-modern art than is possible with, say, the drama film. In doing so, the point is both to locate the avant-garde and to try to engage with it, especially for readers and viewers who find the experimental film so far off the map of cinema, especially the cinema of narrative drama, so aberrant to the norms of viewing a film, that there's no engagement at all. For, by and large, this is filmmaking without story, characters and plot – or in which these elements, considered so essential to cinematic form, are put into new and critical relationships. The book concedes that this negative view might well be right, in certain instances at least, and starts from there – that is to say, at the outer fringes of the map of cinema and even over the borders.

It hopes to be useful to readers who have seen some experimental films and want to know more about them, and also to film- and video-makers who make, or want to make, work of this kind and who are interested in the general background of historic and recent avant-gardes. No more knowledge than this is assumed, and if the book serves either of these two purposes it will have done what it set out to do. The Notes and Bibliography indicate where to find more specialist information, guiding the reader to sources which explore particular topics in more depth.

The first sections of the book briefly survey some basic issues in the light of contemporary arguments about art, film and the mass media. They try to show the current state of play as far as theorisation goes, and where experimental or avant-garde film crosses over into current debates about post-modern art and cinema. The aim here is to set the scene in the present, given that the main purpose of the book is historical. Since absolute chronology is not preserved these sections amount perhaps to a signal that the avant-garde has a non-linear aspect as well as a strictly time-bound one.[2] Arguments recur and boundaries are unfixed.

Next there is a historical review of the experimental film from its origins to the Second World War. This is the broadest part of the book, tracing the birth of experimental art and film back to its roots in early technologies and then to the cubist movement and its aftermath in painting and sculpture. It attempts to show how modern art intersects with the notion of film as an art form, with examples from Dada, surrealism and constructivism. Then it takes up the movement in its rapid post-war development and on to the present day.

The second part focuses on the British scene as it has evolved since 1966. This may be considered parochial, but it seemed a useful idea to fill in some of the lesser-known details of the British scene and 'The Co-op After Le Grice' – to quote a front-cover headline from the *Monthly Film Bulletin* in 1984.[3] The world-wide expansion of artists' work in film, video and digital media since the 1970s has anyhow made it impossible to take the full international overview exemplified in David Curtis's inspired and now classic *Experimental Cinema* (1971).

It is a pity to lose the international perspective,[4] but luckily there is an increasing number of national or 'area' studies of film, video, electronic and digital art to supplement the partial account given here, as well as many current art and design journals and exhibition catalogues which cover these activities. A more positive result of narrowing the field is the chance to review some British work of the last thirty years which has not yet had the attention – and above all the viewing – which it merits.

The book assumes that artists' film and video is a distinct form of cultural practice, with its own autonomy in relation to the mainstream cinema. This diverse body of work, almost coextensive with the beginning of cinema and the birth of modernism, makes up a tradition of a complex and often contradictory kind. A further notion is that avant-garde film and video is a serious art form even when, as with Dada and neo-Dada, it looks as if it is doing something stupid. It is sometimes important to make stupid art (it might not end up that way). John Cage summed up this aspect of the avant-garde – in the context of a documentary film made about him by Peter Greenaway – when he said that 'some people take my work too seriously and some don't take it seriously enough'.[5]

The focus of the book is on films and videos by artists, that is to say by those film-makers for whom film is primarily an art form allied to painting, sculpture, printmaking and other arts both traditional and modern. Other comparisons might be to music or poetry, but for a number of reasons the visual analogy dominates. No attempt is made to define the terms 'avant-garde' or 'experimental' in any rigorous way – they are used according to historical context where possible – but the origins of these troublesome but persistent words are glanced at and their changing uses are borne in mind.[6] In general, they are used as names rather than as descriptions.

Cinema as a whole is of course an art form, of an especially complex kind, but this book concentrates on films which stand apart from the commercial and even the 'arthouse' sectors. It is most concerned with films and videos made outside the mainstream, or at its margins, by single-person authors, whose scales of production and funding are almost as far removed from the radical art cinema of Godard, Wenders, Marker and Straub-Huillet as from the industrial cinema itself. The art cinema can be seen as an avant-garde in its own right, and indeed the mainstream itself has avant-garde directors like Ken Russell and David Lynch. The scope of this book, however, does not for the most part stretch that far. It centres on experimental film and video as an alternative to the major genres, and often in opposition to them.

For the first half of cinema's first century the borders between art, experiment and industry were particularly free. Global commercialisation and media power have changed the picture since then, as have wider cultural changes in the arts. So, without denying that 'avant-garde' has more than one meaning and context, this book concentrates on a loose network of individual authors working outside the industrial sector and the art cinema as a whole. Much of the work discussed here is only tenuously related to the cinema as an industrial culture or a cultural industry.

The book relies on many sources to compile this overview, and tries to account for them in the bibliographical notes which follow the main text – but the selections, prejudices and exclusions throughout the book are my own. Scope and space as well as bias have also limited the films and their makers dealt with here. There are many regrettable omissions on all these scores. Readers will undoubtedly discover this for themselves and remedy the gap. It would of course be possible to write quite a different book on this topic, using the same or many other artists and films and looking at other issues. But this is not that book.

Introduction

Siting the avant-garde

There have been innovative film-makers since film and cinema began, emerging from mainstream and arthouse feature production to push cinema a step further into untried territory.[7] They include individuals like Fritz Lang, Luis Buñuel, King Vidor, Jean-Luc Godard, David Lynch. Such forward-looking directors are sometimes historically linked to film avant-gardes which are far more marginal to the mainstream and unknown to large parts of it; Buñuel to the surrealists, Lang to the abstract film, the Movie Brats to the underground, Godard to the situationists. It is these avant-gardes, a set of diverse individuals and groups at the margins of the mainstream but occasionally intersecting it at acute or oblique angles, which are the focus of this short account.

Aside from its important if often unacknowledged influence on mainstream film and television, the avant-garde cinema itself has only surfaced to wider view at particular moments in its history. Its best-known epochs are probably the abstract and surrealist film in the 1920s, the pathbreaking underground film in the 1960s and (in the UK) the school of Derek Jarman in the 1980s. In these cases the avant-garde broke out of its often self-imposed obscurity to take part in a broader cultural picture. Some films and their makers have become cult or even popular classics, as with Oskar Fischinger, Jean Cocteau and Kenneth Anger. But the movement as a whole has more often looked to alternative, rather than to popular audiences on the margins of the mainstream cinema.

The avant-garde rejects and critiques both the mainstream entertainment cinema and the audience responses which flow from it. It has sought 'ways of seeing' outside the conventions of cinema's dominant tradition in the drama film and its industrial mode of production.[8] Sometimes it does so in the name of 'film as such' or even 'film as film'. It was this aspect of the avant-garde that led the Soviet director Sergei Eisenstein to attack Dziga Vertov for his 'formalist tricks' in the 1920s.[9]

At other times film avant-gardes emerge out of wider social movements to speak for silenced or dissident voices. Dating back to political documentary in the 1920s and 1930s, this wave passes through the civil rights and Beat Era in the 1950s and on to today's cultural minorities. Their search is less for formal purity than for a new language uncompromised by the regimes they resist. At some historical moments the artists and the social radicals meet up in crucial conjunctions (as with documentary and abstract film in the 1920s, the New American Cinema and the underground film in the 1960s, political and structural films in the 1970s and the fusion of music videos with independent cinema in the 1980s).[10] Whether they look to aesthetics or politics for their context, the films of the avant-garde challenge the major codes of dramatic realism which determine meaning and response in the commercial fiction film.

1

But cinema is not the only context for the avant-garde film. Some film-makers, and arguably entire movements, have overturned the codes and iconography of the cinema from far outside the mainstream and in opposition to it. Surrealist and abstract film in the 1920s, like much film and video installation art today, flowed from the artistic currents of the time. As the dominant and industrial cinema achieved higher production values and greater spectacle, the avant-garde affirmed its 'otherness' in cheap, personal and 'amateur' films which circulated outside the cinema chains. In this sense some avant-gardes can be seen to appropriate the film machine on behalf of contemporary art. The gallery or club rather than the movie-house is their site, outside the space and conventions of cinema.

Avant-garde film has also taken over the traditional genres of art – rather than those of the cinema itself. These have been central to its language and rhetoric and have shaped its subject-matter. They include *still life,* such as Hollis Frampton's *Lemon* (1969), Malcolm Le Grice's *Academic Still Life (Cézanne)* (1977) and Guy Sherwin's *Clock and Candle* (1976); *landscape,* from Fischinger's *Munich–Berlin Walk* (1927) to Michael Snow's *La Région céntrale* (1971) and the films of Chris Welsby; *cityscapes,* opening with the Sheeler-Strand *Manhatta* of 1921 and through to Stan Brakhage, Shirley Clarke, Ernie Gehr and Patrick Keiller; and *portrait,* from Andy Warhol through to Stephen Dwoskin and more recent artists such as Jayne Parker, Alia Syed and Gillian Wearing. At the same time, the avant-garde has participated in the expansion and occasional implosion of modern art forms, from auto-destructive art to multi-screen projection. The idea of experimental or avant-garde film itself derives more directly from the context of modern and post-modern art than from the history of cinema.

But the unfortunate and militaristic overtones to the term 'avant-garde' have saddled artist film- and video-makers with a dual legacy. They are rarely by intent an 'advance-guard' of the cinema, as the phrase may suggest, however much they may have influenced the stylisation of such well-known films as Stanley Kubrick's *A Clockwork Orange*, the montage structure of Scorsese's *Mean Streets*, the rapid cutting of Oliver Stone's *JFK* or the layered texture of Lynch's *Lost Highway*. And if the ideal of 'progressive' vanguard film-making was an aspect of the cinema's optimistic first half-century (and a little beyond into the 1960s), the avant-garde since then has turned with the wider culture to doubt and uncertainty. Warhol is pivotal between these two moments. In his portrait films of 1963–5 a fixed camera illuminates and thus reveals the human face, but renders it as indecipherable and blank.

More positively, the notion of an avant-garde asserts that innovation is a main goal of this area of film and video. At the same time, it implies a continuous history, even though avant-gardes appear, decline and are re-born in different national and historical contexts. It thus begs the question of whether the artists' film avant-garde is one or many. Is it one broad movement spanning the century or simply a cluster of fringe activities at a tangent to popular cinema but with little other identity? Significantly, the avant-garde has traded under many other names: experimental, absolute, pure, non-narrative, underground, expanded, abstract; none of them satisfactory or generally accepted. This lack of agreement points to inherent differences and even conflicts within the avant-garde, just as it also implies a search for unity across broad terrain. Because avant-gardes tend to

2

spark off each other, this search is always open. P. Adams Sitney astutely notes that such names as avant-garde or independent cinema 'admirably' bind a 'negative element' into their definition.[11]

Spanning Futurism to post-modernism, and linked to them and to modern art by the nuance of its similarly time-ordered name, the avant-garde cinema is similarly international in scope. This has distanced it from the main context in which world cinemas operate, their production base in the nation-state. Avant-garde films have easily crossed national borders since the 1920s. For the most part they avoid script and dialogue, or approach film and video from an angle which emphasises vision over text and dialogue. The expanded use of new media in the art world in recent years has been just as international, even if the sheer explosion of film, video and installation art ironically makes it more difficult to scan and summarise the field comprehensively.

Using the terms 'avant-garde', or even 'experimental', film at this late date may appear anachronistic or a provocation. For a long time they have scarcely been used without some degree of embarrassment. The earlier history of the avant-garde idea, which first dates from the 1830s, is briefly sketched below. It was applied loosely to artists' film-making from the 1920s, but peaked in the 1970s when it ousted the term 'underground film' as a seemingly more serious name for the then rising structural film movement.

Since then the term as an artistic category has been deconstructed on two fronts.[12] One internal attack dates primarily from 1974, with Peter Bürger's *Theory of the Avant-Garde*, which argues that all contemporary artistic avant-gardes largely rehearse the deeds of their 1920s ancestors but fail to achieve their promise. The second onslaught, from outside the avant-garde and gathering steam since the 1980s, claims that the idea was delusory from the start, a mask or convenient handle for artists and factions in their power struggles for cultural dominance.

The death of the avant-garde, which coincides with the 'death of the author', is in both cases seen as a sign of historic failure. Art which opposed museum culture is now embalmed within it, with Dada as the classic instance. Furthermore, it often follows, the avant-garde in art is now the mainstream itself; there is no establishment against which to rebel, with the final recuperation of modern art (including its supposed avant-gardes) into the cultural and media landscape. Only the newest and most outrageous art attracts the interest of sponsors, curators and advertising agencies.

None of these claims, which separately are all valid diagnoses of art and of cultural criticism at the end of the century, can quite equate with each other. The avant-garde once was, but is no longer; or it never really was, but only seemed to be. It has failed, and been tamed by the museums which feed it; at the same time, it has succeeded too well by making outrage the norm in a current art scene which the avant-garde dominates.

Subtle criticism could no doubt turn these confusing circles into defined squares. It might show that the new, neo- or post-avant-garde from the mid-1970s to the present is only virtual Dada at many removes. Artists and museums pander to each other's fantasies. Art pretends to outrage, and museums pretend to be shocked, to promote the show.[13] But then shock – the most obvious surface trace of the avant-garde idea – has long been written off as either historical debris which no longer works, or as fake from the first, dating back to the 1920s. That the machine seems to roll on is therefore a mystery. Why do shock and sensation, or the pretence of them, seem to keep working when they have for so long been discredited? Who cares? To judge from public response, it seems that plenty do. Since the range of (absorbed?) shocks now ranges from the cool bricks of Carl Andre to the chopped and pickled sharks of Damien Hirst, from the absence of subject-matter to its strident opposite, from sparse neo-constructivism to ripe post-surrealism, it might be no more misleading to speak of shock in this context than of the sculptural and the conceptual traditions which also underlie these works and on which they comment.

Although 'avant-garde' is not an altogether happy term, and many film-makers reject it, its survival in film criticism suggests that it may not yet be drained of all content, including the survival of shock as a cultural agent or catalyst. Often dismissed as a merely juvenile impulse to throw paint at the public (but sanctified by Marinetti, Mayakovsky, surrealism and punk), shock was cast by the sophisticated critiques of Walter Benjamin and Antonin Artaud as the founding moment of cinema itself. Recast in the 1970s by structural film to attack film norms of vision and duration, and then in the 1980s by body-centred Baudelairian taboo-busters, the maligned idea of shock as cultural stimulant, interruption or break is far from exhausted.[14] Robert Hughes's popular TV history of modern art, *The Shock of the New*, has been updated by events themselves since it appeared in 1980. Shock is an idea in art as much as a sensation, to denote the act of stopping viewers in their tracks, however briefly.

This may suggest a cooler look at the avant-garde idea, freed from modernism's past myths and present caricatures. No art exists free of material context, whether conceived in terms of property and patronage (as in Marxism) or in those of market forces and sponsorship (as in libertarianism). Art, which is always a form of social surplus, is a mixed economy even in the most corporate of regimes. The blurring of orders between avant-garde and mainstream is no new phenomenon; it characterises the century. The avant-garde seems temporarily to have stormed the citadel but without stemming mainstream modernism's turnover of boardroom painting and institutional sculpture. The avant-garde has, however, won both notoriety and acceptance on its own terms: making 'impossible' demands, resisting censorship, getting up noses, offending, asking questions, refusing any given definition of public taste. Based on an inherently oxymoronic radical tradition, it looks for the junction-box between modernism's secret languages and the revealed world of the public mass media.

Vision machine

British independent film-maker Peter Greenaway has recently offered an inclusive definition of cinema – or Cinema, capitalised – which attempts to clarify the issues. For Greenaway, Cinema is the sum total of all technologies which work towards articulating the moving image. Cinema is a continuum.[15] It embraces equally the big movie and the computer screen, the digital image and the handmade film, and – importantly – such structures as speech and writing, acting, editing, light projection and sound. The concept is large and ambitious. Like Greenaway's own films and installations it is a grand synthesis of cinema as (in Paul Virilio's term) 'the vision machine'. Furthermore we stand not at the end of its first century but at the opening of its real history – which has just begun.

The idea is stimulating – not to say cheering in an age of post-everything – but focused on the phenomena of visual spectacle which Greenaway celebrates. Much of the historic avant-garde, as will be shown, has been concerned to challenge the supremacy of that spectacle, although it has its own key moments of visual celebration as well, from the 1960s underground to its belated offspring in the rapid-eye techno-art of the 1990s. But visual spectacle rests on illusionism, which the avant-garde generally resists. The idea of the 'moving image' which binds together Greenaway's cinema as total work of art is itself sustained by illusionism. At the heart of this notion is a crucial paradox, for in film the image does not move – film consists of a series of static frames on celluloid. The impression of movement is an illusion. And in video and digital media the image in motion is coded as a scanned electronic signal. Film, video and electronic media are cinematic equations which slide apart even as they draw together.

For Bazin an unassailable realism underpinned his vision of 'total cinema'. Greenaway's totalising vision is by contrast non-realist and post-modern. Nonetheless, like Bazin, who believed that film embalmed time and resisted its passage, Greenaway also turns to the past in the installations and exhibitions which evoke his film myth. For the 'Spellbound' show at the Hayward Gallery in 1996 this took the form of a multi-media spectacle of primal light, sound and film (*In the Dark*).[16] Below the screens, in the gallery, were rows of 'props'. They included live models in glass cases and a ranked archive of household and film objects dating from cinema's heyday (and Greenaway's childhood) in the 1940s. Greenaway's optimistic vision of cinema art contains a latent nostalgia, an embalming of cinema's own myth and cult.

For much of its history the avant-garde has questioned this assumption of cinema as cultural myth and industrial product, and offered a number of alternative ways of seeing. At the same time, the act of seeing – and hence of illusion and spectacle – is itself put in question. This red thread runs through such diverse work as the surrealists (notably Man Ray and Buñuel), the films of Brakhage and Warhol (otherwise incompatible bedfellows), the English structuralists Peter Gidal and Malcolm Le Grice (from two distinct angles), and the feminist film-makers Yvonne Rainer and Lis Rhodes (using wholly different methods).

The technologies which comprise the force-field of Cinema (film, video, sound, digital) and which are dedicated to comprehensive spectacle (Greenaway's 'vision'), at the same time are constellations which cannot align or cohere. They polarise around different ways to achieve their grand illusions; notably filmic discontinuity – 'the flicks', where single images appear to move by time-exposure; and electronic continuity – 'the telly', whose apparent images are streams of signals which record the breaking up of light by scanning. This ruptures it from the real which it attempts to denote.

This doubt or mistrust of apparent continuity, or the refusal to disavow what one knows about illusionism in order to believe in its impression, has impelled avant-garde film-makers to the extremes of film craft and technique. Single framing (Jonas Mekas, Marie Menken), painted or scratched film (Len Lye), extended dissolves (Germaine Dulac), long-takes (Andy Warhol), flicker editing (Shirley Clarke, John Maybury), cut-ups (Anthony Balch, George Barber), fake synch (Gillian Wearing, the Duvet Brothers), outdated filmstock (Ron Rice), found footage (Bruce Conner, Douglas Gordon), out-of-focus lens (Brakhage, Gidal), intermittent projection (Ken Jacobs and Stan Douglas) – these and more are ciphers of resistance to 'normal vision', in a variety of aesthetic contexts but all stemming from a clash between the cinema apparatus and the moment of viewing.

Ironically, many of these devices leak into the wider culture as they are taken up or imitated in filmic special effects or in TV advertising. Here, anti-illusionism turns into its opposite. In its role as 'vanguard', the experimental film has similarly pioneered the manipulative techniques which electronic and cinematic technologies now encode in their software to reshape the appearance of the real and thus to undermine traditional notions of veracity. At the same time, the avant-garde has opposed that simulationist shift *from the other side*, by questioning the image, the spectacle and the presumed authority of both.

The conflicts of this position – the avant-garde as both inside and outside the wider media culture – take on new urgency as the full implications of the digital era become clear. Instead of the truth at 24 frames a second, theorists and film-makers alike are increasingly aware of the dark and blank gaps between those frames, through which the real seems to leak back into the unrecapturable light. Digital imaging adds further levels of mutability. When the French philosopher Bergson critiqued the cinema in 1907 for breaking up time into a sequence of regular units, thus falsifying its unbroken flow, he prefigured the substance of a concern which is now widely and publicly shared.[17]

Time base

If the questioning of vision, and of vision as truth, has been the core of film experiment, to set in doubt the cinema as spectacle which Greenaway affirms, what replaces the authority of the image, an authority on which film's realism is based? The answer suggested here is that time and duration make up that substitute. Instead of the visual image, experimental film centres itself on the passage of time.[18] This has been explicitly recognised by diverse avant-garde artists from Walter Ruttmann and Maya Deren to John Latham and David Hall.

The notion of film as primarily a time-based art is central to the avant-garde, even though the shaping of time is common to all cinema. But the experimental tradition puts film time at the core of its project. Fiction film, in the systems worked out largely from 1906–15, shaped narrative space around a montage framework of edited and elided time. The dramatic unities of the classical and Renaissance drama are preserved in fiction film through the stability of narrative space, plot and acting. Mainstream narrative fiction has itself responded to a 'crisis in representation' with an increasing number of films which play with time as central to plot, just as documentary film today acknowledges its own codes and procedures. But the centrality of film-time to the avant-garde has other roots than realism. They include 'the moment of cubism' which introduced duration and the fragment to modern art.[19] From these are derived the material tropes and codes of experimental film – rapid camera movement and the long-take, film grain and handpainting – which in their separate ways direct attention to film as a material construct and as a time-based medium.

Point of view

Modernism was founded on a new understanding of point of view, both for artist and spectator. Walter Benjamin's essay on 'The work of art in the age of mechanical reproduction', a seminal analysis of 1936 in which cinema is central, traces the fading 'aura' of the individual art object as it is technologically transmitted through the media culture.[20] This aura was originally bound up with the location – church, palace, great house – for which much classic art was made. As aristocracy was succeeded by bourgeois democracy, the work of art became a commodity circulating among collectors in the art market. Eventually, art adapted to its new mobility. The 'personal touch' was valued, lower genres encroached on traditionally higher ones (as in the rise of landscape and still life over history painting), the academies were challenged and independent groups emerged, and the portable easel painting brought with it a naturalism and intimacy which triumphed over the 'great machines' of the nineteenth century.

These material changes underlie the slow decline of the stable viewpoint in art, a regime of vision which the Renaissance had inaugurated through the science of perspective. By the late eighteenth century, the certainty of perspective-ruled sight in art was dissolving under the impact of the baroque. Delacroix and Turner freed colour from its natural base to explode space rather than fix it. Impressionism and Cézanne affirmed viewpoint (the artist's eye), but also destabilised it to incorporate the passage of time (as in the 'serial' paintings of Rouen by Monet, or the overlapping planes and angles of Cézanne). Their followers, such as the Fauves, invented a free, neo-symbolist space, which in the later fragmented vision of cubism turned overtly against the all-embracing eye of naturalism itself. By the time of Mondrian and Klee, and contemporary with the first avant-garde films, abstract artists were making paintings with no central viewpoint at all or one so radically decentred as to defy the fixed gaze. Matisse, a more figurative and phenomenological artist, similarly devised a method of 'all-over' painting in which figure and ground are evened out, 'subsumed into the greater force of the surface-as-totality', as Norman Bryson summarises.

Once the traditional distinction between figure and ground was questioned by abstractionist art, so was painting as imitation of the visible. The scene gives way to the sign. The viewer has no central anchor around which to construct the fantasy of the scene and the gaze. Yves-Alain Bois states that

as long as an opposition between figure and ground is maintained, we remain in the domain of the projective image and transcendence – the painting is always read as an image projected from elsewhere onto its surface, and this imaginary projection is always illusionistic.[21]

Immanent meaning is substituted for the dialectical conflict which underpins modernist abstraction in its battle with 'imaginary projection' (here used by Bois to describe the appearance of forms in space, but also recalling the codes of perspective geometry).

When Bois writes that traditional painting is 'read as an image projected from elsewhere onto its surface' and that 'this imaginary projection is always illusionistic', he could be describing the narrative cinema. Narrative cinema is the archetype of point of view at work in film. The classical tropes or figures of film narrative – varied distance from the camera, cutting at an angle for reverse field matching, not crossing the line – aim to preserve and locate the viewer's stability across dissolves, edits and jump-cuts. The spectator's identification with a character in drama film is locked into a mobile identification with camera and scene, thus constructed. The narrative theme of 'mistaken identity' in the fiction film (from Hitchcock's *The Wrong Man* to de Palma's *Body Double*, Verhoeven's *Basic Instinct* and Lynch's *Lost Highway*) literalises the moment of misrecognition inherent in post-Freudian notions of the self, to enact this trauma as drama.[22] The screen projection is a mirror for the play of figure and ground, but is also a suppressed emblem of the fantasy relation inscribed in cinema's double-reflection of seen and scene.

Modernisms

A crucial change occurred in the definition of avant-garde film around the mid-century when it became associated with artists who made films to the virtual exclusion of other media. By contrast the first film avant-garde was made up of artists, such as Man Ray and Fernand Léger, who 'supplemented' their work in painting, sculpture or photography with a small number of experimental films which are now canonical. These artists engaged in very little film activity after the late 1920s, even though they continued to distribute and show their early films throughout their long and productive lives – Léger died in 1955 and Man Ray in 1976. But after the Second World War a new generation from Maya Deren to Stan Brakhage affirmed that it was possible for film to be an artist's medium in its own right. They went on to construct bodies of work made up primarily or entirely of films, reversing the traditional priority given to the older arts, however radicalised and modernised, such as painting and sculpture.

This was a key historical shift, with consequences which still affect artists and spectators today. It underlies later distinctions between 'video artists' and those artists for whom video is an additional element in their work. It connects to the never-ending debate – since Clement Greenberg's seminal essays of the 1940s to the 1960s – about whether and how far an art form is determined by the media it employs, of which the 'film as film' debate in the 1970s was an outcrop. More generally, it further complicates an already complex set of terms, notably the question of modernism and the avant-garde.

Modernism is a complex and disunified field of activity, even when its constellation is restricted to so-called high art or literature. As many commentators note, the concept of the modern shifts – or indeed slips and slides – between two related contexts. In the first it defines the general culture of the arts in the twentieth century, focusing on 'the moment of cubism' (as John Berger called it) and emphasising a break with the tradition of realism and mimesis in Western art and literature. At the same time it echoes in name and concept a much broader process of social and cultural 'modernisation'. This second sense, known as 'modernity',[23] points to the global rise and hegemony of industrial, urban and technological societies.

Clearly modernism in art and modernity in its social sense are linked, if only because the early twentieth century took itself to be 'the modern age'. But, as used today, modernism and modernity are retrospective terms which date roughly from the mid-century. They draw into focus a diverse range of phenomena, from Dada to action painting, or Futurism to minimalism. They thus provoke analogies and insights which may or may not have been present to the original participants, for whom the simpler terms 'modern' or 'avant-garde' were enough to denote the contemporary nature of their art. But this usage was too all-embracing for later generations, who looked to distinguish the painterly moderns like Matisse and Braque from the anti-art moderns such as Antonin Artaud, Tristan Tzara and Marcel Duchamp.

At the same time, the secondary revision of art and cultural history in terms of retrospectively defined modernism cannot easily be mapped onto the history of cinema. Cinema is an obvious candidate for 'modernity' – in the social sense – because it is primarily urban, industrial and aimed at a mass audience. For many artists, cinema was an emblem of modern times, as the only independent art form to have been invented since the Renaissance. But in other respects the generic code-word 'Hollywood' stands for values opposed to the major tendencies of modern or indeed modernist art. They include the immobile spectator locked into a virtual image, the illusion of absolute presence ('it was just like a film'), predefined structure, narrative continuity, popular appeal, and the ultimate goal of visual pleasure.

The central question for literary and cultural modernism is, perhaps curiously, its relation to the past. Some modernists saw themselves as revitalising outworn traditions or discovering forgotten ones, as in Ezra Pound's rumbustious polemic 'How to Read' (1927)[24] and in his slogan that 'poetry is news that stays news'. Others – perhaps reflecting the impressionist Pissarro's call to 'burn the museums' – recognise in modernism a distinct voice which represents a radical break, or rupture, with the past. More recent deconstructionists argue a third and more conservative case which draws pre- and anti-modernists into an expanded modernist canon. Meredith, Wells and Shaw are among the latest candidates.

Cultural and political radicalism, which so often seem to march together in the twentieth century, are clearly not always allied. Eliot's élitist modernism of the right stresses a high degree of continuity with the past; Adorno's élitist modernism of the left underscores negation and break with the past. Both join in opposition to popular culture, seen as unremittingly commercial and profit-oriented, and to the progressive theories of the 'enlightenment'. Benjamin's position shifts between these two, and he tellingly opened paths between high and popular art by way of surrealism and cinema. His unfinished great project, centred on Paris as the capital of the nineteenth century, proposed a cinematographic method of quotation and fragment,[25] to 'carry the montage principle over into history ..., to build up the large structures out of the smallest ... structural elements'.

Because it is so intimately tied to popular culture, cinema has a complex relation to the concept of modernism, which initially at least derives from such high culture modes as literature, music and the visual arts. This provokes Anne Friedberg in *Window Shopping* (1997) to doubt that cinema has an equivalent to the post-modern revision of the modernist past which was first debated among choreographers and architects in the 1970s. In what sense is a classic Hollywood film 'modernist'? It was challenged as such by innovative films like *Citizen Kane* (1941), and attacked in advance by the Soviet school of the 1920s. Similarly, cultural modernists like Fellini and Bergman rejected the Hollywood cinema, the supposed modernist master-code. It was also questioned by the avant-garde cinema, led by film-makers who were 'otherwise involved in all that modern came to mean in the other arts'.[26]

Friedberg concludes that the distinction between modernism and postmodernism cannot be applied to cinema. She sees 'avant-garde' as a necessary but 'troubling' third term between cinema's ill-defined modernism and the broader sense of modernity, urban and social, which produced cinema and its technical base, or 'apparatus'. The assumed historical link between the modern age and the cinema borders on a 'nominalist quagmire', since Hollywood's modernism – unlike that of the other arts – is openly narrative, representational and often realist. Friedberg turns to the relations between modernism and its avant-gardes to unscramble the knot.

Both Peter Bürger and then Andreas Huyssen (the latter in *After the Great Divide*, 1986) distinguished modernism from the avant-garde, which earlier critics from Renato Poggioli to Irving Howe and Jurgen Habermas had seen as coextensive. In this new historicisation, Bürger argued that while modernism had attacked the conventions of form and language, the avant-garde had gone further to undermine the institutions and even the very concept of art itself. Friedberg uses Richard Abel's extensive research into French cinema to show that the great divide between the avant-garde and modernism does not work for film.[27] Abel argues that narrative avant-garde cinema from 1919–24 (with feature-length directors like Germaine Dulac, Abel Gance and Jean Epstein) and abstract avant-garde film from 1924–9 both fought a common battle to have film recognised as a serious art form, and indeed as a high art. Marcel L'Herbier and Louis Delluc used the term 'impressionism' to link the visuality of film with painterly or musical ideas. In this context, the borders between modern, narrative and avant-garde film are especially fluid.

To take a different perspective, Hollywood was itself eager for cinema to be taken seriously and recognised as an art form, but rejected the methods of modern art in favour of a nineteenth-century realist aesthetic based on the well-rounded story and on closed rather than open forms of narration. Its production systems and technical inventiveness were geared to these ends. Huyssens argues that modernism's high-toned resistance to mass culture – Hollywood included – is in contrast to present-day post-modernist reconciliation of high and low cultures. Paradoxically, the historical avant-gardes emerge as precursors here, precisely because their political intent, from Dada onwards, impelled them to incorporate elements of popular culture rather than to exclude them on grounds of impurity and commercialism.

At the same time, of course, these avant-gardes reject the conformism of mass cinema even as they transgress the formal divisions laid down by modernism and hence look forward (a true vanguard for once) to post-modernism's deliberate blurring of traditional cultural barriers. While this leaves post-modernists seemingly destined to repeat the gestures of their avant-garde forbears – only less effectively, which is Bürger's complaint – it also makes clear that there is no singular history of high art in the twentieth century. But the difficulty here is where to draw the line around the concept of modernism, and thus to define how high is high art. In one sense Mondrian (for example) is very high indeed, dismissing as mere kitsch the flower paintings which he sold in order to be free to paint his pure abstractions. At another level, he had a real zest for urban popular life, and one of his last works is the exuberant and aptly titled *Broadway Boogie-Woogie*. Nearly all the first so-called modernists were also great cinephiles and their enthusiasm for film predated amd partly shaped their work in this medium (see also the following sections on cubism and Futurism).

While this debate resonates through current criticism, it is by no means new. In 1965 the New York art critic Barbara Rose wrote that 'the slick magazines have invented a fictional scene for public consumption', and one of 'the disturbing signs' she notes is that

> among art students, one perceives a 'make-it' mentality conditioned by mass press descriptions of artistic high-life ... As the pace becomes more frantic and distinctions are blurred, values are equally obscured ... Having lost their common purpose on being accepted into the Establishment, and now rapidly losing their centre as galleries and museums and exhibitions proliferate, is it any wonder that avant-garde artists are experiencing a crisis of identity?[28]

Two years later, in 1967, Clement Greenberg asked 'Where is the Avant-Garde?' ('it is a fact that joining up with the avant-garde becomes less and less an adventurous, self-isolating step, and more and more a routine, expected one'), and spoke of 'assimilation' and 'hypertrophy'.[29] Two years further on again, in 1969, he followed up with an essay on 'Avant-Garde Attitudes':

> innovations follow closer and closer on one another, and because they don't make their exits as rapidly as their entrances, they pile up in a welter of eccentric styles, trends, tendencies, schools.

To this confusion, he adds, it seems that the media are 'exploding' and turning into each other, 'scientific technology is invading the visual arts and transforming them even as they transform one another', and 'high art is on the way to becoming popular art, and vice versa'.

Between these two forays, which along with Rose's article are remarkably proleptic of the post-avant-garde world we now inhabit, Greenberg took part in a 1968 interview with the English art critic Edward Lucie-Smith and which was quoted as the lead quotation for this book. Asked for a definition of 'avant-garde', Greenberg replied, 'You don't define it, you recognize it as a historical phenomenon'. At present, he goes on, the avant-garde may be 'undergoing its first epochal transformation' because it has

> taken over the *foreground* of the art scene ... Since what is nominally avant-garde has done this, the term and notion themselves have changed. The question now is one of continuity; will the avant-garde survive in its traditional form? (And there's no paradox in juxtaposing 'avant-garde' and 'tradition').

For Greenberg, an active rather than compromised avant-garde was a necessary factor in the production of high art; he did not (unlike Bürger) see it in opposition to what was being labelled 'high modernism', but as its fundamental condition, and hence he was concerned to defend the avant-garde impulse. The critics were using different maps, then as now.

The first map (Greenberg and Adorno, say) pitched modernism against mass culture with the avant-garde leading the attack, while the second (post-Bürger and Huyssens) shifts the avant-garde into alliance with at least some elements of mass (now 'popular') culture to tear down high modernist élitism. For one group, the avant-garde exemplifies high art while for the other the avant-garde is always oppositional to it. The terms switched gear, so to speak, in the mid-century. Film, and the other media related to it such as video and other 'scientific technologies', always occupied a curious place in these debates and distinctions, wherever the borderlines were drawn. For some, its technical base and mass-culture associations undermined its actual or potential status as an art form; for others, it was simply a new medium to be added to the range of media which an artist could use.

The argument is not only historical, but appears again in later and contemporary times. J. Hoberman's 1984 essay 'After Avant-Garde Film' (the irony is in the title) argued that a new and rebellious clutch of film-makers in the 1970s and 1980s added such post-modernist tropes as appropriation, pastiche and quotation to the inherited language of the classical film avant-garde (construed by Hoberman as high modernists).[30] In so doing, film-makers like Beth and Scott B., Vivienne Dick and Eric Mitchell were also rerunning the New York Underground of the 1960s, in opposition to the 'mandarin' culture of structural film. Camp jokes and popular culture were used as weapons against institutionalised avant-gardisme by Friedberg's 'avant-garde *after* modernism'. Like David Hall in the UK, Hoberman believed that artists must turn to the previously foreclosed space of television, now the leading mass medium in the post-cinema age and as yet uncolonised by the contemporary arts. Although Hoberman does not himself say so, in this perspective it looks as if television plays much the same role for artists today as cinema did for the early modern movement led by Picasso, Marinetti and Malevich.

Contemporary art theory has clearly been much vexed by the overlapping ideas generated by modernism and its aftermath, and which extend to avant-garde film and video as art forms. In *The Return of the Real* (1996) Hal Foster refines and expands Bürger's critique, by similarly distinguishing mainstream modernism from the historical avant-gardes, such as Dada, and from such post-war neo-avant-gardes as Pop Art and conceptual art.[31] Here, minimalist art is the key:

> Minimalism breaks with late modernism through a partial reprise of the historical avant-garde, specifically its disruption of the formal categories of institutional art ... By the same token, it prepares the post-modernist art to come.

In focusing on the minimalists Foster aims to rescue their brand of radical contemporary art from the more conservative modernist tradition and from the post-modern but, as he sees it, regressive revival of expressionism as a counter-avant-garde.

The artist Robert Morris, in his book *Continuous Project Altered Daily* (1993), is more pessimistic about the post-modern attack on the institutions of art, since all art depends on a compromised relation to its social and economic conditions.[32] He slices modern art into three parts or 'discourses' rather than the familiar pairing of modernism and the avant-garde, and looks to the production of art rather than the context of exhibition. Morris first distinguishes the positive concept of 'abstraction' as the leading trend in progress-oriented 'high modernism'. He then turns to political artists who propose the 'address of power' as the key tactic of anti-institutional art. Finally, he describes a 'negative discourse' in modern art, with which he identifies, in which art is an ongoing critique that resists both the positive moment of abstract formalism and the reduction of art to a social programme.

Rosalind Krauss, in documenting her own move from formalist criticism to post-modernism, returns to a binary model of modern art which is almost the traditional coupling, or decoupling, of modernism and the avant-garde.[33] She tracks this along a visual axis, however, rather than wholly through the ebbs and flows of opposing art movements. Firstly, she traces an initial dominance of 'the grid' in modern art, emphasising order, structure and control, as evidenced in cubism. Secondly, she contrasts the grid with 'the matrix', an underlying but ungraspable shape or web made up by the work of art. Unlike the grid, the matrix fluidly resists order and definition. Its transgressive nature is expressed by the dissident surrealist Georges Bataille in his concept of the '*informe*', or non-form, and leads to the hybrid and metaphoric art of the present day.

This contrast of grid and matrix may recall the debate between classic and romantic art led by theorists of art from Goethe and Lessing down to Wöllflin, Hulme and Worringer, that is to say from the birth of Romanticism itself to the dawn of a specifically modern art.[34] It also updates a distinction made early in the twentieth century between formal art (e.g. the constructivist movement after cubism) and the disrupting critique of art offered by surrealism. The contrast was made in Salvador Dali's comment on *Un Chien andalou* (1928): 'With one stroke [i.e. in the famous shot of an eye slashed with a razor] we put paid to the little lozenges of Monsieur Mondrian.'[35] Krauss thus pulls surrealism back into the core of modern art, from which her former mentor Clement Greenberg had expelled it as illustrative, iconic, pre-modernist and neo-romantic.

Foster, Krauss and Morris are all associated with the American journal *October*, named after Eisenstein's famous film. If their different views show a 'family resemblance', they are also not strictly compatible. But for each 'the moment of cubism' is the crucial episode in modern art, just as it is the founding movement for artists' film. Like other art movements, cubism implies a process of artistic change which these writers are concerned to underline in their accounts of contemporary art. A period of *innovation* (1907–25) is followed by *assimilation and consolidation* (1925–35) and then by a new critical or negative *reaction* (in cubism this begins early, with the surrealist revolt from around 1925 onwards although crucially heralded by the long-sighted Duchamp, questioning and probing from within the cubist epoch almost as soon as it began).

This three-stroke model of innovation/consolidation/reaction inevitably recalls a much older neo-Hegelian Marxism. It is, in fact, the logical triad of thesis/antithesis/synthesis found in orthodox Marxism, but with the final two terms crucially reversed. The conventional triad is embodied in both radical and orthodox film theory through the influence of Eisenstein, whose ideas were forged in its climate. The three-shot model is the basis of montage, literally so in the legendary Kuleshov experiment and in many of Eisenstein's own films,[36] and more metaphorically when the clash of one distinct shot with another produces a new concept which is their joint product, whether there is a third synthesising image or not.[37]

Methods and theories of montage have for long focused on the subtle variations which can be spun from a triadic system, which has obvious connections to musical form and to some kinds of abstract painting.[38] Underlying the theory of montage in film is a further division to which all Western art forms are subject, but which film specifically encodes. This is the split between the material conditions of film production and the idealised flow of on-screen images which are their result.

On a Platonic scale which mapped the materiality of art-making from the most minimal to the most tangible, graphic notation on paper (words, scores) would appear at one end and object-making sculpture at the other. It is this range of forms of content, prior to the plane of expression, which much modern and contemporary art has been inclined to explore.[39] Foster's instance of reductive minimalist art as the crucial moment leading to post-modernity is carefully chosen.

Cinema is an especially material art – as the full credits to any feature film will reveal – but at the same time, and because of this very materiality, it is also the most illusionistic or phantasmagoric art form in its final product and effect. As symbolic systems the technologies of film rely on animated still frames while video depends on electronically coded signals. The source of the image is, in either case, strictly invisible to the observer. The separate frames of a film echo the regular cubist grid – an aspect parodied in the serial repetitive format of Warhol's early screenprints[40] – but appear as an intuited and impressionist matrix from the point of view of the spectator. The origins of these complex media, which prove so difficult to match even with the multi-plane categories of art and modernism, are the subject of the next section.

Part One: The canonical avant-garde

Origins of the moving image (1780–1880)

New movements in cultural history rarely have a single and agreed starting date, and to trace either the moment when cinema began or when it became an art is a matter of argument. The emblematic years 1895/6, when the Lumières first demonstrated their machine in Paris and London, are an endpoint as much as anything else, for behind those dates stands a long period of research and development in Europe and the USA. Nor did the Lumère brothers think they were making art. Even more arguable is the relation of cinema to the other art forms of the late nineteenth century, including realist painting and drama, as well as the modernism which is the main subject of this historical review.

Modern art and silent cinema emerged at roughly the same time, after a long period of mutual gestation. Both came at the end of a century which was fascinated by the art and science of vision. It underpins the composer Claude Debussy's notion that 'music is the arithmetic of sounds as optics is the geometry of light.'[41] Cézanne, who surfaced from long years of self-willed obscurity to become recognised as a master of 'post-impressionism' in the mid-1890s, wanted to 'develop an optics, by which I mean a logical vision'.[42]

Photography, which had been born from the science of optics, and is a third point of triangulation between art and cinema, had already made its impact on visual artists from the 1840s onwards.[43] It left its trace on the subject-matter, the style or the method of every advanced artist of the period – including Manet, Seurat and Degas – just as it challenged and redefined the picture-making of more traditional, academic painters and sculptors. But both sides drew different lessons from the photograph. While the Impressionists and their followers were typically struck by the surprise or chance-effect of the snapshot, narrative painters focused on the illusionist realism and surface of the Daguerreotype or photogravure. Both groups were quick to use photography as a visual aid or as a means of documentation, thus adding to that extensive 'archive' of photo-images which now engrosses historians of the early modern period.

Photography may link artists with proto-cinema, but it is necessarily a static form of representation which slices time into fractions to achieve its effect. The paradoxes of photographic time continue to fascinate artists today, just as they stimulated such thinkers as Baudelaire, Bergson, Benjamin and Barthes, but the key and missing element – the 'capture' of movement – had to be added to the scientific study of optics before the diverse arts and technologies which made cinema possible were in place. Here science added a further link to the chain as it turned to ever more experimental procedures. By the mid-nineteenth century, in the influential researches of the scientist Helmholtz, for example, the traditional 'static' medical anatomy of the eye was joined to the more fluid and investigative study of colour and light perception which had been pioneered – along quite different lines – by Newton and Goethe, and then by technologists such as Chevreul,[44] in the century between 1728 and 1839.

Chevreul's analysis of colour harmony appeared in 1839 at the same time as the famous public announcement of photography's invention in France. The next year, 1840, the President of the Royal Academy in Britain, Sir Charles Eastlake, published his translation of Goethe's (anti-Newtonian) *Theory of Colour* (1810). Soon afterwards the 70-year-old Turner painted *Light and Colour (Goethe's Theory) – the Morning after the Deluge*, a title which plays on two senses of vision, the scientific and the sublime. Both Turner and Constable, who studied not only nature but the meteorological research of Luke Howard for his famous studies of clouds,[45] were to affect two generations of French artists from Delacroix to Monet for whom painting was above all an art of light and colour. Constable's influence on French artists was first noticed by the critic Villot in 1857. The early audiences who responded so vividly to the movement of trees and shadows in the background of the Lumières' film *Feeding Baby* – almost an Impressionist subject sprung to life – were thus seeing a complex heritage pass before their eyes, just as the Lumières' film of the *Card Players*, also 1895, unconsciously echoes Cézanne's paintings on that theme.

If the first viewers of film made such unlikely connections (had they gone to both Cézanne's Paris exhibition and the Lumière screenings in 1895, for example), they did not record them. It was not until cubism, and even then at a late stage in its development, that a context was offered in which artists might make films themselves, opening a new option for the modern movement, then also known as 'the avant-garde'. But even early cubism was quickly seen to be 'cinematographic' in its concern for movement and viewpoint, and by a happy chance the French philosopher Bergson used that very phrase in 1907 to describe – not uncritically – the process of perception. A year later two young and unknown painters, Picasso and Braque, were pursuing their 'laboratory research' (Picasso), 'like two mountaineers roped together', as Braque recalled.[46] They were climbing in Cézanne's footsteps, developing his 'passage' or overlap between forms just as Bergson focused on 'passage' in time.[47]

Increased attention to the moving image, the cinematographic, was one crucial aspect of the European arts and sciences as they entwined towards the middle of the nineteenth century. Eighteenth-century rationalism had evolved into a broader 'psycho-physics', as Helmholtz called it, to produce demonstrable results from fleeting effects. Leonardo da Vinci had long ago noted such effects as a whirling firebrand which seems to leave a circular trace in the eye. Simulated movement and the persistence of vision were studied by such early modern scientists as Rouget and Faraday, typically by observing the spokes of rotating wheels. Between 1829 and 1833 Plateau in Brussels and Stampfer in Vienna had mapped the successive positions of a figure in movement around the circumference of a turning disc. These brief 'shots' of moving people, birds and animals were viewed through a sequence of slits and reflected in a mirror. Optical toys were the commercial result of this activity, adding to the kaleidoscope and stereoscope invented by Sir David Brewster. Popular variants such as the stroboscope, phantasmascope and zoescope culminated in Horner's drum-mechanism Zoetrope, highly marketable from the 1860s, and Raynaud's sophisticated Praxinoscope from 1877. A further direction of research, which ultimately passed into synaesthetic art and the abstract film, pursued the equivalence of sound and light. In this period, it goes from Goethe and Turner to Rimington's concert of 'colour music', also in the emblematic year 1895.

Photography

Photography grew along with and often overlapped these developments in the art of motion. Some recent historians have questioned the tendency to treat such optical inventions as merely the stages by which 'proto-cinema' finally led to the real thing. Such genealogies are often traced back to the camera obscura, a closed box fitted with a lens which focused a sharp image onto a flat surface, used as a drawing aid from the Renaissance onwards. But it is also argued, following Jonathan Crary,[48] that the fixed and static framing of the camera obscura is very different from more fluid and active moving-image devices like the praxinoscope, suggesting a different model of spectatorship less firmly centred on the centralised gaze. The career of a pioneer like Daguerre shows, however, that the traditional litany of names and devices making up 'proto-cinema' offers real insight into the period.

Niepce's first successful experiments in photography from 1816–22 expanded after his partnership in 1829 with the more entrepreneurial Daguerre. A year after Niepce's death in 1836 Daguerre perfected a silver and mercury method of printing which led to official recognition of the new art in 1839. Fox Talbot's invention of the negative in 1835, inspired by the French pioneers, was also to change the course of image reproduction. Daguerre, like other businessmen-scientists of his time, was well prepared for the popular spread of photography as a medium for the mass reproduction of images.

A pupil of Prévost, he had designed panoramas and dioramas from 1822, later bringing in live action and sound to enhance the attractions of these large-scale scenes of cities, battles and famous events, painted on translucent linen and transformed by lighting. His first experiments in photography used, in fact, an adapted camera obscura. Just as tellingly for the future, the worldly Daguerre made sure that his contract with Niepce in 1829 enjoined them 'to gain all possible advantages from this new industry'. Daguerre's 'showmanship' – his business flair as well as his sense of public spectacle, from dioramas to ballooning – did indeed connect the new technologies of vision and motion; cinema films are still viewed as panoramas in dark spaces, and remain epic rather than intimate in scale.

Balzac, like Dickens and Zola, charts in his novels the passage from classical stasis to romantic flux in nineteenth-century Europe. Motion was a key concept and emblem of the period, from cities and empires to railroads and mass spectacle. The sense of dynamism which this implied, and of which film was both literal figure and late metaphor, was passed on to later generations by way of the aptly named 'motion pictures' and indeed by a host of artistic and political 'movements' which typically came, like light, in waves.

Crary's revisionism attempts to avoid the dangers of simple teleology, or reading history backwards as a series of inevitable steps from the present to the past. It resists the centrifugal tendency of each period, including our own, to construct the past in its own image. At the same time, the nineteenth century's own ideology of progress and its cult of the 'invention' are an implicit part of its cultural history. In this sense, the making of 'moving pictures', which culminated in the 1890s, was indeed a goal to which many scientists and others consciously moved by diverse and overlapping paths. The concept of progress embodies this 'forward-looking' self-image and led to such real effects as cinema itself.

The span of proto-cinema goes from Philip De Loutherberg's 'Eidophusikon' – exhibited in England from 1781 and combining screen images with sound effects – and the spread of 'Phantasmagorias' in Paris, London and New York from the 1790s to 1800. It does not seem illegitimate to connect the exploits of Daguerre, a photographer and balloonist who started as a designer of dioramas, with Grimion-Samson's 1900 'Cineorama' which took circular 360° views on 70mm film from a balloon, or with James White's panoramas of the World Fairs, or with Edwin Porter's similar use of a fluid-panning[49] tripod for shots of the Buffalo 'Electric Tower' in 1900. Film historian Tom Gunning argues that these and similar scenographic ventures make up a pre-narrative 'cinema of attractions' which the advent of the single-screen drama film forced underground – and partly into the avant-garde – after 1907.[50]

It was in a climate of expanding industry and invention from 1820–50 that the idea of an artistic avant-garde materialised. It was prefigured in the bonds between the painter Jacques Louis David's classicism and the Revolution of 1789, when David was practically the official artist of the new regime, organising popular celebrations, or 'street-art', as well as painting its historical icons. But the avant-garde (named as such in the 1820s) first flourished in a later revolutionary France, erupting in 1848, to which artists and intellectuals were central. 'Barriers are falling and the horizons expanding', wrote a critic at the time. Progressive art and revolutionary politics were emblematically united when Delacroix's inflammatory *Liberty Guiding the People* was exhibited for the first time since the previous political uprising of 1830.

For the next thirty years the term 'avant-garde' denoted radical or advanced activity both social and artistic.[51] The utopian socialist Saint-Simon had coined the term to designate the élite leadership of artists, scientists and industrialists in the new century. At first the avant-garde was led by social rather than stylistic concerns. Later it took on overtones of more extreme rebellion. Courbet embodied the artist as social critic and outcast (he was exiled after the fall of the Paris Commune in 1871), and his influence preserved the link between the avant-garde and social realism through the 1860s and beyond.

But, stripped of its historical quotation marks, as Linda Nochlin recommends, the avant-garde in art can more readily be seen to begin with Manet. Manet's realism was nothing if not critical. His free brushwork, allusive and ironic subject-matter and formal doubling of space and reflection (all of which can be seen in the *Bar at the Folies Bergère*) are far from the social realism of progressive art, even though he shared its republican sympathies. At this point the idea of an avant-garde passes through the crucible of art. By the time of Matisse, Picasso,

18

Stravinsky and Diaghilev, avant-garde simply meant new, the latest modern thing. Fine distinctions between modernism and the avant-garde were yet to come. However, the earlier and socially tinged avant-garde idea was reborn in the radical aspirations of artistic movements (notably surrealism and constructivism) during the 1920s and 1930s.

Realism may have been dropped from the agenda by then, but the social instincts of Courbet, Millet, Daumier and the writers of the mid-nineteenth century harmonised with their times. The practice and dissemination of both art and technology had moved beyond private patronage and scholarship to eminently public or state arenas in which academies, associations, exhibitions and newspapers all had their say. These gave the new art and eventually the new movies a context, at the birth of the mass age, in which the image of 'the people' was giving way to the new notion of 'the public'. This intermediate phase, in which new art forms such as film and recorded sound were developing, while older forms like painting and sculpture were being refashioned, only lasted for a short period. Aesthetic, social and economic divisions asserted themselves, so that when their time came, in the early years of the century, such phrases as 'film art' and, even more so, 'art film', came to mean quite different things in the cultural context.

Such divisions were by then a familiar feature of a rapidly changing cultural landscape. In 1895, the year of the Lumières' first screenings, Paul Cézanne's paintings were seen in public for the first time in twenty years in a large exhibition urged by Pissarro and organised by the art dealer Ambrose Vollard. For much of his life this reclusive artist was seen as a botcher and failure (his old but now estranged friend Emile Zola had typified him as such in an 1886 novel with the ironic title *L'Oeuvre* or *The Masterpiece*), but his paintings were increasingly seen by a younger generation to herald a revolution in art which was well under way by Cézanne's death in 1906.

Cézanne wished to bring together the direct perception of nature with the 'solidity' of classical and museum art.[52] In the event his fame rests more on his concern for transition and movement, expecially in those still lifes or landscapes which incorporate different points of view. In particular this led to the rise of cubism that took place between 1908–12, the very time at which cross-cutting, close-ups and other cinematic devices were in development. Despite the rising barriers between new art and public taste, painters and other modernists were among the first enthusiasts for American adventure movies, the cartoons and Chaplin, finding in them a shared taste for modern city life, surprise and change.[53] By 1912 Picasso was an early fan of the famous *Fantomas* serials.

Art and the avant-garde: summary 1909–20

Films directly made by artists were first discussed by Futurist, constructivist and Dadaist groups between 1909 and the mid-1920s.[54] This 'vortex' of activity, to use Ezra Pound's phrase, included the experiments in 'lightplay' at the Bauhaus, Robert and Sonya Delaunay's 'orphic cubism', Russian 'Rayonnisme' and the cubo-Futurism of Severini, Kupka and its Russian variants in the Lef group. In turn, all of these experiments were rooted in the cubist revolution pioneered by Braque and Picasso.

Cubism was an art of fragments, at first depicting objects from a sequenc shifting angles and then assembling images by a collage of paper, print, paint other materials. It was quickly understood to be an emblem of its time Apollinaire was perhaps the first to evoke an analogy between the new painti and the new physics – but also as a catalyst for innovation in other art forms, esp. cially in design and architecture. The painter Derain (later mentor to the abstract film-maker Viking Eggeling) called this language of visual fragmentation an art of 'deliberate disharmonies'. It parallels the growing use of dissonance in literature (Joyce, Stein) and music (Stravinsky, Schoenberg).

At the same time, the period from 1890 to 1914 was also characterised by the issue of method in art and thought.[55] Both Cézanne and Seurat spoke of the search for method, and Signac continued it in his book on colour after Delacroix. Modern logical philosophy was founded at this time by Frege, Russell and Wittgenstein, as was phenomenology by Husserl and psychoanalysis by Freud. The aeroplane, radio telegraphy, X-rays as well as the atomic physics of Einstein and Planck were also developed in the time of the later Cézanne and the young Picasso, and each of these scientific and analytic discoveries carried a symbolic and even romantic dimension, as they expanded the field of vision to embrace exterior flight and the interior body, radio waves and light rays.

New theories of time and perception in art, as well as the popularity of cinema, led artists to try to put 'paintings in motion' through the film medium.[56] On the eve of the First World War, the poet Guillaume Apollinaire, author of *The Cubist Painters* (1913), explained the animation process in his journal *Les Soirées de Paris* and extolled the planned (but not shot) film *Le Rythme coloré* (*Colour Rhythms*, 1912–14), an abstract work by the painter Léopold Survage,[57] which he compared to 'fireworks, fountains and electric signs'.

Apollinaire, whose promotion of new art was unsurpassed, had a complex artistic heritage. Hermeticism, art nouveau and synaesthesia, augmented by Rimbaud's litany of the 'drunken senses', jostled with his urban and technocratic fervour for the Eiffel Tower, the aeroplane, cinema. In 1918 his call was renewed by the young Louis Aragon, writing in Delluc's *Le Film* that cinema must have 'a place in the avant-garde's preoccupations. They have designers, painters, sculptors. Appeal must be made to them if one wants to bring some purity to the art of movement and light.'[58]

When cubists aimed for purity they meant the goal of autonomy in art rather than the search for essential qualities in the media they employed. Their chosen method was to combine or hybridise media and to override accepted categories and genres. Bergson's vision of simultaneity was glossed by the Futurist Marinetti in 1909 as the triumph of the 'dynamic sensation' over the 'fixed moment', in a typically cinematic analogy (although Bergson himself saw film as a deceptive illusion which broke up the fluid passage of time).[59] Yet cubist modernism was also strongly Kantian in its search for underlying form beyond impression, and here it turned to science.[60]

The principle of simultaneity had been introduced to art long before, in Chevreul's account of colour contrast and harmony, influencing Delacroix and the Impressionists. Now optical theory joined with new discoveries in physics. Apollinaire first referred to 'relativity' in 1911. By 1919, Raynal and others could call on non-Euclidean geometry, Mallarmé and the new science as background to cubism, quoting Malebranche, Helmholtz, Bossuet and Kant to witness the limitations and failings of sense-data. To these high sources were added the popular context which cubism shared with the cinema, its contemporary, and with the visual culture of chronophotography, panoramas and dioramas, slide shows, billboards and the instant snapshot.[61] All these had opened new scope for perception even as they undermined the traditional authority of the image as a substitute for reality. This was now the province of straight photography, which had invaded the painterly genres of portrait and landscape and even named its major formats after them. These are the contexts in which cubism questioned the direct bond of seeing and knowing which painting had traditionally evoked.

The call for purity – an autonomous art free of illustration and story-telling – had been the cubists' clarion-cry since their first public exhibition in 1907, but the goal of 'pure' or 'absolute' film was qualified by the hybrid medium of cinema, praised by Méliès in the same year as 'the most enticing of all the arts, for it makes use of almost all of them'. But for modernism cinema's turn to dramatic realism, melodrama and epic fantasy was questioned, in Lessing's spirit, as a confusion of literary and pictorial values. As commercial cinema approached the condition of synaesthesia with the aid of sound and toned or tinted colour, echoing in popular form the 'total work of art' of Wagnerianism and art nouveau, modernism looked towards non-narrative directions in film form.

Cubist polemics often cast this in the image of battle. Aragon's demand for a pure cinema does not foresee a placid or accommodating art. He calls on 'a new, audacious aesthetic, a sense of modern beauty' to rid cinema of the 'old, impure, poisonous alloy' which binds it to its 'indomitable enemy', theatre. 'Don't be afraid to offend the public', Aragon says; slap its face and make it spit. He offers the image of a blank white screen like a pure white sail, metaphors which also attracted Mayakovsky, Apollinaire, Valéry and Mandelstam. Modern art, *en route* to Futurism and surrealism, associated film with shock from the first.

The cubists

Braque and Picasso worked out what they saw as the lessons of Cézanne in a series of portraits and landscapes painted in Paris and L'Estaque from 1908 to 1910.[62] They related time and space in art in new ways. Instead of a single viewpoint in suspended time, which the photograph had now perfected, the typical cubist portrait showed changing angles and viewpoints on its subject. Visual certainty, as given in appearance, was questioned. Instead of the traditional division between figure and ground, each part of the painting was here given equal pictorial value. At the same time, through a visible grid of surface marks, lines and brushmarks, these paintings showed how they had been made. They were shockingly non-hieratic, an impression underlined by their echoes of non-Western art from Africa and Oceania or the rugged non-classical sculpture of Iberia.

This kind of painting aimed, like Cézanne's, to unite direct visual sensations – which are fluid and unfixed – with a firm structure derived from the artistic tradition (the genres of portrait, landscape and still life were retained). But it was also more revolutionary in two ways: the first in its conceptual leap and the second in its radical expansion of artistic form and material.

The Impressionists had opened their eyes to the raw data of vision in search of pictorial truth. The Fauves (who around 1905 included Matisse, Braque and Derain) raised the banner of pure colour; here, the viewer responded to colours in the painting freed from their source in the visible world. In this, despite their direct and 'wild' colour, the Fauves shared the artistic climate of symbolism, which turned to magic and reverie as the keys to an insight beyond appearances. But Fauvism threatened to become a decorative style while symbolism led easily to illustration, exactly those nineteenth-century pictorial codes which young artists wished to escape.

Braque had been a Fauve, and Picasso a symbolist, and they collaborated to move beyond both options. Their solution was cognitive, and focused on what was known rather than seen. And rather than hide the gap between the object and its appearance, by the classic but artificial means of perspective and foreshortening, they began to include visual ambiguity and indecision into their paintings. As summarised by Norman Bryson, 'the cubist experiment sought a way to break the analogy between picture and perception which had governed most of painting's history since the early Renaissance.'[63]

Cubism therefore gave modern art 'the method' for which many artists had called, but a provisional and unstable one which corresponded to modernity in the early years of the century. It did so by breaking with the pictorial sign as a register of observed, visual fact. The sign itself took on a new autonomy – it stood for itself as well as its object – and painting moved a notch further towards pure abstraction. Writing on 'The Intentions of Cubism' in 1919, Maurice Raynal stated that the autonomous work 'will be, to the objects it represents, what a word is to the object it signifies'. Similarly, as expressed by Kahnweiler, 'these painters turned away from imitation because they had discovered that the true character of painting and sculpture is that of a script'. The sign in painting becomes arbitrary, like the word in language (as asserted by cubism's contemporary, Saussure). Scraps of newsprint and text enter the visual frame which is no longer wholly made up of natural signs as analogues of the perceptual field.

Although the cubists did not take the implied next step, which leads to full abstraction, a new phase of inquiry was pursued by Picasso and Braque from around 1910 to 1914. In contrast to the first stage of analysing and breaking down the object and its forms in art, this second moment of cubism was devoted to synthesising and constructing real and imagined objects from a variety of collaged textures and surfaces. Collage introduced a new set of operations and ideas, from the emphasis on the flat surface to machine art and to cut-out phrases and images from the popular press.

These were mainly aesthetic questions for Picasso and Braque, who stood rather aloof from the broadening interest in their work and the even broader conclusions drawn from it. As the latest and most dramatic shock to public taste in art so far, the new painting became both famous and notorious; a double legacy. The derisory term 'cubism' stuck, however, and wider numbers of artists took up the name and explored the style in a cluster of splinter groups. Their ideas and their shows were encouraged by Apollinaire, poet and publicist of the new spirit in art.

Today cubism is seen as distinctively modern because it is sceptical, investigative, active, eclectic. It was the intellectual and artistic core of the modern movement, and is still seen as its foundation. Most major trends in art later in the century looked back to it, and some still do, as a direction to follow or challenge. The moments of cubism still attract critical debate. Key issues remain unresolved, from anarchist readings of Picasso collages to more familiar problems of order and dating. But cubism remains an open question for more than historical reasons. It did not begin as a movement nor did its founders seek to found one, but the 'researches' of two young painters took on wider importance in a period of artistic change when traditional forms and content were under attack.

Their challenge was made in part by turning to non-Western sources outside the tradition and by identifying with the most radical aspects of that tradition, which is why cubist myth incorporates Cézanne, Jarry and Rousseau in a rhetoric of the innocent or even child-like eye. Echoing the machine age by turning from the central, positioning human eye, cubist collage took city life – from newspaper clippings to household wallpaper – directly into art. Even by collaborating Picasso and Braque undermined the bravura-myth of individual authorship.

Before cubism radical artists from the Impressionists to the Fauves regarded the space of painting as a scene opened to the eye. To this long tradition they added new sensations of colour, texture and form. City-bred cubism questioned this notion of optical truth and of the identifications it implied, chiefly between the object and its image and between viewer and viewed. The compositional unity of what Duchamp later dubbed 'retinal art' fell victim to cubist syntax, which sought conceptual form rather than visible appearance.[64] Low-key materials and ordinary objects from the artisan's workshop or the artist's studio distanced the new art from the idealism inherent in the rejection of the visible, a doctrine that goes back to Plato.

This pushed the cubists away from pure painting around 1912–14 towards collage or assemblages. Behind this stood the experience of city life which cubism looked to represent. Urban patterns and rhythms score the surfaces of cubist and Futurist paintings with multiple perspectives, or jagged lines and phrases torn or quoted from newspapers or billboards. Against the unitary gaze of the Western art tradition, cubism offered fluid clusters of dots, curves and lines – critic Maurice Raynal called them 'a new notation' – to replace visual harmonies with a series of abrupt glances that recall an exchange of looks in the street.

While the influential philosopher Henri Bergson criticised cinema for falsely eliding the passage of time, his vividly cinematic metaphors echo and define modernism's attitude to the visual image: 'form is only the snapshot view of a transition.' This is practically a definition of cubism. Bergson objected to the way in which we think of time in terms of space, depicting it as a straight line marked with 'moments' as its points. He argues that experienced time is pure *duration*, not a succession of moments but a flow of invisible continuity. This flow is in fact characteristic of all experience, which is an organic stream. Language, which is in distinct parts, misleads us to ascribe its own structure onto the world.

Bergson himself was not a champion of the new art, but the writer Gertrude Stein certainly was.[65] An early collector of Braque, Matisse and Picasso, she had been a favourite student at Harvard of William James, who saw Bergson as a precursor of his 'radical empiricism'. James himself, in 1890, had described experience as a 'stream of consciousness'. He criticised the older empiricism for isolating impressions or sensations from the stream, in terms that, like Bergson, recall the contemporaneous film: 'Consciousness does not appear to itself chopped up into bits, it is nothing jointed, it flows.'

Stein looked back in 1934 at her book *The Making of Americans*, written in 1906–8 when she had moved to Paris, and acknowledged her debt to cinema. The book aspires to the universal, envisaging a Warholian 'long book that is a real history of everyone who ever was or are or will be living from their beginning to their ending'. Stein wrote in the continuous present, like film, but claimed that she did not employ simple repetition – a common belief about her work – because of the 'slightest changing' that was also part of her technique. This she compares to the cinema:

> Funnily enough, the cinema has offered a solution of this thing. By a continuously moving picture of any one there is no memory of any other thing and there is that thing existing . . . I was doing what the cinema was doing, I was making a continuous succession of the statement of what that person was until I had not many things but one thing . . . In a cinema picture no two pictures are exactly alike, each one is just that much different from the one before, and so in those early portraits there was . . . no repetition . . . It is not repetition if it is that which you are actually doing because naturally each time the emphasis is different just as the cinema has each time a slightly different thing to make it all be moving.

She admits bravely that

> I of course did not think of it in terms of the cinema, in fact I do not think I had ever seen a cinema but, and I cannot repeat this too often, any one is of one's period and this our period was undoubtedly the period of the cinema and series production. And each of us in our own way are bound to express what the world in which we are living is doing.

If Warhol's 'famous for fifteen minutes' dictum is prefigured in Stein's 'history of everyone', so here are implanted his film-based repeated images and the 'series production' which characterised his art.

Stein's quiet revolution of the word passed down into later modernism, gathering speed at mid-century when John Cage gave it extra spin.[66] At this point it impacted on the young Stan Brakhage for his innovatory film *Anticipation of the Night* (1959) whose structure of slow, Stein-like jagged repetitions was also indebted to Stein's more combative contemporary, Ezra Pound.[67] Pound thought of poetry in visual terms. His 1913 formula for a new poetics of 'imagism' conceived the word as a vortex[68] of action and the image as a snapshot. 'An "Image" is that which presents an intellectual and emotional complex in an instant of time.' Pound defines the image so as to compactly render the hallmarks of modernism: a conversion of the dynamic and the kinetic into the static, of the temporal into the spatial, and of successiveness into simultaneity. It inevitably recalls the cinematicity of Bergson and heralds Eisenstein's analysis of montage and frame.

Primitives and pioneers (1880–1915)

Film may have permeated the thought and gained the excited interest of leading artists and thinkers – but was it art?[69] And if so, of what sort? Authors of the time from Faure to Munsterberg debated this issue, in which the impersonal technology of film and its lack of direct authorship seem to run against the grain of traditional art, an argument which continues today. There were two contexts in which the cinema was described as an art form in the silent era. The first was to apply the term to cinema as a whole, as did Méliès. Ricciotto Canudo and Abel Gance hailed cinema as a 'sixth art' in 1911/12, while for the Polish critic Karol Irzykowski in 1924 it was 'the tenth muse'. For the American poet Vachel Lindsay in 1922 film was like architecture, and that same year the art historian Elie Faure adopted the word 'cineplastics'. This line was also taken up by artists and critics like Apollinaire, the mentor of modernism, whose vision of a synaesthetic cinema was heralded in Canudo's 1911 essay 'Plastic Art in Motion'.

A second conjunction of art and early film was less cultural and more commercial, although it shares a context in which mastery of the technological base was entwined with cultural property and artistic status. Here the growing film industry used the traditional link between art and individual talent (paradoxically set in doubt by the cinema itself) to argue that film-making necessarily entailed creative authorship. This was crucial to their legal battles to establish copyright and ownership. Companies and associations such as Les Films d'Art (1908), United Artists (1919) and the Academy of Motion Picture Arts and Sciences (1927), party to these battles, traded on the name of art for both cultural and legal reasons, dryly summed up by Benoît-Lévy's 1907 definition of film as 'a literary and artistic property'.

It is in the crucial period shortly before the First World War that an eventual division between opposed visions of cinema was seeded. Largely through the vitality of the American cinema, films rapidly passed through a primitive stage when they were brief and often single-shot diversions made by entertainers and showmen for fairgrounds and music-halls.[70] Around 1903 to 1905 they were revived by capital investment and dramatic invention. They became longer, more elaborate and were shown in purpose-built cinemas – the origin of the picture palaces which were to dominate most of the century. Within ten years the fiction film had attained epic proportions as in Griffith's *Intolerance* (1916) and Pastroni's *Cabiria* (1914). The impulse of the early fiction directors was to develop a fluid language of film that would absorb, enchant and finally 'move' its audiences, developing the narrative drive which the novel and the drama had already attained. It is from this branch of cinema, its mainstream, that questions of realism classically emerge.

At the same time, a very different approach to film was developing among a small but influential number of enthusiasts who focused on the cultural implications of the new medium. For some it heralded a new age, a new way of seeing, understood in a positive light by Canudo and Faure[71] but more gloomily by Maxim Gorky[72] in his famous account of visiting 'the kingdom of shadows' in 1905. For others, and these included philosophers like Bergson (and, later on, Moore and Wittgenstein),[73] film offered a new way of understanding the construction and paradoxes of time and duration. For yet a third group, mostly composed of artists such as Apollinaire and Picasso in France, the Futurists in Italy and abstract painters like Ruttmann and Eggeling working in Germany, film was a means of forcing forward the development of avant-garde abstraction along the lines of the controversial new painting and sculpture centred on cubism and its aftermath. Around 1912, his friend Kahnweiler recalled, Picasso was thinking in terms of animated objects. Fifty years later he returned to a 'flipbook' technique for his cycle of drawings *After Manet*,[74] completing a historical cycle to link Manet's modernism and the invention of optical toys a century before with its long aftermath in post-cubist art, as fixed gesture turns to sequential movement.

While early modern artists like the Impressionists were affected by the first machine age and its optics, it is also broadly the case that the later moderns were aware of a more abstract new physics associated with the theories of Einstein. The art critic David Sylvester states that

> there is, of course, a certain correspondance between Relativity and Analytical Cubism, for the overlapping and juxtaposition of a multiplicity of views of an object represents the perceptions of a spectator at different stages in a promenade around the object and therefore implies the notion of space-time ... The main philosophical implication of Cubism is Russell's conception, expounded in *Our Knowledge of the External World* (1914), that what we call a 'thing' is a 'system of aspects': what, indeed, is an analytical cubist picture but a 'logical construction' from a series of appearances? If in contrast there is a connection with Relativity, it is an oblique one.[75]

In 1920 the painter Paul Klee wrote that the activity of the spectator was essentially temporal.

Russell himself was sceptical of Bergson's subjectivism, but Bergson continued to influence the growing theory of cinema through his ideas about time and his strikingly visual metaphors.[76] Hugo Munsterberg's *Film – A Psychological Study* (1916) argues that the spectator's outer world diminishes as film hollows out an inner imaginative world free of linear time, space and causality. Erwin Panofsky's essay on film (1936) describes a mobile spectator who is identified with the shifting lens of the camera, as space is dynamised and time rendered spatial. Bazin's notion of film as a defence against the passage of time is a spirited reversal of Bergson's own view that cinema falsifies duration. During the mid-1970s Gilles Deleuze and Jean-Louis Baudry inserted into the prevailing structuralist ethos some key Bergsonian ideas which focus on film as a 'simulation machine' in which 'representations are mistaken for perceptions', a basic assumption on which classical film drama rests as 'a technique of the imaginary' (Christian Metz) which mobilises and organises a libidinal economy of pleasure.

Futurists[77]

While Bergson is best known today for his ideas about perception, in his own time he was seen as a vitalist philosopher who stressed the role of action. The challenge of cubism was taken up as a vitalist war-cry by the first of the new self-styled vanguard movements, Futurism in Italy and the cubo-Futurists in Russia. The Italians were a definite group with an agenda and a manifesto, the Russians a looser collection centred on the charismatic poet Mayakovsky. Cubism in their view had not gone far enough; art must move beyond painting into life. Freed from the gallery, art was to intervene in the flow of daily events (hence the taste for demonstrations and street scandals) and to affect all aspects of the culture. High and low were merged and barriers between the arts were broken down. This was to be the model for interventionist avant-gardes through to current times. With Futurism, the avant-garde which had begun as the cultural arm of political reform now turned to cultural politics and direct action. Prepared by this before the First World War, the Futurists in the 1920s vied for support from their respectively Fascist and Soviet regimes when the movement was otherwise split in two by its ideological divide. Mayakovsky's suicide in 1930 and Marinetti's gradual sidelining from the centre of Fascist ideology mark the end of these aims to gain official status for Futurism as the vanguard of art.

Even so, the Italian Futurists are arguably the most important of the early vanguard groups. They were the first to storm the public with wild-eyed manifestos and with art as a provocation, announcing a permanent revolution at the heart of museum culture. They turned from art as a private cult to its role in the mass arena. They roamed freely across the arts, inventing new ones such as Russolo's 'Art of Noise' or refurbishing old ones in Marinetti's 'Futurist Cooking'. They took up the contemporary themes of work and street life, formerly a hallmark of the realists but now given a new dynamic style. Their idea of modernity openly embraced war and violence as well as music and the movies. Everything they touched on they ignited: automatic art (which led to surrealism), the painting of light and motion (which led to abstraction), art in the streets (which led to performance art), art as critique (which led to Dada). They broke up text and lettering, severing them from their origin in handwriting and leading to a non-linear print revolution which continues today.

The Russian Futurists have equal claims to innovation in these activities, but were overshadowed by the Italians in their own time and for long afterwards when Russian and Soviet radical art disappeared from art historical view. The Italian version was the model for all later art groups founded on a signed, collective statement of intent. Many admired too the general idea of the rebel artist restyled by Futurism, but few took up its strident machismo and war-fever. Such ideas had wider currency in literature than the visual arts, some linked to Futurism (Wyndham Lewis) and others to Expressionism (Ernst Junger). But the discovery of the self-willed and self-publicising group was instrumental for artists in a period when private patronage had collapsed, state patronage was hidebound and the gallery market an infant.

The make-up of explosive, eccentric and uneven talents in the Futurist group, even its mix of avant-garde and kitsch, resembles very early Hollywood – another cluster of ambitious adventurers using spontaniety, publicity and the machine to create a new art. Certainly the Futurists saw the cinema as a vivid, popular and dynamic metaphor for the age, and an 'autonomous art' as they called it in the 1916 manifesto, *The Futurist Cinema*. Deploring its conventional use as 'theatre without words' (as yet), they claimed that 'the cinema, being essentially visual, must above all fulfil the evolution of painting, detach itself from reality, from photography, from the graceful and solemn. It must become anti-graceful, deforming, impressionistic, synthetic, dynamic, free.' They boldly concluded: 'ONE MUST FREE THE CINEMA AS AN EXPRESSIVE MEDIUM.'

The Futurists were the first modern artists who wanted to make films themselves, as well as among the first to design sets for early 'avant-garde narrative' films such as *Thais* (1916) by Bragaglia. The graphic sets in early art cinema gave an outlet to Futurism's symbolist and even expressionistic side, but very little to its machine-age aesthetic. The inventors of noise-music and automatic art therefore tried to make films of their own. How much they achieved has to be surmised from spare accounts, a few stills and written scripts. But once again, they set a precedent for the avant-garde film to come, for these first experiments were free in style and collaboratively made. The writers played in their own films and enlisted their friends to take other roles. Productions were cheap and unfussy. Stories were minimal enough to prefigure the early films of Vito Acconci, William Wegman and Bruce Nauman in the 1960s, as in a love-story between the painter Balla and a chair, or a 'discussion between boxing-gloves' from Ginna's 1916 *Vita Futurista*. Some of the Futurist films had such story-lines, or more conventional ones, but already there were suggestions that the art of film could go further into abstraction.

Abstract film

The early avant-garde followed two basic routes. One invoked the neo-Impressionists' claim that a painting, before all else, is a flat surface covered with colour; similarly, the avant-garde implied, a film was a strip of transparent material that ran through a projector. The critic and art dealer Daniel-Henri Kahnweiler recalls that the making of an abstract handpainted film was debated among the cubists around 1912,[78] and opened the way to Survage's designs for his abstract film. But even these were preceded by the experiments of the Futurist artists (and brothers) Ginna and Corra, who handpainted raw film as early as 1910 and wrote up the results as *Abstract Film – Chromatic Music* in 1912. The films do not themselves survive, but written notes do, so a tentative reconstruction can be made of these colour sketches. The first begins with a green colour-field. Then a small red star spreads tentacles which cover the screen, until green dots return to absorb the red and return the screen to the original colour. The film lasts one minute. Two further and more elaborate episodes follow, one based on a play of three colours and another on the seven colours of the solar spectrum in the form of small cubes.

Handpainted film is better known for its independent rediscovery – and first surviving examples – in the mid-1930s, when Len Lye made *Colour Box* (1935) for the Post Office film unit, and when Norman McLaren made his first films in Glasgow.[79] Both needed to work cheaply, Lye because he had promised his boss John Grierson a film for £5, and McLaren because he was an art student who only had old junked films from which he stripped the emulsion to work on (much as Ginna and Corra had done in 1910). Later still handpainting and its cousin frame-printing were to be considerable sub-genres in avant-garde film, notably with Harry Smith in the USA from the late 1940s through to Vera Neubauer, Kayla Parker and Stuart Hilton in more recent British work.

The handpainted film is a primal means of film-making, hence the early interest shown by cubist and Futurist painters in extending a traditional medium to a new format. There are two options: the first to paint straight down the transparent filmstrip and allow the projector to impose the frames which give the impression of movement; and the second to divide the strip into frames and paint each one as a separate unit. The process can be reversed – for example, by gouging into an emulsion base rather than painting onto clear film to make shapes and patterns – or further refined by using an optical printer to reprint selected frames and sequences and thus to extend or repeat the drawn images. Lye was to use all of these methods, from the complex colour film *Trade Tattoo* in 1937 to his simplest final works like *Free Radicals*, released in the 1970s and scratched frame by frame to synchronised sound.

The abstract films designed by Gina–Corra and Survage called for sophisticated colour effects which look to tinting and toning of the print as well as directly painting on the original strip. These experiments were hampered by the very limited access which artists had to film equipment and technology. Early experimental film-makers learnt these things by trial and error, and it is not surprising to find that the first outlines for abstract films were sometimes confused about technique, especially in the earliest period around 1909–13 but also into the 1920s. In fact the first fully achieved abstract films after the First World War were not made by direct painting but by adapting the animation process. Here separate drawings or paintings are shot by single-framing them on a rostrum or bench. The drawings are translated into film form with the intervention of the camera, a more sophisticated process. The continuing appeal of handpainting, however, was that it made possible the direct, camera-less film.

It was through animation that abstract film dominated the German avant-garde from 1919–25, stripping the image to pure graphic form with a post-cubist variation of squares, curves and rectangles, sometimes handcoloured and accompanied by adapted or composed sound played live or on disc. This led to a modernist variant of synaesthesia, purging the screen of overt human action while developing rhythmic interaction of basic symbols (square, circle, triangle) in which music replaces narrative as a master code. An early vision of this 'Plastic Art in Motion' is found in Ricciotto Canudo's 1911 essay *The Birth of a Sixth Art*,[80] an inspired if volatile amalgam of Nietzsche, high drama and Futurist machine dynamism.

The comic burlesque

Abstract film was one route by which artists were to engage with the new medium. A second direction led artists to burlesque or parody films which draw on the primitive magic and slapstick film, notably Méliès, before (as many modernists believed) it was sullied by realism. A return to the style of early film drama has characterised much avant-garde narrative ever since. At the same time these films are documents of the art movements which gave rise to them, with roles played by

– among others – Man Ray, Marcel Duchamp, Erik Satie and Francis Picabia (*Entr'acte*, 1924) and Eisenstein, Len Lye and Hans Richter (*Everyday*, 1929). The ironic humour of modernism was expressed in such films (some now lost) as *Vita Futurista* (1916), which starred Marinetti and many others, its Russian counterpart *Drama of the Futurist Cabaret* (1913), its successors in *Glumov's Diary* (Eisenstein, 1923) and Mayakovsky's comic-guignol films, and such later elaborations of cultural slapstick as Clair's classic *Entr'acte* (1924) and Hans Richter's dark comedy *Ghosts Before Noon* (*Vormittagspuk)* (1928). This genre was explored mostly in the Dada and surrealist tradition, which valued dream-like 'trans-sense' irrationality as the key trope of film montage and camera image.

Arguably the avant-garde story film later in the century was founded in the comic and burlesque mode of the artists' cinema from 1913 to the late 1920s. The tradition lived on in the Freudian comic-dramas of Sidney Peterson and James Broughton in the 1950s through to the underground. Even Maya Deren – who aspired to make film into a high and poetic art – praised the slapstick genre of the Keystone Cops as a uniquely cinematic invention and inspiration. Artists remembered Méliès when he was otherwise forgotten. The surrealists were instrumental in passing on the comic tradition of cinema, which figures large in their famous film-lists to 'Do See' and 'Don't See'.

The early film in general, often but not only in its comic side, was to exert a strong influence on the avant-garde. There were two main reasons why the comic burlesque continued to appeal to film-makers. Firstly, it unchained film drama from narrative logic, showing that drama need not pass through realism. It opened the way to parody and to an irrational-comic style, linked to the surrealists' insight into Freud's analysis of wit and jokes as agents of the unconscious and of subversion. Secondly, the magic and early comedy film revelled in film-making devices which realist film largely excluded, such as stop-frame motion and variable speeds. These were markers of 'the road not taken' by the mainstream, but of great interest to film-makers working in basic ways and formats.

The Art Cinema and its circuit

An alternative route to the cinema as an art form (the specific meaning of which overrides the general sense in which all cinema is an art) ran parallel to the artists' avant-garde from *c.* 1912–30 and sometimes overlapped with it. This was the Art Cinema, or the narrative avant-garde as it has been termed by Richard Abel to distinguish it from the artists' avant-garde with its direct origins in cubism and Futurism.[81] It is hard to draw firm lines here, for the very good reason that they did not exist at the time. Individuals moved between the two camps, ideas were exchanged between them, and they were collectively seen as part of a new cinema outside the commercial genres.

The Art Cinema or narrative avant-garde was diverse and multinational. Its admiration for American films was tempered by a fear of Hollywood's domination of the world market, and throughout the inter-war period it took part in attempts to protect the European industry though trade agreements and regulation. America itself found it hard to sustain a cinema outside the powerful industrial sector; US enthusiasts for experimental film found themselves in the unusual position of looking to Europe and beyond for information in the 1920s and 30s. The Art Cinema included such movements as German Expressionism (with *The Cabinet of Dr Caligari*, 1919, and *The Golem*, 1920), the Soviet school of Eisenstein, Pudovkin, Kuleshov and Shub, the French 'Impressionists' such as Louis Delluc, Jean Epstein and Germaine Dulac, the Japanese director Kinugasa, and independent directors such as Gance, Murnau and Dreyer. Like the 'artist' film-makers, they resisted the commercial film in favour of a cultural cinema to equal the other arts in seriousness and depth. In the silent era, with few language barriers, these highly visual films had as international an audience as the Hollywood-led mainstream they opposed. There were many differences, some only seen in hindsight, between this cinema and the artists' film, especially in the question of feature-length drama and literary values. The divisions of later times were, however, blurred for the first generation of film artists and their supporters.

Art Cinema directors were able to take advantage of theatrical release and distribution through national agencies (as with the Soviets) and 'cultural' organisations, as well as through their financial backers. They drew the attention of serious critical writing which backed their cultural circulation. But nearly every art film was a one-off production, rarely backed (except notably in Soviet Russia) by a studio structure. Making Art Cinema was a precarious business even when the distribution chain gave such films a relatively long life which experimental films often lacked. Such films as Eggeling's *Diagonal Symphony* and Lye's *Tusalava* seem to have had one screening each, in 1925 and 1930 respectively, and then waited another twenty or thirty years to be seen again. Hence the importance of the film clubs and societies such as those in Paris, London, Berlin and Warsaw, which made up a non-commercial screening circuit for 'artistic' films of all kinds. These supplemented the small number of arthouse circuits in some major cities, a few of which survive today as repertory cinemas.

With such limited and fragmentary distribution, the dissemination of the avant-garde and the Art Cinema largely relied on the art journals of the period. These were legion, although – as today – many of them published no more than one or two issues. A few concentrated only on film, but at first the avant-garde film was publicised in radical art journals (*G*, *De Stijl*) associated with different factions within the Dada, constructivist and other modernist art movements. Later, there were such specialist magazines as the Swiss-based *Close-Up*,[82] the English *Film Art* and the American *Experimental Film*. French journals were in abundance, and included *Le Film*, *Le Journal de ciné-club*, *Cinéa* and *Le Gazette des septième arts*. Their overall tone was optimistic, their favourite theme the renovation of cinema through visual poetry, which was conceived as a bi-polar impulse sparked by abstraction on the one side and montage-editing on the other. These would enliven the mainstream fiction film, which they saw as prone to moralising kitsch and sentimentalism, and also create an independent film vision and culture on the artists' terms.

As important as the (rare enough) screenings and the energetic journalism of the period were a number of conferences and festivals which featured the avant-garde film. Some of these were 'closed' affairs such as the two famous gatherings of independent film-makers at La Sarraz and Lausanne in 1929 and 1930.[83] Others were pioneering trade shows and expositions, of which the most elaborate was the 'Film und Foto' Exhibition at Stuttgart in 1929. This gave rise to two important books published by the exhibition: *Here Comes the New Photography!* by Werner Graeff,[84] who was also a film-maker, and *Enemies of the Film Today, Friends of the Film Tomorrow* by Hans Richter. *Photo-Eye*, a selection of photographs edited by Franz Roh and Jan Tschichold, was a further spin-off from this show. The upbeat titles, like that of Epstein's *Bonjour, Cinéma* (1923), are absolutely characteristic of the time. Expanding on Epstein's elegant cubist-designed book, Graeff and Richter used the full array of modernist typography, including the photo-essay made up of stills or framestrips, to carry their message that a new way of seeing, based in cinema and the photo-eye, was on the move.

These events sometimes led to the commissioning of new films. An early trade fair, 'Kine-Foto' (1925), was promoted by the short promotional film *Kipho* directed by veteran cameraman Guido Seeber. An astonishing display of self-reflexive invention, in which the spectator is made aware of the act of watching the film itself, it features abstract light-play, split-screen effects, chronophotography and clips from Fritz Lang and others to underline the magic of film. At the same time, shots of young men and women with handheld cameras imply the democratisation of the new media – films made by all rather than the few. *Kipho* sums up the main visual tropes of the avant-garde of its time while heralding the 'promo' genre sixty years later.

Political unions of artists like the November Group in Weimar Germany also supported the new film, and French cine-clubs tried to raise independent production funds from screenings and rentals to plough back into making films such as *La Glace à trois faces* (*The Mirror Has Three Faces*), 1927, by Jean Epstein. Some artists funded their own films, as did Fernand Léger, while in France several important films – including *Blood of a Poet* by Jean Cocteau, *L'Age d'or* by Buñuel/Dali and *Mystères du château de Dés* by Man Ray – were commissioned in the late 1920s by the Comte de Noialles, a patron of modernism close to the surrealists. Len Lye, far from these circles in London during the late 1920s, and recently arrived on a cargo-boat from New Zealand, remembered 'living on fish-heads' for two years while making his first animated film – that same *Tusalava* which had a single screening in 1930 at the London Film Society.

Just as the Futurists laid out a rough grid for avant-garde film to follow, so too these mixed and haphazard funding systems, or improvisations, were to be the pattern for the rest of the century. Film-making is expensive and time-consuming, depending on a network of skills from shooting to editing and lab printing to eventual distribution. The basic choices were to acquire funds and loans in order to hire in experts, including actors, in addition to the usual crop of friends and bystanders willing to take roles. This was the route followed by Clair, Cocteau and Buñuel. It is the standard model for the 'narrative avant-garde' in general, but not only for that genre. Much later Maya Deren and Kenneth Anger – key figures for the US avant-garde – would use camera-operators and basic crews (but professional actors more rarely) in much the same way during the 1940s and 1950s.

The second choice, which appealed especially to painters and photographers with craft skills and a hands-on aesthetic, was to undertake as much single-person direct authorship as the medium allowed. Over time the growing availability of cameras and labs made this easier. At first, collaboration was needed even for the technically simplest film.[85] Man Ray and Fernand Léger made films with the aid of the American cameraman Dudley Murphy, who was eager to work with the new artists of the 1920s (a case can be made for Murphy's co-authorship of Léger's *Le Ballet mécanique*, as indeed the surviving credits announce). Marcel Duchamp worked with Man Ray and Marc Allegret, a young French cameraman, in the mid-1920s, at the same time as the American painter Charles Sheeler and the photographer Paul Strand joined in making the lyrical and observational *Manhatta* in 1921.[86] The period from Buñuel and Dali down to the 1950s has many examples of dual authorship: Bruguière and Blakeston, Watson and Webber, Alexeieff and Parker, Charles and Bebe Barron, and Charles and Ray Eames. Both traditions continue today. Some experimental films will use small crews or teams, assembled for professional or perhaps collectivist reasons. Others are as individually, or 'artisanally', made as films can be. Both lack the hallmarks of the extended drama film, whether arthouse or mainstream. Scripts and scenarios tend to be basic if they exist at all (although Griffith could claim the same for his early films), and production roles and methods are far more fluid and improvised. These impel the avant-garde film to experimentation and to the ascription of direct authorship, as with most of the contemporary arts but less obviously so in the feature or drama film.

For the first decade there were few firm lines drawn by enthusiasts for the 'artistic film' in a cluster of cine-clubs, journals, discussion groups and festivals, which even-handedly promoted all kinds of film experiment as well as minor, overlooked genres such as scientific films and cartoons which were similarly an alternative to the commercial fiction cinema. Many key figures crossed the divide between the narrative and poetic avant-gardes: Jean Vigo, Luis Buñuel, Germaine Dulac, Dziga Vertov, and Kenneth McPherson who edited *Close-Up* and co-directed the aptly-named *Borderline* (1930),[87] starring the poet H. D. (inventor of imagist poetry with Ezra Pound), the novelist Bryher, and the black American actor Paul Robeson.

The division between the narrative and poetic avant-gardes was never absolute, as seen in the careers of Buñuel and of Jean Vigo, especially in his two experimental documentaries *Taris* (1931) with its slowing of time and underwater shots, and the carnivalesque but also political film *À propos de Nice* (1930). Vigo's films were shot by the cameraman Mikhail Kaufman, brother of the Russian director Dziga Vertov. Vertov's own *Enthusiasm* (1930) reinvokes the Futurist idea of 'noise-music', has no commentary, and is unashamedly non-naturalistic despite its intended celebration of the Soviet Five Year Plan.[88]

Cine-poems and lyric abstraction

The idea of the avant-garde or 'art film' in Europe and the USA linked the many factions opposed to mass cinema. At the same time the rise of narrative, psychological realism in the maturing Art Cinema led to its gradual split from the anti-narrative artists' avant-garde, whose 'cine-poems' were closer to painting and sculpture than to the tradition of radical drama.

The short experimental films made by the Futurists around 1913 inaugurate the cine-poem. The Russian variant of Futurism usefully recalls that one of the major distinctions between prose and poetry was formulated in the circles of young linguists and literary critics which included Viktor Shklovsky and Roman Jakobson, both of whom were to be leading voices in defence of the new arts emerging in Russia just before the 1917 Revolution and which rose to prominence in the decade after it. In the West their thinking was paralleled by Ezra Pound and his group, initially as the Imagists around 1910/13 in London, who were similarly concerned to redefine for the modern age the traditional distinction between the continuity of prose and the fragmentation of poetry.

In Jakobson's now classic formulation, poetry and prose divide along a linguistic axis.[89] Prose is founded on metonymy, the elaboration of terms out of an initial series into further levels of description. Poetry is based in metaphor, in which terms from two series are set in contrast to each other. There are many versions of this distinction. Shklovsky's 1927 essay 'Poetry and Prose in the Cinema' states that prose and poetry in film are 'two different genres; they differ not in their rhythm – or rather, not only in their rhythm – but in the fact that in the cinema of poetry elements of form prevail over elements of meaning and it is they, rather than the meaning, which determine the composition.' Jakobson's own examples compare the prose of film drama (metonymic through the connective power of editing) to the poetry of comic film (metaphoric by the disjunctive option within editing).

Here the continuous flow of images which editing permits, and which is the basis of dramatic illusionism in film, is in contrast to the equal power of film editing to enforce breaks and interruptions in that flow. The first method is built on expectation, the flow from shot to shot which confirms 'what happens next', while the second is built on the sudden jump, on surprise, the element of unpredictability in humour. Obviously the two modes are not absolutely distinct – every drama film has its poetics, many avant-garde films incorporate narrative – but in some senses the role of experimental film was to push the distinction to its limits.

The poetry–prose distinction is a helpful guide to understanding the avant-garde project. In the widest perspective, the experimental cinema can be seen to expand the poetic art which the drama film subsumes in its drive to fiction. It has its haiku – short elliptical Japanese poems praised by Pound and his successors for a montage of sudden leaps between images – such as Deren's *A Study in Choreography for Camera* (1945), Baillie's *All My Life* (1963) and Kubelkas's *Adebar* (1957), as well as its epics, notably the large-scale films of Bruce Baillie, David Larcher and Michael Snow. Between them lie all the variants of poetic film form, from ambitious narratives to the random use of junk footage by the underground and punk film.

But Jakobson's dualist contrast of poetic metaphor and prose metonym is not rigid. Two early 'cine-poems' make the point. Henri Chomette, brother of René Clair but hardly known today (he was killed at thirty-one in 1927 when a war correspondent in Rabat), made his *Cinq minutes du cinéma pur* (or *Five Minutes of Pure Cinema*) in 1925/6.[90] Much in the spirit of the first travelogues, but taken to delirious extreme, the film is a high-speed tour of Paris. The camera literally 'shoots through' train tunnels, along the river and roads and back to railway tracks, all without pause. In one sense the film elaborates on the metonym of travel, linked by the continuous flow of the tracking camera, and is therefore prose. In another respect it plays on the metaphor of vision, by cutting across disjunctive spaces with the camera-eye, and is therefore a poem.

What really makes it a poem, however, is its stress on rhythm as an aspect of form, expressed both in variable shooting speeds and in the pace of cutting.

> Thanks to this rhythm [Chomette declared] the cinema can draw from itself a new power which, abandoning the logic of facts and the reality of objects, generates a succession of unfamiliar visions inconceivable outside the union of lens and moving filmstrip; intrinsic or pure cinema, separated from all other elements, dramatic or documentary.

Calling it a 'universal kaleidoscope' or 'generator of all moving vision' – and hence glancing to its roots in earlier scientific optics – Chomette asks 'Why should the cinema not create, with the domain of sound combined with that of light, pure rhythm and pure form?' This vision marks the difference between Chomette's film and a similar sequence in Clair's famous *Entr'acte* of 1924, where a runaway hearse is seemingly chased across city and country by more and more improbable pursuers, on foot, in cars, by boats and down a rollercoaster until they all disappear by camera trickery as Picabia waves a magic wand. Chomette's film, by contrast, reduces the narrative element to search for a 'pure cinema' free of the human touch (the chase, the story as frame, the all-seeing spectatorial eye) which is, of course, the charm and humour of Clair's absurdist Dada comedy. The film 'reduces' itself in order to focus on vision and rhythm as poetic and not dramatic facts.

Chomette's path, shared by other film-makers of the period, was to 'abstract from' the visible world in order to transform it. His *Jeux des réflets, de lumière et de la vitesse* (1923–5) is entirely composed of abstracted shots of water and reflected light, and applies to nature the photogenic eye with which Germaine Dulac – admired by Chomette for her notion of 'visual symphony' – observed the beauty of machines in *Etude cinégraphique sur une arabesque* (1929). This was to be a main tendency of the cine-poem; it no more abandoned referentiality than did the poems of Pound and Eliot or the paintings of Picasso and Braque. Rather it cast them in a new and arguably more material light, even as its theory tended to an opposite idealising direction.

Origins of abstract film[91]

The German abstract film was a switch-station in the alternating currents that flow from cubism and Dada to constructivism. A largely post-war movement, dedicated to rational abstraction, constructivist art emerges from mixed origins in the fertile epoch of early modernism. In the spring of 1914 the painters Kandinsky, Marc, Klee and Kubin took part in a theatre project led by Hugo Ball, then the young producer of Munich's Chamber Theatre and later the founder of Dada. Ball showed work by Klee and Kandinsky in 1917 at his Galerie Dada in Zurich. He lectured on Kandinsky with examples of work which the war had prevented from touring with the expressionist Der Sturm group in Berlin. Klee also exhibited in an expressionist context in Zurich during 1917, but his own direct contact with Dada came only later, in Munich during 1919/20.

The bio-mechanics of Lissitzky and Meyerhold around 1921, the *Dynamic of the City* of Moholy-Nagy in 1921–2 and Schlemmer's abstract *Triadic Ballet* at the Bauhaus in 1922–3 all share roots in an earlier abstraction of the body undertaken in dance and theatre by Dalcroze, Laban and Adolphe Appia. This first movement, however, while it collectivistically saw theatre as free and unalienated space, was hostile to intellectualism. Some of its strands led to post-war Expressionism, notably through Bruno Taut and such 'fantastic' films as *The Golem*. It makes a late appearance in the symbolist prologue to Leni Riefenstahl's *Olympia*, shot by Bruno Ganz (a modernist cinematographer released from Nazi detention to film this sequence) and a Laban-esque dance of fire and water (a style by then absorbed into the state cult of the natural body, in part through the films of the former dancer Riefenstahl herself).

Other strands lead further east to revolutionary Russia, where Meyerhold proposed 'the cinefiction of theatre' and for which Léger illustrated Ehrenberg's *And Yet It Moved*, published in Berlin and Moscow in 1922. Kandinsky, in Russia from 1914 to 1921, was director of the theatre and film section of the state Department of Visual Art under its supremo Lunacharsky. The formalist circle produced theorised accounts of film language (barely known in the West until a half-century later). But despite plans and talk, and the industrial factory links which some exhorted, Russian artists made no experimental films of their own outside the national studio systems of the Russian Federation (later the Soviet Union). Freed from commercial restraint, while subject to official approval, the urge to experiment passed solely through the school of Soviet montage (Eisenstein, Kuleshov, Vertov, Dovzhenko) and its later rivals and heirs. The radicals were bolstered by the unexpected fame achieved by their films in the West, although both Eisenstein and Vertov were to be highly suspect in their independence. While there was no place for a Western-style artistic film avant-garde – which the Soviets themselves disdained, if Eisenstein's rejection of the abstract film is typical – the strict stylistics and determined documentarism of Shub and Vertov, as well as their battles with officialdom, form part of the avant-garde's broader history.

The German writer Robert Musil, in his 1925 'Notes towards a dramaturgy of film' inspired by Béla Balászs, claimed that film language 'curves away' from reality without ever losing it, so that it is 'a frontier between two worlds'. But just as in the early modernist poetics of Kruchenykh and Khlebnikov, pioneers of the Russian avant-garde who split word and sound from sense and reference to inaugurate 'concrete poetry', so too some film-makers turned to 'absolute' or non-referential abstraction. In this case their immediate model was the abstract painting of their time, itself partly inspired by the non-referential art of music.

The absolute film

This was the case around 1916/17 in a series of Chinese-style scroll-drawings made in Switzerland by the Swedish artist and Dadaist Viking Eggeling.[92] Himself the son of a musician and a minor painter in the style of the cubists and Derain, his sequential experiments began as investigations of the links between musical and pictorial harmony. He pursued this analogy in collaboration with fellow-Dadaist Hans Richter from 1918, leading to their first attempts to film their work in Germany around 1920. Then they quarrelled, and Richter turned to a more hard-edge geometrical style closer to Bauhaus constructivism. Eggeling worked on alone, assisted by a young Bauhaus student, Erna Niemeyer. He died in 1925 shortly after completing his *Diagonal Symphony*, which was premièred in the famous November Group presentation (Berlin, 1925) of abstract films by cubist, Dada and Bauhaus artists: Richter, Ruttmann, Léger, Clair and (with a 'light-play' projection work) Hirschfeld-Mack. After that, it was hardly seen again until its re-release by Richter (who had inherited many of Eggeling's scrolls and drawings) in the USA during the 1940s, probably cut to half or possibly a third of its original length.

The ten minutes which remain are unique in the history of abstract film. *Diagonal Symphony* bridges the two kinds of cine-poem of the 1920s and 1930s, the camera-eye films of Chomette and Dulac and the fully abstract films of the German group, although unlike either of these it is strictly flat and frontal. Its forms and shapes, while highly abstract, evoke musical patterns and notation just as they echo the early drawings of 1915–20 in which Eggeling derives abstract forms from the study of landscape. *Diagonal Symphony* is a delicate dissection of almost art deco tones and lines, its intuitive rationalism shaped by cubist art, Bergson's philosophy of duration and Kandinsky's theory of synaesthesia, all of which are referred to in Eggeling's written notes. Here too, Jakobson's dyad is suggestive but not exhaustive. The film metonymically plays on sequences of lines, curves and cones, all of which are introduced early in the film and systematically but not predictably varied until it ends. At the same time it articulates with great clarity its metaphoric relation to musical form through its visual systems of harmony, fusion and disjunction. The metaphor, or analogy, is made the stronger by Eggeling's insistence that his film be shown silent. And here too, as with Chomette, the poetics of the film crucially depend on its absolute control of form and rhythm, its serene velocity, shot with a single-frame animation camera.

Like Eggeling's work, the abstract films of Richter, Ruttmann and Fischinger were based on the concept of painting with motion, but also aspired towards the visual music implied in such titles as Richter's *Rhythmus* series (1921–4) and Ruttmann's *Opus I–IV* (1921–5).[93] Eggeling's *Diagonal Symphony* also announces a musical aspect in its title, as do such key figurative cine-poems as Dulac's *Thèmes et variations* 1928, Léger's *Ballet mécanique* and other films of the period. For the purely abstract (or 'absolute') film-makers, the musical analogy had a special resonance. This wing of the avant-garde was strongly idealist, and saw in film the utopian goal of a universal language of pure form, supported by the synaesthetic ideas expressed in Kandinsky's *On the Spiritual in Art*, which sought correspondences between the arts and the senses. In such key works as *Circles* (1932) and

Motion Painting (1947), Fischinger, the most popular and influential of the group, tellingly synchronised colour rhythms to the music of Wagner and Bach. Although Richter and Ruttmann made advertising films which drew from their abstract experiments, they saw their commercial work as a separate venture. Fischinger, however, used studio-production methods to create the most pleasurable films of the new abstract cinema. He embraced the pop classics and 'light music' as soundtracks which could open his films to wider non-specialist audiences, rather like Norman McLaren in the next generation of film artists. It is no surprise that he exerted a strong influence on Disney films, with which he was briefly associated after he moved to the USA in the 1930s, although to what degree is still unclear, especially in his troubled and brief employment on the production of *Fantasia*.

Fischinger's work was carefully preserved by the artist, his wife Elfriede and – in later years – the American curator William Moritz. He is one of the few abstract film-makers of his generation for whom there is a full archive.[94] Some experiments of the period, by Werner Graeff and Kurt Kranz among others in the Bauhaus circle, were never completed or are lost. Only Eggeling has so far attracted a full art-historical monograph (from his homeland, Sweden). The surviving work has been preserved by the film-makers or in archives. Even the relatively well-known and much-screened films of Richter and Ruttmann exist in varied versions.[95] A specially composed score for Ruttmann's *Opus* by Max Butting exists, but has rarely been played live and never recorded. Some archival prints bear traces of original colour, but the films of the period are generally now seen in monochrome prints without their original sound accompaniment. Léger and Richter often showed their early films in this form to the end of their lives, although Duchamp was more careful to track down unapproved variants of *Anémic cinéma* in circulation. Shorn of sound and colour,[96] the general effect has been to render these films perhaps even more austere than their makers intended (with the exception of Eggeling) although they have always been regarded as a 'peak' of pure film art since they first appeared in the 1920s.

Hans Richter's early abstract films from the *Rhythmus* series, mainly 1923–5, were reissued and re-edited over twenty years later by the film-maker after he emigrated to the USA. Others, such as *Vormittagspuk* (*Ghosts Before Noon*, 1928), acquired new soundtracks. What remains of the originals is enough to demonstrate the vitality of the early work, and his growing and rapid mastery of technique. The first stabs at the new abstract film, preserved in *Rhythmus 23*, are reassuringly rough-textured, as Richter works out a language of basic forms in screen space. Like the cubist painters he turns to cut-outs, graphics and drawing to create sequences of receding and expanding squares and rectangles. Interspersed with this sometimes 'raw' material are linear drawings which echo Eggeling's very different aesthetic of visual music and pure flatness. Like his contemporary Walter Ruttmann, Richter was more concerned to explore the visual dynamics of film. Both their styles are generally more robust and optical than Eggeling's, and they prefer regular clear basic shapes over his delicacy of line and diagonal matrix.

Tonal subtlety is more important to the abstract film than can easily be recognised on the 16mm and video copies which circulate today. Here again, Eggeling pursues a different goal. Influenced by cubist figurative painters like Derain (and perhaps Braque), and by Kandinsky's linear abstraction, he uses film as a medium to record drawing in time. He finds formal equivalents in film for post-cubist ideas. One of these is in the viewer's relation to the projected image. The angular plane in *Diagonal Symphony* reduces the viewer's 'human-centred' fantasy identification with the screen which broader, frontal shapes evoke (Ruttmann wittily plays on this to turn curves into dancing legs at the end of *Opus IV*).

A second formal equivalent taken from cubist drawing is the linear unfolding of small, tonal clusters which suggest the complementary relations sketched by Eggeling in his notebooks: open/closed, dark/light, etc. The carefully graded tonality, and the many kinds of line and form which are used, recall the complex armature of classic cubist art. This is all the more remarkable in that the film is achieved by moving cut-out silverfoil shapes rather than by direct drawing. It is shown in negative to emphasise white on black, so the film-maker had, as it were, to work in reverse tonalities when making the film, rather like a printmaker.

Of the early abstract film-makers, Walter Ruttmann was the most sustained and ambitious up to 1925. Trained as an architect and with professional animation skills, like Fischinger he exploited the technique of the industrial rostrum camera (whereas Richter and especially Eggeling set up makeshift devices in their studios). Ruttmann stands somewhere between Richter's purist constructivism of abstract signs and Fischinger's fully blown anthropomorphism in which shapes and sounds evoke human sensations. His work merges both of these modes. The overt 'narrative' in the sequence *Opus I–IV* is a battle or dance between curves and hard-edge forms such as triangles and rectangles. The Richter–Eggeling programme for a 'universal language', announced in 1919, was implicitly taken up by Ruttmann from 1921 when he embarked on his *Opus* series. Ruttmann shifted abstract film from the purely formal plane towards a 'universal symbolism' of music, myth and the body. These codes animate the forms in abstract play.

At the same time, the *Opus* series explores abstract form in film more thoroughly than did Ruttmann's co-pioneers. More assured in its grasp of screen geometry than most abstract films of the era, it decisively engages with off-screen space and the multi-layered plane. Ruttmann investigates rhythm with the same confidence, including slow and irregular pulsation where the general trend was to go for speed. The sequence ends with an optical display of horizontal flicker and vertical flow. It recalls the 'eye-opening' tropes of frames, windows and camera shutters with which Vertov – the former 'cubo-Futurist' – begins *Man with a Movie Camera* (1928).

Despite the promise of visual revelation with which the *Opus* films concludes, Ruttmann made no more abstract films after 1925. It was the high-point of the movement, which ends with Eggeling's death and the return of the repressed image in 'the new objectivity' and surrealism. The constructivist impulse was about to wane as the chief radical art language, and within a few years suffered both state repression (in Germany and the USSR) and rejection by the documentary-based political left. Ruttmann's later career falls into this history. The shift is symbolised in the opening shots of his now-classic documentary *Berlin* (1927), in which abstract shapes melt into railway tracks and disappear. Only the film's subtitle – 'Symphony of a Great City' – harks back to the musical aspiration of pure abstract film. The expressionist side of Ruttmann, seen in his 'Dream of Hawks' animation for Lang's *Kriemhild's Revenge* (1924), surfaces as melodrama crossed with the naturalism of his Italian co-production feature *Accaio*, made in the 1930s. He also worked with Leni Riefenstahl in Nazi Germany, and ended his career making state-sponsored and army training films before dying, probably in action, in 1945.

Fischinger alone of the German group pursued abstract animation throughout his career, which ended in the USA, when several other German film-makers turned away from this genre after the mid-1920s, partly because of economic pressure (there was minimal industrial support for the non-commercial abstract cinema) as well as shifts in taste. Richter, who also made fashion and advertising films, turned to lyric collage in *Filmstudie* (1926), mixing abstract and figurative shots in which superimposed floating eyeballs act as a metaphor for the viewer adrift in film space. His later films pioneer the surrealist psychodrama.

Cubism and popular film

While cubism sought a pictorial equivalent for the newly discovered instability of vision, the cinema was moving rapidly in the opposite direction. Far from abandoning narrative, it was encoding it. The 'primitive' sketches of the period 1895–1905 were succeeded by a new and more confidently realist handling of screen space and film acting. Subject-matter was expanded, plot and motivation were clarified through the fate of individuals. Most crucially, and in contrast to cubism's display of artifice, the new narrative cinema smoothed the traces of change in shot, angle of vision and action by the erasure-effect of 'invisible editing' to construct a continuous, imaginary flow.

Nevertheless cubism and cinema are clearly enough products of the same age and within a few years they were to mutually influence each other: Eisenstein derived the concept of montage as much from cubist collage as from the films of Griffith and Porter. At the same time, they face in opposite directions. Modern art was trying to expunge the literary and visual values which cinema was equally eager to incorporate and exploit (partly to improve its respectability and partly to expand its very language). These values were the basis of academic realism in painting, for example, which the early modernists had rejected: a unified visual field, a central human theme, emotional identification or empathy, illusionist surface.

Cubism heralded the broad modernism which welcomed technology and the mass age, and its openly hermetic aspects were tempered by combining painterly purism with motifs from street life and materials used by artisans. At the same time cubism shared with later European modernism a resistance to many cultural values embodied in its own favourite image of the new, the cinema, dominated then as now by Hollywood. While painters and designers could be fairly relaxed in their use of Americana, being independent at this time of its direct influence, the films of the post-cubist avant-garde are noticeably anti-Hollywood in form, style and production.

The avant-garde films influenced by cubism therefore joined with the European

Art Cinema and social documentary as points of defence against the market domination by the USA, each attempting to construct a model of film culture outside the categories of entertainment and the codes of fiction. Despite frequent eulogies of American cinema, of which the surrealists became deliberately the most delirious readers (lamenting the growing power of illusionism as film 'improved'), few surviving avant-garde films resemble these icons. Only slapstick, as in *Entr'acte* (1924), was directly copied from the American example, but this too has its roots tangled with Méliès and the primitive trick-film, which was as much a European as an American genre.

Dada and surrealist film

As has been described, in France some film-makers, such as Henri Chomette (René Clair's brother and author of short '*cinéma pur*' films), Delluc, and especially Germaine Dulac, were drawn to theories of 'the union of all the senses', finding an analogue for harmony, counterpoint and dissonance in the visual structures of montage editing. These were fundamental to the birth of the 'cine-poem', a genre also pursued by Storck and Ivens with a documentary twist which is traceable down to the early films of the aptly named 'Free Cinema' (UK) and 'New Wave' (France) in the 1950s and 1960s. But the surrealists in France during the 1920s rejected such attempts to 'impose' order and musical structure where they preferred to provoke contradiction and discontinuity. Perhaps they were made especially hostile by the collective name given to Dulac, Delluc and their followers, who were dubbed the 'Impressionists'.

Surrealism was, like Futurism before it, a fully fledged group of the kind which dominated modern art between the two world wars.[97] It had leaders, notably Louis Aragon, Paul Eluard and André Breton (the moving spirit, and by the end the only survivor of the triumvirate). It had too a quasi-party structure in which group loyalty bulked large, a series of journals, no less than two major manifestos and several minor ones, a theoretical position, political commitments initially to communism and then to Trotskyism, expulsions and heretics (Dali, Artaud, Bataille and many more) and, above all, a project – the overthrow of rational thought and of the barriers between art and life.

The movement was founded in 1924 from the debris of Dadaism. Both groups were directly linked to the devastating world war of 1914–18. Dada was a loose collection of artists who gathered in or around Zurich during 1916, some of them pacifists, others war-wounded or resisting conscription in their native countries.[98] Neutral Switzerland was their refuge, as it was for Lenin – who may have visited the famous dada nightclub, the Cabaret Voltaire – and the young Walter Benjamin, a friend and neighbour of Dada's prime mover Hugo Ball.

Ball's diary, published in 1927 as *Flight Out of Time*, records the rapid and explosive growth of Dada:[99] its improvised performances, its neo-Futurist magazines, its eclectic evenings at the Cabaret, its emphasis on chance and disorder, its invention of the simultaneous poem (random texts chanted, sung and shouted by several performers at once), its tactic of provocation. Dada, a nonsense or transsense word invented in 1916, was even more of a protest movement than the

Futurism which had in part inspired it. Ironically, the Futurists themselves were enthusiastic fighters in the war, which they saw as 'the apotheosis of the machine age'. In this they followed their own logic. Dada was their mirror; a mad art for a mad age.

There were, roughly speaking, two kinds of Dada, one more tough-minded than the other. At moments they merged, which was Dada's aim, but finally they split in two, which is when Ball withdrew from Dada activity. The softer side was drawn to pacifism and mysticism and, despite everything, to 'the demands of art'; it included Arp, Jansco, Eggeling and Ball himself. In Ball's case these concerns took an especially tormented form which led to religious conversion with his companion, the dancer Emmy Hennings. This branch of dada was connected to the Laban–Wigman school of Eurhythmic dance in the nearby colony of Ascona.[100] The harder side of Dada lay mostly with politicised radicals such as Richard Huelsenbeck and Wieland Hertzfelde who were soon to take part in the revolutionary uprisings and agitation in their native Germany between 1919 and the mid-1920s. As may be guessed, the ideas of Nietzsche – but in different aspects of his thought – lay deeply within both kinds of Dadaism. He too had acclaimed the birth of 'joyful irrationalism'.

It was in this milieu that Eggeling and Richter began to study the art of movement, which eventually led them to film. At first, film was simply the best (if as yet purely notional) means to articulate the unfolding rhythmic patterns which they drew out on scrolls – long rolls of paper, like ancient texts. For Eggeling, film stayed a means and not an end, an austere and purist position of great personal integrity. Richter, a more expansive artist, was however to become an influential and diverse maker of abstract and experimental films which explored the visual language of cinema, as well as one of the avant-garde's first chroniclers and historians. In 1919, with Europe still in turmoil, they published together a booklet on film as a potential 'universal language', to seek industrial and cultural sponsorship for their work. Amazingly enough, they succeeded; a German manufacturer lent Eggeling a camera for 'research purposes' and this enabled him to complete *Diagonal Symphony* over the next five years.

It would be inaccurate to call Eggeling and Richter's films 'Dadaist' except in the special historical sense outlined here, which leads back to their discussions and speculations in wartime Zurich within the Dada milieu. Just as the first 'cubist' films were only able to materialise many years after the event, notably in Léger's *Ballet mécanique* of 1924, so too it makes sense to see Eggeling and Richter in the broader context of abstract film and art from 1921 to 1925. For the authentic Dada flavour it is necessary to turn to René Clair and especially to Man Ray, who notably did not pass through Zurich or the Cabaret Voltaire. As an American he only arrived in Europe in 1921, just in time to take part in the post-war 'Paris Dada' manifestations led by Tristan Tzara (an original Zurich Dada) with the dynamic Francis Picabia and the 'eminence gris' of modern art, Marcel Duchamp. Both Picabia and Duchamp had spent the war years in the USA where they had participated in 'New York Dada', a more playful and ironic offspring of the original branch. Man Ray was, importantly, a photographer. He soon obtained one of the new 'amateur' cine-cameras, marketed in the wake of Europe's economic and social recovery.

Man Ray's first films, made on the cusp of Dada and the new surrealist group which was to supersede it, anticipate the next phase of film art in surrealism, even as they evoke a Dadaist anti-aesthetic.[101] The major films of the surrealists turned away from the retinal vision of form in movement – explored variously by the French 'Impressionists', the rapid cutting of Gance and L'Herbier, and the German abstract avant-garde – towards a more critical and contestatory cinema. Vision is made complex, connections between images are obscured, sense and meaning are questioned.

Man Ray's emblematic 1923 Dada film – its title *Return to Reason* evoking the parody of the enlightenment buried in the name *Cabaret Voltaire* – begins with photogrammed salt, pepper, tacks and sawblades printed on the filmstrip to assert film grain and surface. A fairground, shadows, the artist's studio and a mobile sculpture in double-exposure evoke visual space. The film ends, after three minutes, in a shot of a model filmed 'against the light', an allusion to painterly Impressionism, printed first in positive and then negative. Exploring film as indexical photogram (objects placed directly on the filmstrip), iconic image (representational shots of objects mainly in the artist's studio) and symbolic pictorial code (the nude as sexual and artistic image of desire), its Dada stamp is seen in its shape, which begins in flattened darkness and ends in the purely cinematic image of a figure turning in 'negative' space.

Return to Reason was an 'occasional' piece, assembled in one night, so Man Ray tells us, to fill out the programme for what turned out to be the last Paris Dada event before the dissolution of the group, 'The Evening of the Bearded Heart'. Man Ray's later film *Étoile de mer* (1928), loosely based on a script by the poet Robert Desnos, refuses the authority of 'the look' when a stippled lens adds opacity to an oblique tale of doomed love, lightly sketched in with punning intertitles and shots (a starfish attacked by scissors, a prison, a failed sexual encounter). Editing draws out the disjunction between shots rather than their continuity, a technique pursued in Man Ray's other films which imply a 'cinema of refusal' in the evenly paced and seemingly random sequences of *Emak Bakia* (1927) or repeated empty rooms in *Les Mystères du château de Dés* (1928).

While surrealist cinema is often understood as a search for the excessive and spectacular image (as in dream sequences modelled on surrealism, as in some films by Hitchcock), the group were in fact drawn to find the marvellous in the banal, which explains their fascination with Hollywood as well as their refusal to imitate it. Their technique of watching films has since become famous, moving from one cinema to the next and leaving in the middle of the show when they lost interest – a kind of cinematic channel-hopping only possible in the days of cheap movie-houses.

The surrealists' own films only rarely invoke the 'special effects' and high-grade illusions with which their name is often associated (these appear more often in directors influenced by them, such as Walerian Borowczyk, the Quay Brothers, Terry Gilliam and David Lynch). Surrealist visual hallmarks are, rather, a scathing documentary eye, 'trick-effects' in the simple and direct manner of their admired 'primitive' cinema (often made in the camera) and an avoidance of overt montage rhythm (seen as too seductive). Man Ray, Duchamp and Buñuel–Dali also encode post-Freudianism in ways which cannot be reduced to a triumphalist or uncritical masculinity. Images that evoke castration and loss are central to all the surrealist classic films, which resist any simple notion of (male) narrative pleasure.

Duchamp cerebrally evoked and subverted the abstract film in his ironically titled *Anémic cinéma* (1926), an anti-retinal film in which slowly turning spirals imply sexual motifs. These 'pure' images are intercut with words on rotating discs; the letters spell out scabrous and near-indecipherable puns (e.g. 'Inceste ou passion de famille, à coups trop tirés' – 'Incest or family passion, with too much stroking'; ' Avez vous déjà mis la moëlle de l'épée dans le poêle de l'aimée?' – 'Have you already put the marrow of the sword in the oven of your beloved?'). The word-play echoes Joyce's then current and likewise circular 'Work in Progress', *Finnegans Wake*. Less reductively than Duchamp, Man Ray's films also oppose passive 'visual pleasure' and the viewer's participation. In *Emak Bakia* montage is used to slow down or to repeat actions and objects which both invite and defy thematic connection (spirals, words and phrases, revolving doors and cartwheels, hands, gestures, fetish objects, light patterns). The tactic of the film is seemingly to frustrate narrative and elude the viewer's full grasp of the fantasies which film provokes. This austere but playful strategy challenges the rule of the eye in fiction film and the sense of cinematic plenitude it aims to construct.

Seen today the films of the surrealists have gained a certain 'patina' or perhaps 'aura', due to the sheer fame and continuing popularity of surrealism itself. Seen art-historically, in the context of museum and exhibition screenings, the films are documents of their epoch and of the surrealist movement as a whole, from which they cannot be disengaged. At the same time, and partly through this mixed circulation, they have a continuing half-life in contemporary culture and the mass media. Surrealism has a cult value in a variety of subcultures, from modern myth-and-magic (based on surrealism's appeal to the occult) to MTV. Surrealism is not only the most popular and widely known of all modern movements, but also one of the most influential on the fashion, advertising and cinema industries. To this extent it has long been 'recuperated'; Man Ray himself was a successful and stylish fashion photographer. And yet, in addition to its historic role and to its effect on mainstream and subcultures, it also exerts a powerful influence on new and contemporary art. American 'action painting' of the 1940s, European 'New Image' painting of the 1970s and the current heterogeneous art scene worldwide all have a surrealist dimension.

So too has much critical thought, especially when it passes through Lacan's revision of Freud. Here the connections are direct. Lacan was a friend and associate of the surrealists in the 1930s. His wife Sylvia Bataille (who stars in *The Seashell and Clergyman* by Dulac and Artaud, described below) was previously married to the dissident surrealist writer and thinker Georges Bataille. The intellectual direction taken by French thought in the post-war period, and especially since the 1960s, is permeated by this cultural milieu, which coincidentally includes Bataille's friend Walter Benjamin for whom surrealism was a central moment of modernity. To the extent that present-day art criticism still engages with the surrealist critique (notably in Rosalind Krauss, Hal Foster, Suzi Gablik and David Sylvester – a very diverse list of critics!), coupled with the seemingly evergreen allure of surrealism on the formation of young artists, it remains a living cultural force in a sense not true of the other art movements of its time.

Viewers may therefore encounter surrealist cinema in a variety of contexts: in museum repertory, as clips and quotes on TV, in mixed programmes of avant-garde film. In the following section some key surrealist films of the 1920s and 1930s are loosely linked with other French experimental or art films of the epoch to suggest some relations and differences between them in the growth of a radical approach to film language.

The French avant-garde 1924–32

Three major French films of the period – Clair's Dadaist *Entr'acte* (1924), Fernand Léger's cubist *Ballet mécanique* (1924) and Buñuel–Dali's surrealist *Un Chien andalou* (1928) – celebrate montage editing while also subverting its use as rhythmic vehicle for the all-seeing eye.[102] In *Entr'acte* the chase of a runaway hearse, a dizzying rollercoaster ride and the transformation of a ballerina into a bearded male in a tutu, all create visual jolts and enigmas, freed of narrative causality. *Ballet mécanique* rebuffs the forward flow of linear time, its sense of smooth progression, by loop-printing a sequence of a grinning washerwoman climbing steep stone steps, a Daumier-like contrast to Duchamp's elegantly photo-cinematic painting *Nude Descending a Staircase* of 1912, while the abstract shapes of machines are unusually slowed as well as speeded by montage.

Léger welcomed the film medium for its new vision of 'documentary facts'; his late-cubist concept of the image as an objective sign is underlined by the film's Chaplinesque titles and circular framing device – the film opens and closes by parodying romantic fiction (Katherine Murphy sniffs a rose in slow-motion). Marking off the film as an object suspended between two moments of frozen time was later used by Cocteau in *Blood of a Poet* (*Le Sang d'un poète*, 1932), where the action takes place between two shots of a falling chimney which open and close the film. The abrupt style of these films evokes earlier 'purer' cinema: farce in *Entr'acte*, Chaplin in *Ballet mécanique* and the primitive 'trick-film' in *Blood of a Poet*.

These and other avant-garde films all had music by modern composers – Satie, Auric, Honneger, Antheil – except *Un Chien andalou* which was played to gramophone recordings of Wagner and tangos. Few avant-garde films were shown silent, with the exception of the austere *Diagonal Symphony* for which Eggeling forbade sound. According to Richter they were even shown to popular jazz. The influence of early film was added to a Dada spirit of improvisation and admiration for the US cinema's moments of anti-naturalistic 'excess'. Contributors to a later high modernist aesthetic of which they – like Picasso and Braque – knew nothing at the time, these avant-garde films convey less an aspiration to purity of form than a desire to transgress (or reshape) the notion of form itself, theorised contemporaneously by Bataille in a dual critique of prose narrative and idealist abstraction. Their titles refer beyond the film medium: *Entr'acte* ('interlude') to theatre (it was premièred 'between the acts' of a Satie ballet), *Ballet mécanique* to dance and *Blood of a Poet* to literature – only *Un Chien andalou* remains the mysterious exception.

The oblique title of *Un Chien andalou* asserts its independence and intransigence. Arguably its major film and certainly its most influential, this stray dog of surrealism was in fact made before its young Spanish directors joined the official movement. A razor slicing an eye acts as an emblem for the attack on normative vision and the comfort of the spectator whose surrogate screen-eye is here assaulted. Painterly abstraction is undermined by the objective realism of the static, eye-level camera, while poetic-lyrical film is mocked by furiously dislocated and mismatched cuts which fracture space and time, a post-cubist montage style which questions the certainty of seeing. The film is punctuated by craftily inane intertitles – 'Sixteen Years Later' inserted within the same sequence, for example – to aim a further blow at the 'silent' cinema, mainstream or avant-garde, by a reduction to absurdity.

The widely known if deliberately mysterious 'symbolism' of the film – the hero's striped fetishes, his yoke of priests, donkeys and grand pianos, a woman's buttocks that dissolve into breasts, a death's-head moth and ants eating blood from a human hand – for long dominated critical discussion, but recent attention has turned to the structure of editing by which these images are achieved. The film constructs irrational spaces from its rooms, stairways and streets, distorting temporal sequence, while its two male leads disconcertingly resemble each other as their identities blur.

For most of its history, the avant-garde has produced the two kinds of film-making discussed here: short, oblique films in the tradition of Man Ray, and the abstract German films, which broadly set up a different space for viewing from narrative drama, in which stable perception is interrupted and non-identification of subject and image are aimed for. *Un Chien andalou* sets up another model, in which elements of narrative and acting arouse the spectator's psychological participation in plot or scene while at the same time distancing the viewer by disallowing empathy, meaning and closure; an image of the disassociated sensibility or 'double consciousness' praised by surrealism in its critique of naturalism.

Two further French films expand this strategy, which came with the sound film era and the end of the first phase of avant-garde film-making before the rise of Hitler: *L'Âge d'or* (1930) and *Blood of a Poet* (1932). Almost feature-length, these films (privately funded by the Vicomte de Noailles as successive birthday presents to his wife) link Cocteau's lucid classicism to surrealism's baroque mythopoeia. Both films ironise visual meaning in voice-over or by intertitles (made on the cusp of the sound era, they use both spoken as well as written text). Cocteau's voice raspingly satirises his Poet's obsession with fame and death ('Those who smash statues should beware of becoming one'), paralleled in the opening of *L'Âge d'or* by an intertitle 'lecture' on scorpions and later an attack on ancient and modern Rome; Buñuel links the fall of the classical age to his main target, Christianity (as when Christ and the disciples are seen leaving a chateau after, it is implied, a Sadean orgy). The film itself celebrates 'mad love'. A text written by the surrealists and signed by Aragon, Breton, Dali, Eluard, Peret, Tzara and others was issued at the first screening: *L'Âge d'or*, 'uncorrupted by plausibility', reveals 'the bankruptcy of our emotions, linked with the problem of capitalism'. The manifesto echoes Jean Vigo's endorsement of *Un Chien andalou*'s 'savage poetry' (also in 1930) as a film of 'social consciousness' which he gave in a speech to introduce a screening of the film. 'An Andalusian dog howls,' said Vigo. 'Who then is dead?'

The poet, artist and film-maker Jean Cocteau was scathingly attacked by the 'official' surrealists in his own time. He was both an unabashed aesthete and prominent in the post-war period for a classicist 'return to order' shared with Picasso and Stravinsky. Cocteau nonetheless shares much in common with surrealism, from the use of ironic symbolism to a sardonic wit. In his first film, *Blood of a Poet*, the poet-hero is first seen in a burlesque of eighteenth-century décor, drawing a portrait. The mouth of this image takes on a life of its own, calling for 'air, air' in the voice of the film's female lead, the photographer and pupil of Man Ray, Lee Miller.

Materialising as the poet's Muse, she leads him 'through the mirror' – in a spectacular trick-shot – to a series of encounters with archaic art, fake suicide, magic, ritual, voyeurism, opium and transvestisism. In his final adventure, he encounters a scene from his own past: a snowball fight in which his childhood self is killed. The poet finally dies on stage in front of an indifferent audience when he loses an emblematic game of cards. His transformation complete, the poet, crowned with laurels, enters the 'eternal glory' which he desires and which has so far eluded him; at the same time, it ambiguously fixes him forever in the image of the past and of tradition.

Cocteau's film finally affirms the redemptive power of the classic tradition, but the dissolution of the hero's personal identity also undermines the Western fixation on stability and repetition, asserting that any modern version of classicism was to be determinedly 'neo' rather than 'post'. It inaugurates a new genre in the avant-garde, the psychodrama, in which a central character undergoes a series of ritualised trials which typically end in either death or transfiguration. This subjectivist thematic had an especial appeal to American film-makers a decade later, with Cocteau's film in circulation through the US arthouse circuit. By then, Cocteau was embarking on the larger-scale art films which make up his 'second period' as a director. While many of them are as personal, emblematic and inventive (and as sarcastically funny) as *Blood of a Poet*, they are also more elaborate in scale and production values. This links them more closely to the films of Franju and to the post-war French Art Cinema than to the low-budget artists' avant-garde, although in another perspective Cocteau's entire film output over three decades makes up a distinct body of authored work.

Voice and vision in the pre-war avant-garde

The now legendary conflict between director Germaine Dulac and poet Antonin Artaud, over the making of *The Seashell and the Clergymen* (*La Coquille et le clergyman*, 1927) from his screenplay, focuses some key issues in avant-garde film.[103] The differences between them were manifest in the film and its reception. Often cast as a crude misogynistic attack by the surrealists on a famous woman filmmaker outside the movement, the issues were more complex. Artaud and Dulac began from different points on the modernist map and their divided principles gradually emerged as the film was being made.

Dulac made both abstract films such as *Étude cinégraphique sur un arabesque* (1929) and stylish narratives, of which the best known is the pioneering feminist work *Smiling Madame Beudet* (*La Souriante Madame Beudet*, 1923). These aspects of her work were linked by a theory of musical form, to 'express feelings through rhythms and suggestive harmonies'. Artaud opposed this aesthetic vehemently, along with representation itself. In his 'Theatre of Cruelty', Artaud foresaw the tearing down of barriers between public and stage, act and emotion, actor and mask. In film, he wrote in 1927, he wanted 'pure images' whose meanings would emerge, free of verbal associations, 'from the very impact of the images themselves'. The impact must be violent, 'a shock designed for the eyes, a shock founded, so to speak, on the very substance of the gaze' (*le regard*). (Coincidentally, Georges Bataille acted in *La Coquille*.) For Dulac too, film is 'impact', but typically its effect is 'ephemeral ..., analogous to that provoked by musical harmonies'. Dulac fluently explored film as dream-state (expressed in the dissolving superimpositions in *La Coquille*) and so heralded the psychodrama film, but Artaud wanted film only to keep the dream-state's most violent and shattering qualities, breaking the trance of vision.

La Coquille is a film of cinematic flow centred on an Oedipal clash between an older male ('the general'), a young priest and a desired woman. The Freudian scenario is near-literal as older and younger man chase the 'vanishing lady'. This play of desire is signalled in the subtly dream-like shifting of scene to scene. The film is located in imaginary and distorted space, but far from Artaud's hyper-aggressive view of film language, or counter-language. This is perhaps better reflected in the Buñuel–Dali *Un Chien andalou* of the following year which contains some of those images which Artaud describes, notably the 'shock designed for the eyes' in its most notorious 'cut', the slicing of an eye by a razor. But its ironies and parodies appear less suited to Artaud's deathly serious vision, which favours the grotesque over the slapstick and comic-absurd, both of which are at the core of Buñuel and Dali's masterpiece.

Here the avant-garde focused on the role of the spectator. The Artaud–Dulac conflict, which was expressed in two quite different visions of modernist cinema, is one of the starkest examples of aesthetic choices during the late 1920s. The issues are not always so clear-cut, but often overlap as the problems are worked out over a series of films and polemical essays. In the abstract film, analogies were sought with non-narrative arts to challenge cinema as a dramatic form, and this led to 'visual music' or 'painting in motion'. The German 'non-objective' film took this in one direction, the French 'Impressionists' in another. Both in their different ways sought a 'pure' cinema which stands to the narrative film as poetry does to prose. Insofar as surrealism rejected absolute abstract art, it promoted in painting a kind of dream-image or magic iconography – in Dali, Ernst, Tanguy – which for later critics such as Clement Greenberg revealed its literary bias and its anti-modernist streak; its favoured artists did not go through the crucible of cubism, which tried (it will be remembered) to 'pass beyond' literature, symbolism and illustration. But in cinema the surrealists took a harder line. Their major films (those made close to the movement if not from within it) resist the lure and pleasure of dream in favour of its more purely disruptive elements.

In Jean Goudal's 1925 surrealist account film-viewing is seen as akin to 'conscious hallucination', in which the body – undergoing 'temporary depersonalisation' – is robbed of 'its sense of its own existence'.[104] We are nothing more than two eyes riveted to ten metres of white screen, with a 'fixed' and 'guided gaze'. This forward-looking critique (only the size of the screen has changed) was taken further in Dali's *Abstract of a Critical History of the Cinema* (1932), which argues that film's 'sensory base' in 'rhythmic impression' leads it to the *bête noire* of harmony, defined as 'the refined product of abstraction', or idealisation, rooted in 'the rapid and continuous succession of film images, whose implicit neologism is directly proportional to a specifically generalising visual culture'. These directions of which he disapproves clearly include the abstract film of any kind as well as the narrative cinema. Countermanding this, Dali looks for 'the poetry of cinema' in 'a traumatic and violent disequilibrium veering towards concrete irrationality'.

The goal of radical discontinuity did not stop short at the visual image, variously seen as optical and illusory (as by Buñuel, whose weapon is disruptive montage) or as retinal and illusionist (as by Duchamp, who attacks it with the 'precision-optics' of his rotor-reliefs filmed in *Anémic cinéma*). The linguistic codes in film (written or spoken) were also employed, as in films by Man Ray, Buñuel and Duchamp which all play with punning or interruptive intertitles to open a gap between word, sign and object. The attack on naturalism continued into the sound era, notably in Buñuel's documentary on the Spanish poor *Las Hurdes* (*Land Without Bread*, 1932). Here the surrealist Pierre Unik's commentary – a seemingly authoritative 'voice-over' in the tradition of factual film – slowly undermines the realism of the images, questioning the depiction (and viewing) of its subjects by a chain of *non sequiturs* or by allusions to scenes which the crews – we are told – failed, neglected or refused to shoot. Lacunae open between voice, image and truth, just as the eye had been suddenly slashed in *Un Chien andalou*.

Paradoxically, the assault on the eye (or on the visual order) can be traced back to the 'study of optics' which Cézanne had recommended to painters at the dawn of modernism.[105] This was characteristically refined by Walter Benjamin in 1936, linking mass reproduction, the cinema and art: 'By its transforming function, the camera introduces us to unconscious optics as does psychoanalysis to unconscious impulses.' Benjamin was interested, like Richter – another member of the informal 'Brecht circle' – and the surrealists, in the power of shock to break the viewer's 'absent-minded' stare and induce self-conscious 'apperception'. A decade earlier Artaud had put the case *in extremis*, calling for a cinema that was a 'total reversal of values, a complete overthrow of optics, perspective and logic' – the reverse too of Cézanne's cherished hope for a 'logic of sensations'.

Unlike Artaud, for whom shock was visual, optical and physical ('founded on the very substance of the gaze'), Benjamin argued that cinema was uniquely determined by temporality and not by the image. His concept of shock is therefore expressed in terms of time: film is 'dynamite at a tenth of a second', which frees the spectator from the fixed space of the nineteeth century. It is the victory of the panorama and diorama, the arts of controlled light, over solid architecture. His position is close to Vertov's theory of montage, in which the gaps or 'intervals' between frames are as important as the frames and their contents in making up the shot.

The discontinuity principle underlies the avant-garde's key rhetorical figure, paratactic montage, which breaks the flow, or 'continuity', between shots and scenes, against the grain of narrative editing. Defined by Richter as 'an interruption of the context in which it is inserted', this form of montage first appeared in the avant-garde just as the mainstream was perfecting its narrative codes. Its purpose is counter-narrative, by linking dissonant images which resist habits of memory and perception to underline the film event as phenomenological and immediate. At one extreme of parataxis, rapid cutting – down to the single frame – disrupts the forward flow of linear time (as in the 'dance' of abstract shapes in *Ballet mécanique*).[106] At the other extreme, the film is treated as raw strip, frameless and blank, to be photogrammed by Man Ray or handpainted by Len Lye. Each option is a variation spun from the kaleidoscope of the modernist visual arts.

This diversity – reflected too in the search for non-commercial funding through patronage and self-help co-operatives – means that there is no single model of avant-garde film practice, which has variously been seen to relate to the mainstream as poetry does to prose, or music to drama, or painting to writing. None of these suggestive analogies is exhaustive, in part because of the avant-garde's own insistence that film is a specific if compound medium, whether basically 'photogenic' (as Epstein and others believed) or 'durational' (film was firstly defined as 'time-based' by Walter Ruttmann in 1919). The modernist credo that art is a language brought the early avant-gardes close to Kuleshov ('the shot is a sign'), to Eisensteinian montage, and to Vertov's 'theory of intervals' in which the gaps between shots – like silences in post-serial music – are equal in value to the shots themselves.

A very special sense of opticality was developed during the 1920s by the first avant-garde. In attenuated form it has survived among many later groups of filmmakers. It does not simply *reject* the visual, nor the pleasure of sight, but insists on sieving or filtering the sense of vision through the material constraints of the medium. This is one of the reasons why the experimental cinema can be seen as medium-specific, as long as it understood that the medium is not the same as the technology of film. To take two terms from painting as a metaphor, the medium is equivalent to the surface, or what is presented, while the technology is the support, or the means of production. The implication of the one through the other is the core of what artists and critics have called the materiality of the medium, and which some are still concerned to elicit even as the digitalisation of the image questions the lucidity of the distinction. And this is yet another manifestation of what Lucy Lippard in 1977 referred to as the dematerialisation of the art object. By focusing on absence (gaps between frames, breaks between shots, disjunctions in editing and nonsynchronous sound) rather than the illusion of presence which these phenomena can also yield, the historic avant-gardes passed a complex legacy of ideas to later movements in film, video and digital art. These ideas were manifested not only in the advanced texts of Benjamin, Eisenstein, Brecht, Artaud, Dali and others, but in a series of films which are aesthetically and philosophically inexhaustible.

Transition: into the 1930s and documentary

Many of the 'extended' avant-garde films of the later 1920s and early 1930s had integral soundtracks. Experimental sound, modernist music scores and minimal synchronised speech in these films expanded the call for a non-naturalistic sound cinema in Eisenstein's and Pudovkin's 1928 manifesto and explored by Vertov's *Enthusiasm* (1930) and Ruttmann's *Symphony of the World* (1930). This direction was soon blocked by the popularity and realism of the commercial sound film. Background music and synched speech were prime contributors to this new naturalism of the mainstream feature film, exactly as the Soviet directors and the surrealists had predicted and lamented. An important branch of the avant-garde defended the silent – hence purely visual – cinema for many years to come. The birth of the sound film also of course led to a new branch of specialist technical production and to higher financing. Rising costs of film-making and the limited circulation of avant-garde films contributed to their decline in this period.

Such problems were not simply economic, but also political.[107] The broadly leftist politics of the avant-garde – both surrealists and abstract constructivists had complex links to communist and socialist organisations – were increasingly strained under two reciprocal policies which dominated the 1930s: the growth of German nationalism under Hitler from 1933 and the 'popular front' opposition to Fascism which rose belatedly, under Moscow's lead, in 1935. The attack on 'excessive' art and the avant-garde in favour of popular 'realism' were soon to close down the international co-operation which made possible German–Soviet co-productions like Piscator's formally experimental montage-film *Revolt of The Fishermen* (1935) or Richter's first feature film *Metall* (abandoned in 1933 after the Nazi take-over). Radical Soviet film-makers as well as their 'cosmopolitan' allies abroad were forced into more normative directions.

The more politicised film-makers recognised this themselves in the second international avant-garde conference held in Belgium in 1930. The first more famous congress in 1929 at La Sarraz, Switzerland, at which Eisenstein, Balászs, Moussinac, Montagu, Cavalcanti, Richter and Ruttmann were present, had endorsed the need for aesthetic and formal experiment as part of a still growing movement to turn 'enemies of the film today' into 'friends of the film tomorrow', as Richter's optimistic 1929 book had affirmed. One year later the stress was put emphatically on political activism, Richter's 'social imperative': 'The age demands the documented fact', he claimed.

The first result of this was to shift avant-garde activity more directly into documentary. This genre, associated with political and social values, still encouraged experiment and was – despite claims for its objectivity – ripe for development of sound and image montage to construct new meanings. Finally, the documentary did not use actors or, if it did, they were not star vehicles. In the first full age of the film star, acting was one of the final barriers between the avant-garde and mainstream or arthouse cinema.

The documentary – usually used to expose social ills and (via state or corporate funding) propose remedies – attracted many European experimental film-makers, including Richter, Ivens and Storck. In the United States, where there was a small but volatile community of activists for the new film, alongside other modern developments in writing, painting and photography, the cause of a radical avant-garde was taken up by magazines such as *Experimental Film* and seeped into the New Deal films made with Pare Lorentz and Paul Strand (a modernist photographer since the time of *Camerawork*, New York Dada and his own early short film-poem *Manhatta*, made with Charles Sheeler).

In Europe, notably with John Grierson, Henri Storck and Joris Ivens, new fusions between experimental film and factual cinema were pioneered. Grierson's attempt to equate corporate patronage with creative production led him most famously to the GPO, celebrated as an emblem of modern social communications in the Auden–Britten–Coldstream montage section of *Night Mail* (1936), which ends with Grierson's voice intoning a night-time hymn to Glasgow – 'let them dream their dreams . . .'. His legacy is still hotly debated. For some Grierson compromised too far with his sponsors and especially with their statist and imperialist ambitions. Such critiques also focus on Grierson's realism, here cast as reactionary. An alternative view looks to his attack on commercialism and his championing of modern artists, poets and film-makers even when – as with Humphrey Jennings – they were too 'arty' for his own taste. On this account, Grierson's cinema was the British avant-garde movement of its time.

This is not solely a British issue – American and European documentarists faced similar conflicts under government or private sponsorship, as they do today. But certainly there was a peculiarly British dimension due to the reaction against 'élitist' modernism of the 1920s by a young generation of artists in the 1930s. They ranged from the social poets led by Auden to the 'apocalytics' headed by Dylan Thomas and George Barker. Eliot, Pound, Joyce, Stein, abstract art and serial music were, in different ways, found wanting. There were few abstract painters and sculptors, and even these (Moore, Hepworth, Nicolson) saw their sources in 'natural forms' and landscape. The novel especially swung against modernist experimentation, in Graham Greene, Evelyn Waugh and Aldous Huxley.

But 'Grierson's gang', which agreed with this general trend, and indeed took part in it, also breached it. This was for two reasons. The first was their belief that film's language was basically montage, which came directly from the theory and practice – and, on occasional visits, the person – of an arch-modernist, Eisenstein. Grierson, who cut in the English intertitles for *The Battleship Potemkin* when it was shown in London in 1928, said that he learnt editing by studying this film. Secondly, they were inspired by figures such as Brecht, Weill and Eisler – then in exile from Nazi Germany – who similarly tempered 'abstract' modernism with social art and who were strong anti-realists. Added together, these radical and international connections were points of resistance to a 'little Englander' rejection of modernism.

Many of Grierson's productions were indeed standard enough, centred on the role of the post office. Others more ambitiously anticipate the forms of TV drama and documentary to come (the first TV broadcasts in the UK were made in this period, 1928–36). Of these the most hard-hitting was made independently (funded by a gas corporation) by Edgar Anstey, *Housing Problems* (1935). Cumbersome sound trucks were taken to London's East End to record people's stories, spoken directly to the camera, of poverty in the rat-infested slums. The film mixes interviews, documentary shooting and studio models (of improved estates) with a social punch which is still the basic strategy of TV reportage. It recalls such European radical social films as Buñuel's *Land Without Bread* (1934) and Ivens's *Misères aux Borinage* (1929).

The most famous of British artist-documentarists, Humphrey Jennings, did not easily fit Grierson's earthy approach to film: his major works, mostly edited with

Stewart McAllister (another ex-painter from Glasgow School of Art, like McLaren), were made in wartime for the Crown Film Unit after Grierson's departure to North America. But he did complete *Spare Time* (1939) for the GPO, with a laconic commentary written and read by the poet Laurie Lee, only recently returned from the Spanish Civil War. This short study of three British regions focuses less on their industries than on 'what people do with their leisure – the time they call their own', from cycling, strolling, drinking and choral singing to playing the kazoo. *Spare Time* has always been an enigma. For many, including Grierson, it seems to sneer at its subjects from a smugly élitist high angle; for others it is an intensely observed, emblematic celebration of dailiness and the submerged magic of ordinary events. It can't be both; but which? Fittingly, Jennings was a member of the English surrealist group with Roger Roughton, Herbert Read, David Gascoyne and Charles Madge. Here again, the radicalism of continental Europe – suitably naturalised – approaches the core of British culture by feeding in from the margins.

In a comparable but distinct category is a film like *Coalface* (1935). Here the theme is fully industrial. The work of British miners, and their living conditions, are seen – with the aid of maps, diagrams and chanted statistical information – and also questioned. Its stance is not neutral. It does not flinch from details of working hours, poverty, injury and death rates. With sound by Benjamin Britten and a poetic choral text by W. H. Auden (both still in their twenties), this is the most indebted of the GPO films to the radical and 'Brechtian' ethos. Again the European link is direct, for it was directed (or primarily assembled from existing footage, some of it shot by Flaherty for *Industrial Britain* in 1931) by Alberto Cavalcanti. Grierson invited the young Brazilian director to join his team after Cavalcanti had completed such films as *Rien que les heures* (1926).

Alberto Cavalcanti and Len Lye were hired to bring new ideas and techniques to the documentary movement. Lye's uncompromising career as a film-maker, almost always for state and business patrons, showed the survival of sponsored funding for the arts in Europe and the USA in the Depression years. His cheap and cheerfully handmade colour experiments of the period treat their overt subjects – parcel deliveries in the wholly abstract *Colour Box* (1935), early posting in *Trade Tattoo* (1937) – with a light touch; the films celebrate the pleasures of pure colour (including technicolor) and rhythmic sound-picture montage. The loss of Grierson, Lye and Norman McLaren to North America after the 1940s marked the end of this period of collaboration.

Reviewing the first avant-garde

Cubism had set the tone of later modernisms by stressing that the role of process in art was as important as the result and should be indicated in the work. At the same time, the work was to be autonomous and non-mimetic (i.e. 'pure') to resist final interpretation through logic or verbal language. The emphasis on surface and form was attacked by surrealists as mere formalism. Cubist collage was given new content in the chance-based methods of the Dadaist Jean Arp or in the cut-up dream montage of 'Dada-Max' Ernst. A sense of process was thus preserved in collage, automatic writing and chance procedures, all of which distinguished the surrealists from the 'return to order' and classicism during the 1920s. The surrealists, for whom the formal autonomous image was anathema, proposed instead to seek the 'marvellous'. By this they meant an image (better found than made) which was rich and disturbing in its associations but was severed from rational meaning. The film still, detached from its context and rendered enigmatic, was a rich source of these. Plucking images from their context to reveal a latent and unintentional magic was like the cinema of mind created by the surrealist drifting from one movie-house to another.

A mutual enthusiasm for the new film linked apparently diverse movements such as Dada and constructivism, and indeed the surrealists. Unexpected fusions between these groups appeared in the European borderlands such as Hungary, Holland, Czechoslovakia and especially Poland.[108] Even the supposedly unified constructivist movement was made up of distinct traits, from extreme rationalism to theosophy. It included the Russian factory-based productivists, the theory of 'cinematology' (Malevich), the proto-structural films of Charles Dekeukelaire in Belgium, the Dada-flavoured films of Stefan and Franciszka Themerson (whose *Adventures of a Good Citizen*, 1937, inspired Polanski's 1957 surreal *Two Men and a Wardrobe*), the abstract film *Black-Grey-White* (1930) by László Moholy-Nagy as well as his later documentary shorts (several, like a portrait of Lubetkin's London Zoo, made in England), the semiotic film projects of the young Polish architect and political activist Mieczysław Szczuka and the light-play experiments of the Bauhaus.

For these and other artists film-making was an additional activity to their work in other media. Poland had an especially thriving film culture, in the main provincial cities as well as in Warsaw. Film clubs and groups for the 'artistic film' grew among enthusiasts for modern art. Polish modernism uniquely fused constructivism with Dada-surrealism, a vividly internationalist blend for the beleaguered inter-war years. This fusion of seemingly opposite artistic directions had a strongly social caste in an age of post-war rebuilding and industrialisation. Much activity centred on the 'constructive' role of architecture and the city theme, also the subject of several now-lost films. The range of screenings, published journals and film-making from the late 1920s to 1937/8 was rooted directly in the first era of the avant-garde, transmitted notably through figures like Eggeling's friend and contemporary, the Polish artist Henryk Berlewi.

It was probably through Berlewi, and the Western European art journals, that the leftist constructivist designer Mieczysław Szczuka was inspired to make his first drawings for an abstract film in 1925 (like Eggeling, using long scrolls). The film was never shot, for Szczuka's death at twenty-seven in a climbing accident prevented both this and a second project being realised. The later work was more ambitious and original, a semiotic play or permutation of three dramatically descriptive phrases ('I kill, you kill, we kill') which were to be seen in different typefaces and sizes. Well in advance of the 1970s structural film, it anticipates the 'word movies' of Sharits and Snow as well as the typographic imaginary of post-modernist design.

Key surviving films from this era include those by Stefan and Franciszka Themerson. Rooted in Dada-futurism, their early films were either sponsored commercials or promotional documentaries. Their influential *Adventures* carries a strong anti-war message. The 'good citizen', uncertain whether to go 'left' or 'right', overhears a foreman instructing two removal men to carry a wardrobe backwards – 'The sky won't fall if you walk backwards!' Inspired by this novel idea, the citizen encourages others to do the same. An angry crowd, offended by this unconventional gesture, chases them, but they escape to Parnassus in the skies. In a rare moment of synchronised sound, a pipe-player in a field then speaks directly to camera and says 'Ladies and Gentlemen, you must understand the metaphor.' This shot is followed by an image of a child crawling in the grass, which ends the film.

The Themersons' last films, made in wartime London, exemplify the playfully didactic spirit of the Polish group. *Calling Mr Smith*, 1944, is a propagandist attack on Nazi brutality, with highly manipulated colour and sound. *The Eye and the Ear*, 1945, by contrast is a lyrical evocation of synchronisation and counterpoint between musical and visual forms. In each of its four sections songs by the Polish modernist composer Szymanowski are explored though abstract photograms, graphic diagrams and photogenic camerawork. These films end the epoch emblematically, with a return to the origins of the abstract film in the 1920s. They embody the goal of a modernist synthesis in abstract art, and affirm a postsymbolist surrealism in the context of the social documentary. The Themersons' films, with typical modern infusions and influences from formal film, contemporary music, abstract art, complex notation, abstract graphics and direct address to the audience in voice-over, mark the close of this kind of vision of experimental film. Even the sponsored funding which made them possible was on the way out.

The inter-war period also closes emblematically with Richter's exile from Nazi-occupied Europe to the USA in 1940. Shortly before, he had completed his book *The Struggle for the Film*, in which he had praised both the classic avant-garde as well as primitive cinema and documentary film as opponents of mass cinema, seen as manipulative of its audience if also shot through (despite itself) with new visual ideas. In the USA Richter became archivist and historian of the experimental cinema in which he had played a large role, issuing (and re-editing, by most accounts) his own early films and Eggeling's. The famous 1946 San Francisco screenings 'Art in Cinema', which he co-organised, brought together the avant-garde classics with new films by Maya Deren, Sidney Peterson, Curtis Harrington and Kenneth Anger; an avant-garde renaissance at a a time when the movement was largely seen as obsolete.

Richter's influence on the new wave was limited but important. His own later films – such as *Dreams That Money Can Buy* (1944–7) – were long undervalued as baroque indulgences (with episodes directed by other exiles such as Man Ray, Duchamp, Léger, and Max Ernst) by contrast to the 'pure' and to a later generation more 'materialist' abstract films of the 1920s. Regarded at the time as 'archaic', *Dreams* now seems uncannily prescient of a contemporary post-modernist sensibility. David Lynch selected extracts from it, along with films by Vertov and Cocteau, for his 1986 BBC *Arena* film profile. Stylish key episodes include Duchamp's reworking of his spiral films and early paintings, themselves derived from cubism and chronophotography, with sound by John Cage. Léger contributes a playful skit on the act of viewing, in which a semi-hypnotised audience obeys increasingly absurd commands issued by the film they supposedly watch. Ernst's episode eroticises the face and body in extreme close-up and rich colour, looking ahead to today's 'cinema of the body' in experimental film and video. Richter's own classes in film-making at the New School for Social Research were attended by, among others, another recent immigrant Jonas Mekas, soon to be the energetic magus of the 'New American Cinema'.[109]

Two decades earlier, the avant-garde had time-shifted cubism and Dada into film history (both movements were essentially over by the time artists were able to make their own films). By the 1940s, a new avant-garde again performed a complex, overlapping loop, re-asserting internationalism and experimentation, at a time as vital for transatlantic art as early modernism had been for Richter's generation. Perhaps the key difference, as P. Adams Sitney argues, is that the first avant-garde had added film to the potential and traditional media at an artist's disposal, while new American (and soon European) film-makers after the Second World War began to see film-making more exclusively as an art form that could exist in its own right, so that the artist-film-maker could produce a body of work in that medium alone. Ironically, this generation also re-invented the silent film, defying the rise of naturalistic sound which had in part doomed its avant-garde ancestors in the 'poetic cinema' a decade before.

Origins of the post-war avant-garde

The avant-garde film movement before the Second World War was international in scope, although Europe was its cultural epicentre. From Paris, Berlin and Munich the idea of an abstract and surrealist cinema spread outwards to Holland, Belgium, Poland, Czechoslovakia, the USA, Britain and Japan. The rise of naturalistic sound cinema closed this chapter in modern art. The political strife of the 1930s also propelled radical film-makers away from purely artistic concerns towards the 'social imperative' of the documentary film.

European avant-garde film was reborn surprisingly soon after the war, in the 1950s, with the provocative neo-Dada of Fluxus, Lettrisme and Action-Art.[110] It was unexpected. Reviewing the French avant-garde of the 1920s for Roger Manvell's brave (but mostly historical) *Experiment in the Film* (1949), veteran cineaste Jacques Brunius praised it as a precursor of Clair and Renoir, but lamented its 'excesses' in the era of cinema's 'adolescence'. He saw no signs of a new emergent avant-garde, but only two years later, in 1951, the Lettriste poets Isidore Isou and Maurice Lemaitre, soon joined by Guy Debord, made their first films, described by Tony Rayns as 'a rediscovery of the founding spirit of Dada and surrealism in the years after the First World War'. Aggressive and physical, they reduce the screen to found footage, raw colour and bursts of black and white frames. 'Excessive' even in their length, these films answer Brunius' hopes and fears for a new avant-garde, as they reclaim the radical heritage of the first one.

As in the original *Cabaret Voltaire*, and for similar reasons, mockery and 'excess' were weapons of social and cultural protest. The post-war period, marked by violent decolonisation, the nuclear threat and the Korean War, was dubbed 'the age of anxiety'. But film as an aspect of 'bomb culture' was often defiantly marginal, even after the aptly named underground surfaced to public view in the 1960s. It was in this climate that (in Bürger's view) a neo-avant-garde was born. If, as many argue, this finally led modernism tamely into the museum, its radical aspirations safely defused, there were artists who resisted direct recuperation. Film, still a marginal medium for artists, was perhaps attractive for that very reason.

During the 1950s and early 1960s a small number of European radical artists used film as a medium in live performance or other events, and a small number explored its more 'minimal' properties. Post-Dada artists in Paris recycled 'treated' found-footage to undermine its original message and more formalist artists in Austria turned to experiment in basic sound, light and montage. These were important strands which in some ways lead straight to art today, where found-footage, installation and 'basic' video are much employed. But in sheer output and in eventual wider influence, these developments were overshadowed by the rise of the experimental film movement in the USA, beginning in the early 1940s. The American avant-garde is still the best known and most sustained example of all similar movements, and remains a paradigm for independent film-making.

It meant that the US took the lead role in avant-garde film, as it did with painting when New York replaced Paris as the cultural capital of modernism. As Abstract Expressionism triumphed in the 1940s, new waves of experimental film-makers began to explore film as an art form.[111] The Americans, in a climate of cultural growth, were more positive than the Europeans about their shared Dada–surrealist heritage. They wanted to make art, not abolish it. Their hallmark was personal vision, the basis of both the California-based abstract film and of the short film-poems made in the artists' colonies of Los Angeles, San Francisco and New York.

Many currents ran together to produce this extraordinary period. They comprise the wartime presence of modernist writers and artists from Europe, a new self-confidence, a need to emerge from Europe's shadow (once European modernism had been absorbed into the bloodstream), an economic boom, the availability of equipment and cameras, a generation of artists prepared by the public funding and commissioning of the Roosevelt years, and of course the model (or counter-model) of American Hollywood cinema as a leading home-grown industrial and cultural industry. At the same time, many of the films which were made did not directly reflect the optimism and 'new birth' which is such a strong feature of much post-war US art, dance and music. Often they were dark and parodic, as in the psychodrama, and expressed elemental fear and anxiety. The avant-garde in part was equivalent to 'film noir' articulation of these themes in narrative fiction, but in a strongly subjective mode and made by individuals outside the commercial sector.

This personal stance was as much material as ideological. Portable 16mm cameras with variable lenses and shooting speeds could be found on the war surplus and amateur film markets. Most major cities had laboratories and sources of film-stock. Cheap and flexible technology literally put the means of production in the film-maker's hands. As 16mm became the regular projection format in colleges, cine-clubs and arts groups, new circuits opened for the avant-garde. Like the live poetry readings which grew in this decade, film-makers often presented and discussed the films in person. At a time when auteur theory was controversially being applied to the mainstream, the avant-garde here underlined personal and direct authorship, and audience response, to challenge the regime of commercial cinema, from production to reception.

On the West Coast Oskar Fischinger presided over the revival of abstract *Motion Painting*, the title of his 1947 film. Like his fellow-exile Len Lye, his work became more purely absolute as his commercial career foundered (Fischinger's watershed crisis was seemingly Disney's rejection of his abstract designs for *Fantasia*). A handful of native pioneers also explored abstract animation.[112] They include the pioneer of electronic visual art Mary Ellen Bute, who made her first films in the 1930s, while Douglas Crockwell and Dwinnel Grant used wax and paint respectively to construct bio-organic abstractions from the 1940s. Harry Smith handpainted his early abstract films, while the Whitney brothers turned to technology and light-play experiment to explore Duchampian 'chance operations'.

Along with the revival of synaesthetic abstraction, US film-makers reinvented the narrative film-poem. The 'psychodrama' (or 'trance-film') was modelled on dream, lyric verse and contemporary dance. Typically, it enacts the personal conflicts of a central subject or protagonist. A scenario of desire and loss, seen from the point of view of a single guiding consciousness, ends either in redemption or death. Against the grain of realism, montage-editing evokes swift transitions in space and time. The subjective, fluid camera is more often a participant in the action than its neutral recording agent. Jean Epstein's theory of 'photogénie', itself an expansion of Louis Delluc's original concept, and which refers to the specific character of camera vision by which 'the camera transforms what it depicts', was as it were reinvented.

Narrative and abstract directions in the avant-garde have often coexisted, sometimes closely linked and at other times dividing. While abstract film can grow directly from an engagement with the plastic material of film and light projection, as it does for the basically 'painterly' tradition of cubism down to – in this context – Harry Smith and the Whitneys, avant-garde film narrative almost inevitably looks to non-painterly sources as well. For Deren and Anger these included anthropology and magical traditions as well as literature (Deren's college thesis was on Yeats and symbolist imagery). Other film-makers were poets and writers: Sidney Peterson, Willard Maas, Jonas Mekas. Brakhage, who broke most radically with narrative to inaugurate abstract montage, was strongly influenced by Pound and Stein on compression and repetition in language. Deren, Anger and Mekas were writers and journalists for much of their career, while Brakhage has published at length. The literary traditions which this generation absorbed were themselves 'cinematised'. As well as Pound, Eliot and the imagists, the key influence (on Peterson, for example) was probably Joyce. Among the proposed adaptations of his novel *Ulysses* (Eisenstein, Ruttmann and Ford were variously mooted as directors), the poet Louis Zukovsky prepared a full scenario in 1937.[113]

This new narrative avant-garde was symbolised in the now-classic *Meshes of the Afternoon* (1943) by Maya Deren and Alexander Hammid. Its Chinese-box narrative form entraps the young protagonist (played by Deren) as much as the disjointed domestic space around her. Both evoke her alienation. An emblematic knife and key elude her grasp. Actions are interrupted; a record plays in an empty room, a phone is off the hook. A fantasised pursuit of a glimpsed figure ends in violence, perhaps suicide. Erotic, and irredeemably Freudian (despite Deren's protestation at the label), the film combines its spiral structure with pictorialist camerawork and intricately crafted matte shots (as when the sleeping woman faces her other 'selves' who replicate within successive dreams). Both protagonist and spectator search for connecting threads, as the quest theme resonates equally in the film's subject-matter and its style.

The 1940s renaissance of film was part of a wider revolution in American culture. It included the rise of 'American-type' painting, in the sense defined by Clement Greenberg, of competing schools of post-Poundian poets and post-Joycean writers, and of the innovative Merce Cunningham and John Cage in dance and music. As Duchamp's associate (and film composer for his contribution to Richter's 1947 compilation film *Dreams*), Cage linked the European war *émigrés* with their younger US followers. He has a walk-on part in Deren's *At Land* (1944), while Duchamp appears in her uncompleted mid-40s 'feudal magic' film *Witches Cradle*, and her last work, *The Very Eye of Night* (1959), employs Antony Tudor's avant-garde choreography.

The mixture of the arts at this point was promiscuous rather than programmatic. If some Europeans were exploring the meltdown factor in mixed-media assemblage, the Americans wished less to blur the edges between the arts than to freely discover their limits. In this light the reappearance of film drama in a cultural milieu led by purely abstract art, music and dance is less aberrant than it looks. It rehearsed the old argument between film-as-painting and as camera-eye vision, each claiming to express film's unique property as a plastic art form. By turning to the poets and writers of experimental modernism – Pound, Eliot, Joyce, Stein – the film-makers distanced themselves from the direct drama and narrative tradition in realism. The climate, broadly, was surrealist and poetic.

Some film-makers (such as Harry Smith) moved between both modes, but many held to absolute non-figuration (like the Whitney brothers) which yet others saw as denying the camera's ability to depict 'the way things are' (Deren). For Deren, film had an objective aspect which the other arts innately lacked. At the same time, the manipulation of time and space was equally a property of film form, so that editing could undermine the surface realism of cinematography to create a new language that was film's alone.

If Cocteau laid down the paradigm for psychodrama in *The Blood of a Poet*, it was found useful by less sophisticated film-makers who used basic technology to make personal statements. Psychodrama often offers a sexual as well as mythic quest. In many films this has Oedipal overtones: the struggle between the mother and the diver-son in Peterson's *The Lead Shoes* (1949), the encounter between the searching woman and the bedridden patriarch in Deren's *At Land*, the self-blinded youth in Brakhage's *The Way to Shadow Garden* (1955). Such films turn to multiple devices which evoke splits in vision as divisions in the self (a triple matte-shot portrait of Deren in *Meshes of the Afternoon*; negative film used to evoke transcendence, by Brakhage and also by Deren in *Rituals in Transfigured Time*, 1949; the fish-eye lens to distort appearance, as by Peterson). Just as important are rapid edits to break the flow of events (*Mr Frenhofer and the Minotaur*; 1948 by Peterson; *A Study in Choreography for Camera* by Deren) and slow motion, widely used by all of these film-makers to evoke strangeness and to incarnate camera-vision.

All of these tropes are found in the classic films by Cocteau and Buñuel which were now recirculated in the USA. Deren denied their initial influence on her work, but it was largely her effectiveness as promotionist and distributor of artists' films which made them more widely seen. She founded the Film Artists Society (later the Independent Film Makers Association) in 1953, which met monthly until 1956. From 1955 to her death in 1961 she organised the Creative Film Foundation to try to secure grants for film-makers. Prints of Léger's and Duchamp's films had been acquired by the Museum of Modern Art under the curatorship of Iris Barry (an English-born devotee of Ezra Pound and an early member of the London Film Society). Hans Richter re-released versions of the early abstract films which he had brought to the USA from pre-war Germany. This network drew together – as in pre-war Europe, and sometimes with the same participants – the various strands of an art cinema opposed to purely commercial values. It survives today most directly in the collecting and screening policies of Anthology Film Archives, a linear descendent of the post-war revival.

When Abstract Expressionism was promoted as an all-American art in the 1950s – with some of its practitioners colluding in this guise – it obscured the European roots which bound Pollock, Gorky and others to modernism. Cubism and surrealism fused in the new art. In the same way the unique ascent of the American avant-garde film grew from these baselines. The cinematic language of 1920s Europe was reinvented and reshaped, as was the idea of an experimental film circuit and a vibrant journalism pioneered by Tyler, Deren and Mekas.

Many of the first US psychodramas refashion not just the style but also the manner of their predecessors. Classical figures, statues and motifs are mimed, post-Cocteau, in key films by Deren, Peterson, Markopoulos and Anger. As with all movements which aim for the new, such links to pre-war surrealism provoked charges that these films simply reran the past. Their real innovations, such as intense subjectivity and the incarnation of camera as viewpoint, took longer to emerge, largely when these devices were radicalised (or 'infantilised', as Parker Tyler put it) from 1958 to 1968.

Rejecting the refinement of myth in narrative psychodrama, an apparently cruder but more direct mythopoeaia emerges in the dressing-up and body-painting which are hallmarks of child-play regression in Austrian performance art, the American Jack Smith and the English collage film-maker Jeff Keen – burning dolls are an iconic feature of all their live-art performances. Ironically, these films were later still to influence the structural movement, which cared less for their transgressive values than their exuberant editing and key use of film-time.

The first period of post-war experimentation included films by Kenneth Anger, James Broughton, Curtis Harrington and Sidney Peterson. Their keynote was black humour and Oedipal crisis. The fleeing son of Harrington's *On the Edge* (1949) is literally hauled back to mother by her knitting yarn, while in Broughton's *Mother's Day* (1948) the roles of children are played by adults. Peterson's *The Lead Shoes* (1949) features a distorting anamorphic lens, a Californian Kali of a mother, her diver-suited son and a raucous 'scratch' rendition of old ballads ('What's that blood on the point of your knife, Edward?', chants a dissonant chorus). Peterson made the film with San Francisco art students who were also war veterans and survivors. Regressive play here embraces catharsis and release.

By contrast, the fantasy sailors of Anger's *Fireworks* (1947) who savagely beat its hero (played by the film-maker) are culled from Eisensteinian montage as well as the US Navy, to both of which the film pays homage along with 'American Christmas and being seventeen'. The film was shot silent at home (sound, as with most of Anger's films, was added later, usually to re-release a print). Classic cinema is invoked in close-up faces and noir-ish scenography, as when the hero stands smoking on a balcony at night, while a street light blinks in the background. Burning illumination leads the dreaming protagonist to trauma and death, from which he is redeemed by the seminal pouring of milk over his body and the showering of light from a phallic firework. The dreamer awakes to a new consciousness, still in bed but 'no longer alone'.

Marie Menken had already taken a crucial step to free the camera from the centralised human eye assumed by all narrative film, even the most radical psychodramas. In *Visual Variations on Noguchi* (1945) – originally planned to accompany the Cage–Cunningham ballet *The Seasons* – her handheld camera pans round an abstract sculpture to create an improvised dance in film space. Fluently bridging the abstract and the figurative, it seeks lyric form without narrative mediation. Her later experiments in the transformation of 'dailiness' by camera, light and pixillation are compiled in *Notebook* (1963). She and her husband Willard Maas are the models for Martha and George in Edward Albee's *Who's Afraid of Virginia Woolf?*, but 'the mother of the Underground' was also commemorated in Andy Warhol's *Chelsea Girls* (1966), in which she stars. Menken's liberation from film drama – unlike most of the avant-garde she was a painter, not a writer – inspired the young Stan Brakhage to adopt the free camerawork of his transitional *Anticipation of the Night* (1958).

Deren and Anger also moved away from psychodrama in the 1950s. Their films became more gestural and abstract. Both were drawn to magic and became experts on their founding myths, Haitian Voudoun for Deren and Aleister Crowley for Anger. However, their films were also rooted in a tradition which gave primacy to photogenic sight and montage structure. Anger stressed the first of these, most elaborately in his *Inauguration of the Pleasure Dome* (1954–66), which occupied him for most of the 1950s and which he issued in different versions – including triple screen projection – for twenty years. The soundtrack changed from Janáček to rock and back again. Even 'unfinished' (although less so than many of his films), *Inauguration* is a lavish tribute to film as the art of light and colour. Dissolves and superimpositions of the Magus's sparkling rings and regalia lead to an orgiastic initiation rite, in which masks, body-paint and ham acting serve to deflate and ironise the film's high mannerist style.

Myth and dance were central to both Anger and Deren. In Deren this took classical form, as in the final film of her psychodrama trilogy, *Ritual in Transfigured Time*, in which Anaïs Nin also appears. Here a cocktail party becomes a children's game (by freeze-frame rhythms), statues come alive (by stop-motion) and the two female protagonists – played by Deren and the black actress Rita Christiani – change identities in an underwater closing scene, 'the passage from widow to bride', shown in negative.

Her final films no longer psychologise the trance state. In *Meditations on Violence* (1953), trance is embodied in the balletic ritual gestures of a Chinese ritual boxer. His slow-building solo performance displays the sinuous geometry of unarmed combat to flute music. The pace quickens with drumbeats until a sudden montage cut from interior to rooftop shows the whirling boxer now with robes and sword. The first sequence is repeated, this time in almost imperceptible reverse-motion. Overshadowed by her early brilliance, the formal minimalism of Deren's later films anticipate the structural film a decade later, while looking even further ahead in their hybrid mixture of cultures and in Deren's explicit articulation of 'a woman's voice'.

Anger's romantic myth, by contrast, embraced mannerism and even nostalgia in the films he shot or planned after moving to Europe at Cocteau's invitation. This followed the success of *Fireworks* at the important Knokke Festival of 1949. *Eaux d'artifice* (1953) – the title is possibly cod-French for 'waterworks' – is especially baroque. A figure in eighteenth-century dress, apparently female but in fact a male dwarf, darts between the fountains and statues of a palace garden. Rhythmic montage is set to Vivaldi's music. Shot in monochrome by daylight, the blue-toned film evokes night by 'artifice', a tonal effect broken only by a hand-coloured shot of a fan unfolding.

A decade later, Anger made a surprising (and for him unique) turn to contemporary life – vividly mythologised – in *Scorpio Rising* (1964), a response to the new rock and youth culture he found back in the USA after his fifteen-year absence. This heralded for Anger an imminent Luciferian age, whose symbols were encoded in the narcissistic rites of the 'bike boy' cult. The film opens with a cool, documentary invocation of these demonic brothers, later seen donning Nazi-style gear and posing in hieratic shots. Slowly, the montage becomes subjective: a glue-sniffing biker 'sees red', scenes of Brando (*The Wild One*, on TV) and Christ (from a silent religious film) are intercut with comic-strips and flash-frames (Fascism and sex). After clan inititation and church desecration, the film ends in a rapid montage of racing bikes and death, sirens and police lights.

Scorpio became an underground cult classic, partly due to its transgressive theme of 'doomed Youth'. Unusually open-textured for Anger, but in the now preferred style of the underground, it incorporates found TV and film footage, stylised portraits, improvisation and documentary (within a formal structure that moves from inside to outside, opening and closing with artificial light). Above all, and preceded only by Bruce Conner's *Cosmic Ray* (1961), the soundtrack is made up of contemporary rock music (including *Blue Velvet*, later the title for a film by David Lynch). The idea spread to the mainstream young; Scorsese saw it at a loft screening around 1966, the year that his own early films were praised by Andrew Sarris ('a wit capable of talking features') along with Anger and Warhol. *Scorpio* finally led to the birth of the music video (partly through Anger's UK admirer Derek Jarman). Typically, a rock soundtrack in film or video both celebrates and ironises its subject, as does *Scorpio Rising*.

Underground

The 1950s institutionalisation of modern art under its newly acquired name ('Modernism') bred a reaction from disestablished or oppositional artists. Aiming to keep art outside the museum and its rules, they looked back to earlier times (especially to Dada) when its 'negative moment' – art as a critique of reality – was most heightened.[114] This movement later became the 'counter-culture' or, more popularly, 'the Underground'. The shift of emphasis is telling; one military term – an 'advanced guard' scouting ahead of the pack – is replaced by another which reflects clandestine resistance, tunnelling rather than charging, to echo a post-war identification with partisans and prisoners. Jeff Nuttall's punning phrase for this epoch – bomb culture – is a typically double-edged demand as well as a description.[115]

The underground was made up of loosely affiliated groups and individuals who mixed humour, iconoclasm and intransigence: from 'bad painting' (Asger Jorn) to automatic painting (Pino-Gallizio), the Beat Poets, aggressive performance art (the Vienna Institute of Direct Art, the Japanese Zero Dimension Group), John Latham's burnt book constructions, the San Francisco Mime Troupe, the Berlin Commune 1, the Destruction in Art Symposium and the 'prepared' pianos and violins of 'random music' in Cage and Fluxus. Most of all, the word was spread by the 'Underground press', which included *Residu*, *Now Now*, *Merlin*, *Marawannah Quarterly*, *City Lights*, *Poesie Vivante*, *Wild Dog*, *East Village Other*, *International Times*, *Berkeley Barb*, *Klactoveedsedsteen*, *My Own Mag* and *Fuck You – A Magazine of the Arts*.

The roots of the underground which flowered in the 1960s lay in the aftermath of world war. During the early 1950s films were again made in France by fringe dissidents, hostile to the 'culture industry'. The assault on culture began with the Lettriste group in Paris, led by Isidore Isou from 1947. Its attacks on meaning and value look back to Rimbaud, Nietzsche and Dada, and anticipate William Burroughs. Among their tactics of '*detournement*', or subversion, Isou and Maurice Lemaitre cut commercial found footage literally to pieces, scratching and painting the film surface and frame, adding texts and soundtracks to further dislocate its original meaning. These often very long works joined a Lettriste armoury of collage-poems, manifestos and provocations.

Art as a form of social 'intervention' was taken further (at least theoretically) by the situationists, an international grouping which included disaffected Lettristes who followed Debord after his 1952 schism with Isou. Their journal *Internationale situationniste* (1958–69) influenced Godard by its unique attack on the 'society of the spectacle' with a mixture of collage, invective and urbanist theory. For the situationists, however, Godard was 'just another Beatle'. Debord's own six films (1952–78) are rigorously collaged from found footage, with added voice-overs largely made up of quotations. Rarely screened, Debord withdrew them altogether in 1984, in protest against the unsolved murder of left-wing publisher Gerard Lebovici. After Debord's death in 1994 some surfaced again in Paris and London to commemorate (in 1998) the students' and workers' uprising of May '68.

In Vienna, radical artists in the immediate post-war period (*c.* 1948–55) were similarly hostile to the 'commodification' of art but did not reject artistic activity (as the SI eventually did).[116] One such group included the artists and film-makers Felix Radax, Peter Kubelka, and Arnulf Rainer. Their experiments with formal and mathematical systems drew on the spartan music of Webern and the pre-war Vienna School, as in Kubelka's sound and kinetic montage for *Mosaik in Vertrauen* (*Mosaic in Confidence*, 1954–5). This is his only semi-narrative film, interspersing 'disaster footage' such as a motor race crash with a highly oblique love story. His purely abstract film *Arnulf Rainer* (1958–60) used a graphic score to predetermine its alternating patterns of black and white frames, while *Adebar* (1957) and *Schwechater* (1958) employ cyclic repetition of small human movements and fluid colours. Several of Kubelka's films were commissioned, in spite of their purist ambitions – *Adebar*, with its strobe-flattened dancers, was an advert for a café of that name and *Schwechater* uses brief shots of people drinking as an advert for a brand of beer.

A second group of Viennese artists, led by Hermann Nitsch and Otto Muehl, explored confrontational 'live-art' performance under the banner of 'Material-Action'. These became public – and notorious – between 1958 and 1968. Violent and desacrilising, but laced with pastiche, they inaugurated still current controversies on the role of self-mutilation, catharsis and transgression in art. Kurt Kren recorded Muehl's events in films which simultaneously explore perception and film-time. He also made over thirty short films which permutate shots in a strict series (*TV*, 1967) or use rapid motion and cutting (*48 Faces from the Szondi Test*, 1960). Yet others take a new look at the everyday, as in the witty and self-explanatory *Eating, Drinking, Pissing and Shitting Film* (1967), or view nature through time-lapse and multiple exposure (*Trees in Autumn*, 1960; *Asyl*, 1975).

Kren and Kubelka were later to influence the structural film, but US films of the later 1950s initially rejected strict form along with high art. The American underground was broader than the European and less easily defined. Avant-gardism had entered the mainstream partly with the immigration of European exiles from Nazi Europe, such as Breton, Brecht and Richter. This was combined with a native 'tradition of the new', the absorption of new cultural ideas, from early New York Dada (1913) to the 1940s, when Hollywood composers took instruction from the iconoclastic Schoenberg.

Underground film in the USA at first encompassed a range of non- or anti-commercial activities, which challenged Hollywood's grip and commercialism. Pennebaker, Leacock, Wiseman and Clarke reinvented documentary cinema, turning to directly social themes and 'non-interventionist' style. They emphasised spontaneity, as did the fiction films of John Cassavetes. In 1960 the New York artists' avant-garde joined with these other independents to form The New American Cinema Group: 'We don't want false, polished, slick films – we prefer them rough, unpolished, but alive', ran their manifesto. 'We don't want rosy films – we want them the colour of blood.' The mood of the epoch is ironically cued in Cassavetes's *Shadows* (1957), where street-wise toughs confront an exhibition of modern art and argue about it. The mask-like style of one neo-cubist sculpture evokes mixed feelings in an African-American youth.

Similarly semi-improvised was Robert Frank and Alfred Leslie's *Pull My Daisy* (1958), which stars the Beat poets Ginsberg and Corso (and, sheltering under a pseudonym, the young Delphine Seyrig), with voice-over commentary by Jack Kerouac.[117] Equally playful and anecdotal is the quasi-narrative Beat film *The Flower Thief* (1960) by Ron Rice, starring Taylor Mead. But even these looser narratives were soon abandoned. Rice's *Chumlum* (1964) and Jack Smith's *Flaming Creatures* (1963) visually celebrate the orgy as *opera bouffe*, shot in delirious dissolved colour (by Rice) or on grainily pallid outdated stock (by Smith).

Film Culture was founded by Jonas Mekas in 1955 to support the new documentary and fiction film, and later took up the cause of the experimental film artists. In the end, these routes parted; the documentary and narrative branches of New American Cinema were committed to forms of realism which the artists' avant-garde rejected. By 1962 the balance of forces had swung the other way for Mekas, and his magazine was thereafter devoted mainly (but not exclusively) to the experimental film, post-Deren and Brakhage, as was his influential column in *The Village Voice*. Mekas, a Lithuanian war refugee, made the Beat era narrative *Guns of the Trees* (1961) before turning to more personal film-making. In *Diaries, Notes and Sketches* (1964–9) fragments of New York life are glimpsed with a hand-held Bolex camera. As with Andrew Noren, David Brooks and Warren Sonbert, the 'diary film' maintains the quotidian spirit of the NAC; films shaped by daily life rather than by scripts.

The underground's reputation for sexual explicitness heralded the social revolution of the 1960s, but the art critic Calvin Tomkins argues that its major achievements were less to do with subject-matter than with an investigation of the film medium itself. These include the abstract collage of Robert Breer, who began making films from his paintings in Paris during the late 1940s; the mythopeoic animation of Stan VanDerBeek, Harry Smith and the Whitneys; direct documentary by Richard Leacock, Don Pennebaker and the Maysles; the fugal montage of Brakhage and Kubelka; and, later, the structural films of Michael Snow, Hollis Frampton and Ken Jacobs whose first films all emerge from the underground ethos of improvised art. These films were also based on perception, like the other arts of the time. Kubelka and Tony Conrad made systematic or 'flicker' films which reduced film to its primary elements of light, dark, sound and silence. At the other extreme, West Coast film-makers were already exploring video and computer imaging in quest of 'expanded cinema' and lyric vision.

Mekas's role in all of this was crucial, in part through *Film Culture* and the *Village Voice* in which his 'Movie Journal' reviews praised and encouraged the new cinema. Mekas came from a rural but highly literate community in Lithuania. After forced labour in Germany he and his brother Adolfas entered the USA as 'Displaced Persons' in 1949 and began to make 16mm films. Mekas believed film could be a human and universal language. Living on low-pay jobs and learning English he discovered Amos Vogel's 'Cinema 16' screenings (1947–63) and the Russian-born but Smith College-educated Maya Deren who led the 'creative film' circle. Mekas notoriously attacked this latter group in 1955 for its adolescence, shallowness, incomprehensibility and 'conspiracy of homosexuality'. He soon recanted and ironically became a leading spokesman for experimental film, but Deren wanted to sue him and others denounced him.

By 1958 Mekas was defending the avant-garde in the *Voice* and supporting a variety of new ideas on shoestring budgets. A new turn was taken in 1961 when Vogel, the director of Cinema 16 (a regular screening venue as well as the main theatrical distributor of artists' films), rejected Brakhage's *Anticipation of the Night*. He disapproved of the film, and although he was prepared to accept it for rental, he was unwilling to show it himself. Angered at this, the gathering of film-makers at Deren's funeral in 1961 led to the founding of Mekas's Film Makers' Cooperative, a library and distribution centre for avant-garde films. Unlike

Cinema 16, there was to be no selection. Film-makers deposited the prints, set the hire fee, wrote a catalogue note and took the main part of any rentals that came in. It was set up the next year, and Vogel's group folded soon after; in 1963 he went on to start the New York Film Festival with Richard Roud.

Mekas's film reviews for the *Voice* were as non-selective as the Co-op. He praised everything avant-garde that moved, on the grounds that only strong encouragement could make the new art grow.

> Even the mistakes, the out-of-focus shots, the shaky shots, the unsure steps, the hesitant movements, the underexposed and overexposed bits are part of the vocabulary [he wrote]. The doors to the spontaneous are opening; the foul air of stale and respectable professionalism is oozing out.

Within a few years the first sentence could be printed without the justifying word 'even', as the mistakes (here compared to the professional film) became the intention (as film slid further away from the art cinema to the art world). Later to be the hallmark of the structural film, the cinema of 'mistakes' first appears in the deviant 'Baudelairian' films of Jack Smith, Ron Rice and Ken Jacobs. Smith's *Flaming Creatures*, glimpses of nudity and general orgiastic mayhem in the film had attracted obscenity charges, was banned at Knokke in 1963, and an angry Mekas was ejected from the projection booth when he tried to screen it. The next year saw Mekas, beset in New York by police raids on screenings of films by Smith and Genet, reorganising his screening programme under the title of the Film-Makers Cinematheque and finding ingenious ways to get them shown in theatres and lofts.

The publicity around the censorship of Smith – whose films parade the very qualities of camp infantilist chaos which Mekas had denounced in the avant-garde almost a decade before – raised the profile of the underground but unwittingly gave it a reputation at the edge of the sexploitation market which many anti-commercial artists (including Brakhage) rejected, especially when from 1966–7 Mekas and Shirley Clarke tried to promote feature-length films by Warhol, Markopoulos and others on the arthouse circuit. Despite the financial support of Elia Kazan and Otto Preminger, this plan collapsed when Warhol decided to distribute his own films and and eventually to suppress them altogether. At the supposed height of the movement Mekas was ironically deep in debt and struggling to find a regular screening venue. But in 1970 Anthology Film Archives initiated a new phrase of repertory and historical screenings (led by Mekas, Sitney, Brakhage and Kubelka). By this time, and partly in the wake of the student and anti-war movement, Millennium Film Workshop and Film Forum were regularly showing avant-garde films in new York; and so were prestigious galleries and museums like the Whitney and MOMA.

'Part of the early battle has been won,' Mekas said. 'Films are more readily accepted as an art form on a formal basis.' This was at the end of the period which began in the mid-1950s when 'Action painting', as 'cinematised' by Brakhage, impelled the avant-garde film to engage with process and the act of making. This then expanded into gestural, mixed-media live art, pioneered by Jacobs, Smith and Warhol. An important link was made by the neo-Dada Fluxus movement. Fluxus films (1962–6) are typically tongue-in-cheek explorations of extreme close-up (Chieko Shiomi's *Disappearing Music For Face* – a slow-motion smile), permutation (Yoko Ono's 'Bottoms' film), repetition (John Cale's *Police Light*), cameraless films (George Maciunas), single-frame films (Paul Sharits) and banalised humour (George Landow's *The Evil Faerie*). Some of this group peeled off to join the film avant-garde in its structural period, notably Sharits and Landow. Others turned to non-objective art making and conceptualism, and a few kept to the original Fluxus aim of creating anarchy, jokes and games.

Although he began to make film long before Fluxus, Bruce Conner works in a similar vein. His films are all made by re-editing archive footage and putting new soundtracks to the results. His milestone work is *A Movie* (1958), which moves from the hilarious (crazy races, a chase scene with cars and cowboys) to the disturbing (shivering refugees, an execution, air crashes). The act of viewing is questioned by the film's montage just as it plays on the sense of 'a movie' as both kinetic event and emotional affect. Conner maintains his scepticism in *Report* (1963–7) – on Kennedy's assassination – to satirise the FBI, while *America is Waiting* (1982) lampoons the military machine (with a rock soundtrack by Brian Eno and David Byrne).

Self-expression, in psychodrama's sense, was also no longer a goal for Jacobs when he chose junk footage for *Blond Cobra* (1963) (which also calls for live radio soundtrack when screened) nor in Peter Kubelka's savage montage of 'safari' footage commissioned from him by Austrian tourists. His *Unsere Afrikareise* (*Our Trip to Africa*, 1966) documents and subverts the voracious eye. Its complex editing system is quasi-musical, linking shots by duration, shape and analogy. But the film is far from purely formal (the aspect stressed by Kubelka himself). Scraps of folk-song and banal conversation are cut to images of hunted or dead animals, and universal myth (evoked by tourists admiring the moon) is undercut by neo-colonial reality. Its final sardonic line – 'I hope I can visit your country one day, man' – is spoken (in English) by an African, as another is seen walking off naked into the distance.

The romantic strain in film-making was most strongly maintained by the prolific and influential Stan Brakhage. His first films were encouraged by Parker Tyler, Joseph Cornell (best known for his surrealist collage art) and Maya Deren. In his early psychodramas his typically abrupt editing style is used to elicit quasi-symbolist metaphor. In *Reflections on Black* (1955), a blind man 'sees' events behind closed tenement doors, an illicit kiss is intercut with a coffee pot boiling over, and a final hand-scratched image makes light appear to stream from the blind man's eyes. Similarly, *The Way to Shadow Garden* (1955) ends with the inner vision of an Oedipally self-blinded hero, shown in the unfamiliar reverse form of negative filmstock. Sight is restored but transfigured.

In *Anticipation of the Night* (1958) this concern for poetic myth and illumination was displaced onto the formal plane of light and colour, away from fictional diegetic space and the singular narrative subject. The break with psychodrama was not final; *Anticipation* evokes the suicidal state of an unseen protagonist. But the camera treats this genre theme with a fresh and painterly eye, hovering freely over the surface of domestic, daily objects. At times, diffused light and focus draw attention to the physicality of the film medium. Elsewhere, the imagined dreams of sleeping children are elicited by direct shots of 'the real' (a fairground, landscape, animals) and subjective point of view replaces even the vestigial reverse-field editing of the earlier films. Yet immediate empathy is punctuated by repetition, cluster-shots, darkness and erratic movement. These devices, which both construct and distance, draw on Gertrude Stein's prose and on Menken's camera style.

Brakhage's films challenge film conventions even by their extreme contrasts of length, from 9 seconds in *Eyemyth* (1972) to 5 hours in *The Art of Vision* (1965). They include intimate portraits of friends and family, film-poems, landscape films, autobiography and more recent collaborations with composers and writers. His personal creation myth centres on the act of shooting and editing. Equally, the objective side of his films – their rhythms, metrics, camera-style, subject-matter – make uncompromising demands on the viewer to elicit and construct meaning, thus shifting attention from the author's voice to the spectator's eye. Viewing avant-garde film is here very close to the process of viewing modern painting.

Lyric films – short, poetic and visual – flourished in this decade, more often on the West Coast than in the metropolis. Important centres appeared in San Francisco (Canyon Cinema) and Los Angeles. Pat O'Neill and Larry Jordan explored collage and colour, Bruce Baillie matted and superimposed the stately freight trains of *Castro Street* (1966), and Brakhage's prodigious output included his 'birth-film' *Window, Water, Baby, Moving* (1959) – Anthony Balch told William Burroughs it made him faint – to films about the seasons (*Sirius Remembered*, 1959), childhood (*The Weir-Falcon Saga*, 1970) and light (*Riddle of Lumen*, 1972). By contrast, *The Act of Seeing with One's Own Eyes* (1971) unflinchingly documents the work of a Pittsburgh morgue; the title is a literal translation of the Greek word 'autopsy'. But the main output of these film-makers reflects the rural environment, from mountains and forest in Brakhage's *Dog Star Man* (1964) to the Western desert in Pat O'Neill's *Saugus Series* (1974).

Nonetheless, the rural landscape of the avant-garde is industrialised and humanly shaped, often ruthlessly so. It is rarely romanticised as the sublime, although sometimes it appears as a lost arcadia. This new subgenre in the avant-garde was largely an American invention, shared with a native ruralist tradition in nineteenth-century painting and the broad sweep of landscape-format action-painting in the 1950s. It also draws from poets in the line of William Carlos Williams, Charles Olson, Robert Duncan and Gary Snyder. Developing at a slight tangent to the Beat era, whose films are more in the 'crazy capers' mode of *Pull My Daisy* and *The Flower Thief*, some experimental film-makers such as Bruce Baillie were similarly taken by the image of the hobo (as in his road epic *Quixote*, 1967) – or the cowboy-as-bum (*Quick Billy*, 1971).

Defiantly stateside in this use of the native landscape, and filtered by earlier poetic myths which it has generated – from American Indian art and song to modern poets, painters and photographers – these films expand the avant-garde cinema in three ways. Firstly, they aesthetically recharge the near-exhausted landscape tradition, as in Brakhage's Pudovkin-like shooting of ice and rivers in *Creation* (1979) and his rhythmic glimpses of tree, roads and sky in *Machine of Eden* (1970). The titles of these films allude to the nature myth of origin and metaphor. Secondly, they lead into the mainstream genre of 'the road movie' pioneered in the 1970s by German and US 'new wave' directors (Wenders, Jarmusch), in which plot is randomised and to a degree replaced by visual space. And finally, they evince ecological and historical themes then marginalised from, but now central to, the wider culture.

But for some newer film-makers, in the run-up to 'post-painterly abstraction' and minimal art, both the lyric mode and Brakhage's visibly handheld camera (index or trace of the artist's response to experience) were too uncritically subjective. Brakhage's daunting output since the mid-1950s dominated his contemporaries. The new structural direction drew on his modernist montage, as from his bravura collaging of mothwings, pollen and leaves for *Mothlight* (1963). These were printed directly as 'found objects' packed between layers of 16mm film. But the main mentor of structural film was Andy Warhol, whose brief film-making career also dated from 1963, and whose urban, disengaged and impersonal art challenged Brakhage's Romanticism.[118] Warhol's tactics – static camera, long-take, no editing – opposed current avant-garde styles and avoided personal signature (literalised by Brakhage's hand-scratched name on his films of this period).[119]

Warhol's laconic 'I just switched on the camera and walked away' sums up his attack on film as dream and metaphor. In *Sleep* (1964), for example, Warhol parodies the trance film: we see a man sleeping for 6 hours, but not his dreams. In contrast to most of the avant-garde, Warhol's films parody the pursuit of authenticity and selfhood. Improvisation and confession, often hallmarks of realism, here undermine the certainty of seeing and knowing. By withholding (the illusion of) direct access to the real, ambiguity even leaks into Ondine's seemingly spontaneous outburst of anger in the elaborate two-screen colour and sound film *Chelsea Girls* (1966), or Edie Sedgwick's baiting by off-screen insults in *Beauty #2* (1965).

Like Gerard Malanga's acting, cultivated by Warhol in such films as *Vinyl* (1965), Warhol's films displayed a mixture of aggression and cool, camp and tough. At the same time, Warhol's objective camera-eye inspired a turn towards the material aspect of film. With loop-printing, repetition and blank footage – devices unique to the film medium – Warhol made works of extreme duration. He also subtly manipulated time, questioning the seeming simplicity of the long-take. *Empire* (1965), filmed in near-darkness, provokes the eye to scan the screen for nuances of change, leading persistent viewers to examine their own experience of viewing the film.

Warhol's entry into the avant-garde, on which he had a crucial and lasting impact, was strategic and well prepared. By 1963 he was already famous (one of his favourite words) as a leading painter and pop artist. He attended screenings of films by Anger, Brakhage, Markopoulos and Jack Smith before making his own intervention. His parodies and reversals of the major tropes of the avant-garde followed his assimilation of this work. Significantly, he rejected the lyric and expressive modes, notably those of the arch-romantic Brakhage, and adopted a deliberate attitude of cool distance towards his subject-matter. At the same time his subject-matter was still within the well-honed world of the underground film. It focused on outsiders, on playfulness, on sexual themes and on alienation from mainstream society. *Couch* (1964) embodies all of these.

Two avant-gardes (mark 1)?

Other artists besides Warhol were attending Co-op and Anthology Film Archive Cinemateque screenings at this time, 1962–4, when the Judson Memorial Church in Washington Square was the centre for weekly dance-based collaborations which included Meredith Monk, Merce Cunningham, Yvonne Rainer, Steve Paxton, Lucinda Childs, Trisha Brown, James Tenney, Carolee Schneeman, Robert Rauschenberg, Cecil Taylor, LaMonte Young and Robert Morris.[120] The presiding spirit was John Cage, as he had been in the Black Mountain College experiments a decade before. As part of the Judson events, the young Brian de Palma shot *Woton's Wake* (1963), a 30-mimute 'trance film' with parodic quotations from Ingmar Bergman, Maya Deren, *The Bride of Frankenstein* and *King Kong*.

A number of other young artists who went to Anthology screenings in the later 1960s, such as Bruce Nauman and Richard Serra, were soon to be the founders of mimimalist, process or conceptual art. Their first, or in Nauman's case their major, films and videos date from the end of the decade rather than its beginning. These include Robert Morris's *Mirror* (1969), which blurs a landscape with its reflections, and such performance-based works with self-explanatory titles as *Walking in an Exaggerated Manner Around the Perimeter of a Square* (1967–8) by Nauman and *Hand Catching Lead* (1969) by Serra. Like the similar *Adaptation Studies* (1970) of Vito Acconci, Serra's film is a 'test': a fixed frame shows a hand trying to catch pieces of lead dropped into the space of the image. The falling lead coincidentally imitates the activity of the filmstrip passing down through the projector gate.

These process-based works are related to Warhol's films in their grainy, rough-edged quality and their simple use of duration – most of them were shot in a single take. As such, they expand the range and concept of artists' film, as do similar pieces by Joan Jonas and others. In Jonas' *Wind* (1968), for example, a group of huddled dancers on a beach attempt to coordinate their movements against the disrupting power of a strong gale. Her films, like those of Serra and Nauman, are closer to performance art and to sculpture than to the medium-specific avant-garde. They are less concerned to explore the film medium in the narrow sense than to deploy film within a broader context of gallery and site-related art which makes up the totality of their work.

Such films renew a tradition already rooted in the pre-war avant-garde with such artists as Man Ray, Moholy-Nagy and Léger, who are primarily known as photographers, sculptors and painters but who made significant films. A key difference, however, is that conceptual or process artists were now challenging the traditional divisions between media, and were working between rather than across those divisions. In this sense they stand opposed to the film avant-garde, who were precisely concerned to assert that film itself (or in itself) was a valid medium for making art. Brakhage, Deren, Sharits, Frampton and others implied that it was possible to be an artist-film-maker as such, rather than their using film to break down old barriers between art forms or to expand traditional notions of what constituted painting and sculpture. Each side of the argument could enlist Warhol's example to their aid, because – tellingly ambiguous and prodigious as ever – he could be interpreted to support either case. His insistence on playing his films at silent speed, rather than the sound speed at which they were shot, asserts film's specificity; while by joining rolls of film end-to-end with fogging and leader he affirms the material of film as a painterly and even sculptural medium whose 'givens' are to be accepted, shaped and framed.

The differences between the film avant-garde and other artists who used the film medium did not especially materialise in open debate in the 1960s (in some ways, the debate is more relevant to our own times than it was thirty years ago). There were several reasons for this. One is the sheer level of artistic activity in the period, one of the most prolific of the century, in which the discovery of ideas was more important than their fine tuning. Secondly, artists like Bruce Nauman, Richard Serra and Joan Jonas were making videotapes as well as films in the late 1960s and early 1970s, and this largesse cut them off from the more purist film-makers who at this stage were able to ignore the new video medium (a phase which lasted until the next decade and perhaps still lingers on). A third reason is internecine, and relates to arguments inside the two major blocs. The underground film movement was challenged by a new wave of structural film-makers, while the painters and sculptors were breaking into at least three divisions: broadly, these were Pop Art, post-painterly abstraction and the latest addition, concept art. In this vociferous and dynamic context, a confrontation about film (i.e. between medium-specific film-makers and the expanded-media pop or conceptual artists) was not on the agenda, and there was no good reason for it to be. To this extent there were 'two avant-gardes' in film which co-existed and to some extent overlapped aesthetically and in their audiences. But while one group (roughly centred on the Co-op and Anthology) saw film itself as an avant-garde activity, the other (whose core was the Judson Church) embraced film as an aspect of being avant-garde.

It was however in this climate that Michael Fried produced a crucial and much-debated essay, 'Art and Objecthood' (1966), which approached that agenda, even though it was devoted to a single but large issue for the post-modern arts and, incidentally, denied that film was an artistic medium at all.[121] Fried was writing from the view-point of the one group of artists who pointedly did not make films and who asserted the specific values of their own chosen media – painting or sculpture strictly defined in terms of colour abstraction (for the former) and spatial integrity (for the latter). These artists, notably Frank Stella, although seemingly close to the new minimalists such as Serra, Andre, Judd and Morris in reducing art to pure surface and support, were in fact radically divided from them, according to Fried. While his preferred 'post-painterly abstractionists' gave their viewers a sense of real presence and non-illusionism in art, the minimalists offered them only 'theatre' – because, when the barriers between painting and sculpture are broken down and objects assert themselves in space, the result is spectacle. The spectator is outside the work, a loose presence, free to roam. Here, Fried spied decadence and rejected it. Art was not entertainment.

'Art and Objecthood' is a complex, controversial essay and has had a long-lasting effect. It alludes to ideas and obsessions in American culture which the global image-bank now makes universal: the icons of the highway (later materialised in road movies from Wenders to Lynch), the taste for 'experience' over contemplation, the apparent closing of distance between art and spectator and, above all in the contemporary arts, the tendency to collapse levels of media and meaning into an all-embracing theatricality. It was perhaps only in the late 1980s and through the 1990s that the full blast of Fried's suspicions was fully manifested in the fusions of live-art, environmental art and video in a newly dominant form, 'installation art', which does indeed trace back its ancestry to Fried's main culprits, Marcel Duchamp and minimalist art.

It is always possible to give Fried's negative vision a positive twist or spin and turn his vices into virtues. The important issue is not only his own far-sightedness but the pertinence of his 1967 critical manifesto for understanding art today, and the dominance of new media within it. The wide appeal of artists such as Bill Viola, for example, is easily located within Fried's model of 'theatricality' and visual spectacle. And although Fried rejects film as art (whether commercial or experimental) the structural film which was flowering at the time was explicitly anti-theatrical in its own right. A current revival of interest in this phase of film-making is a similar signal that mixed-media art and installation, dominant for the last decade, are now due for re-evaluation and honing in the digital age. For structural film, from the early 1960s, asserted a new vision beyond the underground scenario; and for the first time since the 1920s it also offered a critique of film-as-vision.

Structural

When structural film led the avant-garde to the high ground, after the underground's populism, it sought to explore visual and cognitive ideas of structure, process and chance then appearing in the other arts (especially in the more conceptual side of Cage, Rauschenberg and Johns).[122] It turned away from visual sensation and towards the kind of self-reflexiveness posited in the 1930s by Walter Benjamin (but in the context of Soviet montage), later glossed by Annette Michelson as 'epistemological' film. In structural film, form became content. The viewer's identification with the 'dream screen' was disrupted. The structural film rejected the cinema of pure vision. It posited viewing as an act of reading, literally so in films by Michael Snow, Hollis Frampton and George Landow.

Ken Jacobs's *Little Stabs At Happiness* (1963), starring Jack Smith, expressed a tragi-comic underground 'aesthetics of failure', but the more abstract *Soft Rain* (1968) looks to film as a medium for the registration of light. Jacobs took up questions unresolved since the Abstract Expressionist era which neither psychodrama nor traditional abstract film had dealt with: what was the relation between the physical filmstrip and its projected immaterial image? Together with Brakhage's continued exploration of film colour and form ('Imagine an eye unruled by the man-made laws of perspective', he wrote in 1964), the experimental film shifted into new philosophical territory. Underground sensation gave way to structural investigation.

Like Warhol and Breer, Jacobs had been a painter. Frampton, Snow and Gehr were photographers before they made films.[123] In part, film-makers were responding to a new wave of minimalism and self-referentiality in the arts during the 1960s. This included the post-Cagean music of Philip Glass and Steve Reich, and the post-Fluxus performance art (and later film-making) of Yvonne Rainer and Meredith Monk. Michael Snow, a Canadian artist, developed a counter-montage aesthetic in films, photography and sculpture. The early *New York Eye and Ear Control* (1964) had sound by 'advanced' jazz musicians like Rosswell Rudd, Sonny Murray and John Tchicai and is intuitively shaped in comparison to the rigorous *One Second in Montreal* (1969), in which twenty-four static shots of that city are held for increasing lengths of time. His best-known film – *Wavelength* (1967) – explores the illusion of deep space. For 45 minutes, a camera slowly and irregularly zooms into the far wall and windows of a loft, accompanied by a rising sine wave. The zoom is interrupted by colour changes induced by filters and filmstock, and also by some minimal sub-drama (a conversation, a hammed death, a phone call) which the lens literally passes over in a casually anti-narrative gesture. The film ends in extreme close-up – a photograph of sea waves. A decade later Snow issued its short counterpart, *Breakfast* (1972–6), where the moving camera physically smashes all before it; 'a continuous zoom traverses the space of a breakfast table', wrote Deke Dusinberre, 'serving as a grand metaphor for indigestion.'

Snow's taste for puns and word-picture play was elaborated in the labyrinthine *Rameau's Nephew* (1974), which explores different literal structures of mapping film, drama and fiction; in one sequence, actors speak their lines backwards to imitate a tape played in reverse, in another they all use different languages. This semiotic side of Snow's work continues in *Presents* (1981), where the apparent realism of the stage set is literally taken apart (by fork-lift trucks) and in *So Is This* (1982), which is wholly made up of words and phrases interrogating the act of watching the film.

Elsewhere, Snow made strictly visual and perceptual work which underlines the phenomenology of viewing and the experience of film time. The ambitious *La Région centrale* (1971) consists of pans and zooms of a mountain landscape, shot with a multi-pivot remote control camera and composed in a complex matrix of alternating movements. Later films such as *Seated Figures* (1989) – 'a landscape from the perspective of an exhaust pipe!' (J. Hoberman) – similarly explores visual space close to the lens, where objects turn into fragments of texture and light.

Snow's long films between 1970 and 1978 coincided with the grand, contemplative scale of 'Land Art' (Smithson, Di Maria), and with Brakhage's magisterial 5-hour montage film *The Art of Vision*. While Brakhage's very title celebrates the authority of the image, others used extreme duration to challenge Brakhage's intuitionism as well as the structure of mainstream narrative. A major example is Hollis Frampton's *Straits of Magellan*, unfinished by his death in 1984, conceived as an epic cycle of films (one for every day of the year). A late example of the American sublime (from Melville to Hart Crane and Pound), its grand scale ironically incorporates the ideas on serial minimalism Frampton discussed in 1962/3 with Carl Andre, when both young artists were seeking to undermine Pop Art.

Like Snow, Frampton was drawn to systems, numbers and linguistics. *Zorns Lemma* (1970) – the mathematical title alludes to an 'axiom of disorder' – is again based on the number 24, linking film speed to the letters of the Roman alphabet (without 'j' and 'v'). An early American ABC – a moral as well as linguistic primer – is read over a blank screen. The film then permutates 1-second shots of the alphabet with images which gradually replace each repeated letter. Some images are static or repetitious (a tree, a shop sign) while in others a continuous action is completed at the end of the cycle (a wall painted, a tyre changed, an egg cooked). Finally, women's voices read a mediaeval text on light, each word cued to a metronome beat, while two small human figures and a dog are seen walking across a wintry landscape until they 'white out' in snow and film-flare.

Few film-makers approved of the term 'structural film', introduced in the early 70s by Sitney to describe post-Warholian film-making in which 'the film insists on its shape, and what content it has is minimal and subsidiary to its outline'. Perhaps fearing an onrush of academic theory over artistic practice (later justified), they were unwilling to see the parallel rise of 'structuralism' in 'the human sciences' as more than coincidence (or bad news), even as Frampton, Snow and George Landow were forging links to it by their semiotic or linguistic turn. In a 1972 statement Frampton joked that the term structuralism 'should have been left in France to confound all Gaul for another generation', while as late as 1994 Brakhage lamented that structuralism was the worst thing that happened to artists' film. Like other antis, such as Steve Dwoskin, he exempts the key practitioners, notably Kren, Snow and Le Grice.

Structural film proposed that the shaping of film's material – light, time and process – could create a new form of aesthetic pleasure, free of symbolism or narrative. It typically combined predetermination (for example, camera position, number of frames or exposures, repetition) with chance (the unpredictable events that occur at the moment of shooting). Sitney had specified four characteristics of structural film: fixed camera position, flicker effect, loop-printing and re-photography from the screen. Few structural films had all of these features and some (Snow's *La Région centrale*, for example) had none. The point of the concept was to distinguish this particular direction from the broader 'formal film', defined as 'a tight nexus of content, a shape designed to explore the facets of the material ... Recurrences, prolepses, antitheses and overall rhythms are the rhetoric of the "formal"'.[124]

One film which contains all of Sitney's structural hallmarks, while at the same time evoking the formal film's 'tight nexus of content', which is here the act of viewing the film itself, is George Landow's *Remedial Reading Comprehension* (1970). The phrase printed over a shot of a running man – 'This is a film about you, not about its maker' – alludes to the goal of eliminating personal expression and eliciting the active participation of the viewer in the film. The running man in this case is played by Landow, so the statement equally applies to him (as another image, or 'you'). Landow parodies trance-film to suggest that viewing is more like reading or thinking than dreaming.[125]

Up to then the avant-garde film tradition, from the cubists to Deren and Brakhage, had been essentially pictorial ('Visionary Film') and often silent. This made it both cheap and (so Brakhage affirmed) 'pure', an alternative to naturalistic sound film and 'filmed drama'. A more demotic visuality came with the 1960s, at the underground's height, when it broke taboos on sexual imagery, as in the much banned *Flaming Creatures*, dubbed by Mekas 'Baudelairian Cinema'. Warhol (*Couch*, 1966), Carolee Schneeman (*Fuses*, 1968) and Barbara Rubin famously explored erotic vision. At the same time the West Coast avant-garde (Jordan Belson, Bruce Baillie, Pat O'Neill, Scott Bartlett) were celebrating Tantric symbolism and desert landscapes. Their richly pictorial colour-music was highly romantic and yet commercially adaptable, influencing mass culture from adverts (a growing genre) to mainstream film (often in 'psychedelic' sequences, notably Kubrick's *2001: A Space Odyssey*).

For Frampton and Snow's generation, hostile to Pop Art's easy accommodation to the market, film's attraction lay in its non-commodity form, as a quasi-performance art with inbuilt resistance to museum culture and the private collector. Warhol approved of patronage and significantly made no films after 1967, simply lending his now-famous name to Paul Morrissey as he had to the Velvet Underground rock group. He finally withdrew his films from circulation, perhaps because he was looking to larger-scale production and felt that the reputation of the earlier films would count against him. In the event, the big budgets were not forthcoming.

Because Warhol's films were rarely screened after the mid-1960s, they were known more by description than acquaintance. A few semi-legal prints and dupes circulated and odd clips appeared in Warhol documentaries. Their legendary anti-aestheticism encouraged European film-makers, at the end of the decade, to explore aspects of film which did not simply reflect the American example of 'visionary film', then at its height. The link was made by Hollis Frampton in 1972, discussing the controversial 'structural film': 'I said to Sitney at dinner in July: I have found your structuralists, P. Adams, and they are in England. Complete to the diacritical mark, influence of Warhol, the whole number.'[126]

Part Two: Britain, 1966–98

English structuralists

The English structuralists had in fact seen very few of Warhol's films, and were generally not aware that many of them had been shot at sound speed but shown at slow, silent speed. This enabled them to make some interestingly creative mis-readings of Warhol as a film-maker.[127] For Le Grice, who argued that duration in film was a 'counteract to illusion in the representation of time', Warhol's 'nearly one-to-one equivalence between shooting and projection' was to provoke a radical series of anti-montage investigations based on the real-time relations between maker, film and viewer. Warhol's slowed-down projection speed, an interesting distanciation effect in its own right, actually evoked a quite different experience of film time – more like one-and-a-half to one – but the 'false' inference further inspired Le Grice to take an independent route on which he and others had already embarked. Duration became a hallmark of British structural film, a 'road not taken' by the mainstream cinema or by the lyric direction in avant-garde film, but which linked it to the advanced arts in Europe and – by way of Snow and Frampton – back to the post-Warholian film avant-garde in North America.

The London Film Makers' Cooperative grew from partly American roots between 1965 and 1969, as the Co-op principle spread from New York into Europe.[128] London attracted American artists (like Steve Dwoskin and Peter Gidal), and films arrived from New York or on tour with P. Adams Sitney and other visitors. Another American expatriate, Carla Liss, ran the Co-op's growing distribution archive. But English film-makers quickly found their own direction. The radical student movement and the campaign against the Vietnam War were a key point of focus for the London counter-culture. Screenings of underground films at poet Bob Cobbing's Better Books in Charing Cross Road, where he was manager, led to the formation of the LFMC there in October 1966.

Its first aim was open screening and distribution, and early founding members included Dwoskin, Simon Hartog, David Curtis and film journalist Ray Durgnat. It held a 'Spontaneous Festival' and showed films at the UFO club on nearby Tottenham Court Road until October 1967, with loops and cut-ups played to Pink Floyd and the Soft Machine. UFO then decamped to the Roundhouse in Camden Town, a huge empty engine-shed which Arnold Wesker and others had tried to turn into an arts centre. Cobbing was sacked by the Better Books management at the same time, and the Co-op moved to the Arts Lab in Covent Garden, where new ideas were being invented, explored and disseminated by a variety of artists and activists outside the cultural establishment.

Here new members like Le Grice gave the group a new and unique twist. Led by film-makers whose main aim was production, the Co-op set itself the task of opening access to film-making as well as film availability. Printing and processing facilities were key to this, as a way of cutting costs and escaping commercial pressures. The closure of the Arts Lab in October of 1968 left the Co-op homeless for a year until it moved into successive workshop spaces in north London: Robert Street, the Old Dairy, the Old Laundry. Regular screenings resumed, and the first International Underground Film Festival was launched at the NFT in 1970. By 1975, and now centred on structural film-making, the Co-op had its first production facilities grant from the BFI, to which it had first applied in 1968. This support was to continue (as it still does).

With the aid of its first (home-made) printing machine, constructed by Le Grice, the London Co-op originally took up direct film-making in the craft ethos of the art schools from which most of its film-makers came. Many films reflected the abstract, minimalist concerns of the day: Annabel Nicolson's *Slides* (1971) has '35mm slides, light leaked film, sewn film ... dragged through the contact printer, directly and intuitively controlled'. Others explored time-lapse, shooting systems and – in John Du Cane's *Lensless* (1971) or Lis Rhodes's *Dresden Dynamo* (1974) – direct light and colour.

Structural film in Europe generally showed more concern for film's 'material substrate' – its physical qualities – than for the image or shot, the province of the North Americans. For example, *Rohfilm* (*Raw Film*, 1968), by Wilhelm and Birgit Hein, uses collage, wandering framelines and sprocket holes to affirm 'the film's substance and its physical presence in the projector' (David Curtis). As here, early structural film shared the underground's libertarian and anarchic credo, seen in Steve Dwoskin's 1975 book *Film Is* (subtitled 'the international free cinema'), where praise of the 'wild' Ron Rice and Jack Smith sits alongside close analysis of structural films by Kurt Kren and Peter Gidal.

Such unions were short-lived, as schism grew between the American and the European avant-gardes. Links were never severed, but were often strained. Similarly, film-makers like Jeff Keen, David Larcher and Dwoskin himself – who kept up the anarchic underground tradition – were for a time marginalised by the Co-op structuralists. It was a clash of spirit as much as of substance, signalled in the switch of name from the liberatory 'underground' to the more theoretical 'avant-garde'. For some the Co-op's turn away from the films of Dwoskin, Larcher and Keen was a sign of a new scholasticism. But celebratory cinema was not much in evidence during the post-euphoric 1970s, when the major choices for young film-makers lay between the purist avant-garde and the agit-prop collectives like Cinema Action, Politkino, the London Women's Film Group and the Berwick Street Collective. For much of the decade the visionary film-makers of the first Co-op continued to add to their extensive bodies of work regardless, often ironically enough using the techniques and tropes of structural film, although these efforts were more often appreciated in France, Germany and Holland than at home.

Internationalism – in screenings, festivals, exchanges of films – was vital to the arterial networks that made up both the 'free' underground and the new structural avant-garde, but one potential constellation, lurking in London, did not occur – at least, not then. For several years, during the late 1960s and early 1970s, just as the Co-op film culture was gathering around the Arts Lab and its successors, Kenneth Anger and William Burroughs were living in London (and also in Paris). Both made films there. Anger shot *Invocation to my Demon Brother* (1969) – with a soundtrack by Mick Jagger – and material for the ill-fated *Lucifer Rising* (most of the original footage was destroyed). Meanwhile, Burroughs was working with the film-maker Anthony Balch. Their best-known film is perhaps *Towers Open Fire*, but the more inventive is the exhaustive and semi-structural *The Cut-Ups* (1967). This film permutates four brief statements on its 20-minute soundtrack, along with staggered and repeated shots of a 'medical', a hypnotic 'dream-machine' whose strobe effect links back to Victorian optics, Brion Gysin drawing in single-frame shots and Burroughs walking in three cities which are 'intercut' as in Kuleshov's idea of 'creative geography'.

Although Anger's films and the Burroughs/Balch experiments have a structural edge, and Balch was in contact with the Fluxus artists while he ran some small but crucial London cinemas (which is how Yoko Ono's 'Bottoms' film made it to the West End), their independent worlds did not connect with the London film avant-gardes, or even with each other. Both were already alienated from the New York Film Co-op, and from Jonas Mekas. Anger's main British supporter, the incisive critic Tony Rayns, had limited time for the earnest structuralists at the Arts Lab and Camden Town. The London Co-op and its video offshoots were led by former painters (such as Le Grice) and former sculptors (such as David Hall), while the expatriate Americans and their afficianados were intensely literary – their mistrust of the word, as with Burroughs, was expressed quite differently from the visual silence which is characteristic of the structural film. Both Anger and Burroughs were inclined to the political right (sometimes in mockery, but maybe not always) while the film avant-garde were broadly (sometimes narrowly) Marxist. Some went further: Mike Dunford, one of the early structural film-makers, rejected its aestheticism and turned to social cinema, as Stuart Marshall was to do a generation later. Temperament, taste, background, politics and even age kept these two avant-gardes apart, so that Anger and Burroughs did not connect with the new structuralists.

Yet it almost happened.[129] Jeff Nuttall reports Balch's fainting-fit when he saw Brakhage's 'birth film', and his sense of 'the direct impact' it made. Brakhage was a key if much-debated film-maker for the new Co-op. Through Balch and others, Fluxus was also close at hand in London, Paris and New York, although its founder George Maciunas had been one of the first to reject Sitney's term 'structural film' in a brilliant one-page diagram of 1969, so strife was always at hand too.

In the event, the meeting of the Anger and Burroughs world with its British counterparts was postponed. When it happened, it bypassed the Film Co-op of the time. The connections were made partly through Ken Russell (who admired Anger's early films) and hence to Derek Jarman, who worked on the sets of his film *The Devils* while making his own neo-Brakhagian 8mm film diaries. Performance artist and musician Genesis P-Orridge, co-founder of the 'transgressive' group Coum Transmissions (1969–79), and its band Throbbing Gristle, contacted Burroughs in London in 1973. P-Orridge was effectively driven out of England by police raids and prosecution threats in 1991, but has become the effective archivist of the Balch/Burroughs film legacy through his friendship with this axis of the underground. The Jarman and P-Orridge tendencies fused in the

1980s, when younger film-makers such as John Maybury were drawn to their world of free play, extremist imagery and a hallucinatory 'dream-machine' cinema. In 1982 David Dawson (of the B2 gallery) and P-Orridge held a four-day event called The Final Academy in London, with an offshoot at Manchester's Hacienda club, to celebrate Burrough's work; Nuttall took part, and Balch's films were shown.

The after-effects of this punk-era revision of the underground are taken up later, for eventually it was to lead a rebellion against the structural avant-garde which preceded it as a distinct aesthetic direction. Like many aspects of the avant-garde, however, the works which they revered (in this case, Burroughs and – less directly – Anger) circulate in diverse contexts and yield many codes of meaning. The 'new' punk underground had no more final claim to the old underground than the structuralists did, or indeed artists yet to come.

The film *Bill and Tony*, for example, which dates from 1970–2, is a hilarious and crafted 'interchange' of voices and personalities between Burroughs and Balch, as they 'lip-synch' for each other while facing the camera. The film is coincident with early structural cinema, and shares its ethos even as it exceeds its technical limits (Balch was a shoestring 'independent' of a different ilk from the Co-op artisans). It also shares the 'hallucinatory' breakdown-ethos of post-punk a decade later. At the same time, and seen today, it looks forward to the contemporary taste for lip-synch and frontal cinema seen most recently in the videos of Gillian Wearing (though seemingly without direct influence). Experimental films can share in many contexts, none of which will completely exhaust or absorb their form and content.

The early structural film was especially concerned with the relation between the form of a work and its subject-matter, often theorised as a cinematic relation – and disjunction – between signifiers and signifieds. Typically, experimentation with film's raw substance was combined with the English landscape tradition.[130] In *Whitchurch Down (Duration)* (1972), Le Grice alternates three views, each in different tones and colours. Gidal's *Clouds* (1969) loops a shot of the sky in which a glimpse of an aircraft wing sets the scale. Chris Welsby's *Park Film* (1972) uses time-lapse to compress three days on a busy walkway into six minutes of film time. *River Yar* (1972, with William Raban) is a two-screen study of water, light and colour. In Welsby's *Streamline* (1976) a camera travels on remote wire inches above the water. Elsewhere (as in *Windmill II*, 1973), the camera is wind-powered by blades attached to the lens. Their mirrored surfaces add a literal 'reverse field' to the image obtained, including occasional glimpses of the film-maker behind the camera.

Welsby's doubling of the image was explored in a different way by William Raban's *Time Stepping* (1973).[131] As Le Grice described it, two cameras 'play a rhythmic space-time game, shooting alternately and panning away in opposite directions down the street from the same central point, two doorways at the front of an old row of houses'. The footage from both cameras is cut together and alternated to make up a single film in which gaps in shooting – when the clockwork motors ran down – are shown by blank spacing, while overlaps of shots from both cameras are superimposed. The process of making the film is visible in the act of viewing it, as with David Crosswaite's *Man With the Movie Camera* (1973), which expands the image by placing a circular mirror in front of the lens, to reflect the camera-operator's manipulation of such effects as changing focus. Gill Eatherley's *Dialogue* (1973), explores two shots – from a window and inside a room – as its two camera operators engage with each other's subjective viewpoints, just as Marilyn Halford's *Footsteps* (1974), is a game of catch-and-freeze between receding performer and advancing cameraman.

But the camera's iconic image, single or double, was not in itself the central concern of the early Co-op which – with Mike Dunford, John Du Cane, Roger Hammond, David Parsons and Annabel Nicolson – took film-making further into live events, the handmade film print, procedural systems and expanded cinema (or 'making films with projectors') to question the given definition of film as a representation rather than, as the Co-op saw it, an investigation of its identity as a performance in which viewers as well as makers were engaged. Such films seek film equivalents for natural light and motion. They aim to renew perception by using the whole register of film language, underlining its normally invisible aspects – frame, surface, printstock – and its 'mistakes' (flare, slippage, double-exposure). For Le Grice this constituted a 'politics of perception' (he hopefully titled a series of films in the early 70s *How to Screw the CIA*). The 'pure' landscape films of Raban and Mike Leggett (for example; *The Sheepman and the Sheared*, 1970–5) also allude to the passage of historical time, later explored by Raban in the neo-documentary *Thames Film* (1986) and in colour-field studies of Docklands (*London Film*, 1992). Welsby, an 'unrepentant dualist', followed a more philosophical concern for eye and mind, while Gidal sought to align critical theory and formal film through 'structural-materialism'.

These films had no fictional narrative content; they seem to leap over the history of film, and back to the experiments of Demeny, Muybridge and Lumière. Here a line of descent is traced from the earliest cinema, with narrative as a grand detour. Bypassing the industrial norms of production and division of labour, the primitive or artisanal mode also led to 'expanded cinema'. Le Grice's *Horror Film I* (1970) is a 'live shadow performance' in which a naked figure in front of the screen plays with coloured light. In Guy Sherwin's *Man with Mirror* (1976), live action duplicates multi-screen illusion, while in Annabel Nicolson's *Reel Time* (1973) a projected loop film of the film-maker at a sewing machine is slowly destroyed by passing the film through an actual sewing-machine and re-projecting it. The film alludes neatly to the technology from which the film claw was derived. All of these films wittily expand film (a fixed medium) into the realms of chance; they underline transience and challenge the illusion that 'real time' is ever suspended in the act of viewing.

One of the most succesful longer ventures of the period was made up of 3-minute films, mainly investigating a single perceptual event, which could be combined in any order. This was Guy Sherwin's *Short Film Series* which he undertook between 1976 and 1980. Eventually he issued about thirty of them. Some are single studies of light, focused on the reflections in an eye shot in close-up. Others are domestic, as in the *Portrait with Parents* or *Breathing* (where a pregnant belly rises and falls to change the aperture and focus of the light entering the window in the background). Many deal with two rates of time measurement, as in *Clock and Candle*, or construct visual paradoxes, as in the shuddering stasis of

Metronome – an illusion caused by the clash between the spring-wound mechanisms of the Bolex camera and of the metronome itself. In *Barn Door* the semi-strobe effect of light pulsations flattens the distant landscape. Sherwin's mastery of the hand-cranked camera to perform complex manipulations (including inversions of the shot and a play on focus to register and then dissolve the image) is both a form of pure perceptual cinema and an encoding of the passage of time. Interestingly, Sherwin has recently returned to the series after almost twenty years, with studies of animals and insects which in part recall the fascination with the 'invisible' side of nature felt by the surrealists, and seen in the scientific writing of Roger Caillois and the films of Jean Painlevé during the 1930s.[132] These short films are a particularly subtle questioning of the illusionist image.

The most extreme opponent of illusionism in this group, and with Le Grice its most articulate advocate, was Peter Gidal.[133] Unlike the others Gidal avoided landscape and multi-screen. The handheld camera is not used to expand vision but to shoot bare interiors stripped of personal domestic reference. Film rhetoric is similarly abjured, aside from the cannily rough-edged flourishes of colour, grain and print surface in a series of films that explore duration, repetition and close-up. For Gidal film has three prime moments; shooting, printing and projection. These frame his polemic and underpin his reduction of 'content' to images that defy fixity and registration. In *Flare Out*, for example, the camera blurs shots, photographs of the same spaces, reversing the principle of certainty implied in the trajectory and final image of Snow's seminal *Wavelength*, a photograph of the sea.

'My arguments have been directed all along against reproduction in any form,' he stated in 1979, but of course these ideas grew over a long period of time. Le Grice maintains that the Co-op film-makers began with no theories; theory was applied to the films after they were made, as analysis of what had been made. Ironically, both he and Gidal were associated with theory-building throughout the decade. Gidal added the word 'materialist' to 'structural' film in the mid-70s to signal his Marxist revision of Sitney's primarily aesthetic definition. His work is a political and cultural attack on representation in its varied ideological, social, economic and sexual forms. In this context, cinema exemplifies passive consumption.

Gidal's first and in some ways most notorious expansion of his ideas came in the *Structural Film Anthology*, to coincide with a series of related screenings at the National Film Theatre in 1976. His polemical introduction does not mention Fried's 'Art and Objecthood' essay,[134] but in some ways it seems to answer Fried's objection that 'the cinema, even at its most experimental, is not a modernist art'. Fried did not give reasons for this bold assertion, but his point is possibly that film, by its very nature, is time-based and cannot reveal itself all at once to the viewer – as can the abstract painting and sculpture he was concerned to defend. It consequently 'absorbs' the viewer in a negative or dominating way, and by its illusionism it lacks the real presence which was for him a condition of art.[135]

Gidal's introductory essay *Theory and Definition of Structural/Materialist Film* of 1975 opens mildly enough by claiming that it 'attempts to be non-illusionist', but he unpacks this ambition in strongly didactic terms to successively attack all the major forms of cinema, including classic films, documentaries, dramas, political films and even experimental films in the 'visionary' mode of Brakhage. For him, film is very clearly a 'modernist art', defined by 'flatness, grain, light, movement', in a state of tension with its representational content and with the viewer. The construct or 'shape' of the film is not primary, but rather 'the film is a record (not a representation, not a reproduction) of its own making'. It asserts its real duration and its 'coming into presence' through 'the mental activation of the viewer'.

These key points implicitly reply to Fried's own implied objection that films are inherently illusionistic and are passively watched. Gidal's attack on the 'repression' of time and space in the narrative cinema embraces all forms of fantasy identification. More radically than any other theories of the time, it proposed film as a contemporary art which politically needs to share nothing with the cinema. Far from film being a polysemic or mixed medium, Gidal's vision asserts that its properties were as specific as those of painting or sculpture. Ironically enough, Fried gave up contemporary art criticism in favour of art history just when the structural film in England was attempting for film what his own post-Greenbergian ideas had tried to achieve for the other visual arts, even though he himself had denied that they could be extended to cinema.

Gidal's iconoclasm, however, sets high demands on an audience, a risk he was perfectly willing to take. His films set up a dialectic with the viewer who must actively work at apprehending it – or who walks out. Hence in some ways the film is not as autonomous as it seems. It provokes a politicised questioning of passive consumption and leads to a degree of interaction with the viewer. Le Grice agreed with the tactic, stating that 'my predominant concern has been with the spectator', but by the later 70s he no longer shared Gidal's fervent refusal of all storytelling. Rather as Frampton was to do, he asked if 'all aspects of narrative [are] irrevocably embroiled with the repressive social function it has come to serve?' For Gidal, there was no question that this was so. In 1979 he issued his essay 'The Anti-Narrative' in the leading film theory journal *Screen*.[136] Le Grice, meanwhile, completed the second part of his narrative trilogy in *Emily – Third Party Speculation*.

Primitives and post-structuralists

In both the USA and Europe the avant-garde's interest in early film form coincided with a revisionist history of the primitive era.[137] Historians as well as filmmakers saw primitive cinema as an alternative to the mainstream, not just an ancestor. These interests coincided between 1977 and 1984, as a 'new film history' emerged alongside coverage of the (now intellectually respectable?) avant-garde film in journals from *Screen* and *Afterimage* to *Studio International* and *Art Forum*. Annette Michelson promoted 'epistemological' film-makers who sought in film 'a metaphor for consciousness' (primarily Brakhage, Snow, Frampton, Landow). Speculative and factual histories were written by Le Grice, Wyborny, Frampton and the Heins, and the movement attracted archivists (Peter Kubelka, Enno Patalas, John Hanhardt, Wulf Herzogenrath). From 1970 Anthology Film Archives in New York built its controversial pantheon of classic and experimental filmmakers.

These conjunctions are heralded in Ken Jacobs' deconstructionist *Tom, Tom, The Piper's Son* (1969–71), which scrutinizes texture and motion in a 1905 Billy Bitzer film; re-shooting from the screen expands it from four minutes to two hours. Equally ambitious, Klaus Wyborny's *Birth of a Nation* (1973) ironically explores pre-Griffith film space, here reduced to a few actors in a bare landscape. The viewer is kept at a distance by long-shot and ellipsis. In Brakhage's *Murder Psalm* (1981), an instructional film is re-cut and tinted to evoke an eerie childhood dream. The austere and magisterial *Eureka* (1974) by Ernie Gehr simply slows down an early one-shot film, in the 'Hales Tours' genre, to 8fps. The frontal 'view' is taken from a streetcar heading down a busy San Francisco Street until it reaches the Terminus. Extreme slow-motion sharpens perception, just as the film distils complex metaphor (journey, history, movement, closure) from seemingly chance images. The pun in the title ('I found it!') hints at this.

By scanning early films, bringing together the 'primitive' and the 'advanced', Jacobs and Gehr sought to unlock their meanings by a process of self-revelation. European film-makers showed less respect for the authority of early footage. Le Grice's *Berlin Horse* (1970) alternates two brief shots, one of a horse running in a circle, the other a fragment from Hepworth's 1900 film *The Burning Barn*. With colour added in the printer, the two shots merge in blended rhythm to a Brian Eno soundtrack. The film can be shown on one, two or four screens. In *Kali Film* (1988) Birgit Hein collages early porn with war films and sexploitation movies, finding resistance as well as oppression in films made at the anarchic fringes of 'official' culture.

Structural film had begun as strongly anti-narrative, as were most contemporary arts at this time. Le Grice's first film, *Castle One (The Light Bulb Film)* (1966), was basic cinema. Here, a real light bulb flashes next to the projected film (showing another flashing bulb and a collage of TV documentary shots, mainly industrial or political). But a decade later, his trilogy (*Blackbird Descending*, 1977; *Emily – Third Party Speculation*, 1979; *Finnegans Chin*, 1983) elaborated on point of view and narrative space. The environment is domestic, the tone personal and allusive, the style more baroque in colour and vision. Le Grice has made no films since this long statement, with its implication that 'the spectre of narrative' (Frampton) always haunts the film medium. He has since returned to electronic and computer-based art, areas he first explored in the 1960s, with their more open formats and pliable software systems for the manipulation of source material.

The political roots of the international Co-op movement (and hence of the structural film which dominated it) lay in the campaign against the (heavily televised) Vietnam War. The 'politics of perception' were a weapon of politicised art to 'demystify' media power. In the UK the avant-garde was vocal from 1974 in campaigns for public access film workshops and innovative TV.[138] Channel 4 (from 1983) was partly shaped by these debates, but by then the context had changed. The renewal of a youth-oriented mass cinema by the 'Movie Brats' – including such late-underground progeny as Cronenberg, Scorsese and Lynch – was followed by a 'New Spirit' in painting, largely atavistic and expressionist in the shape of Beuys, Clemente and Baselitz. With a combination of a powerfully boosted 'commodity culture', suspicion of new media in the arts and a now fractious political left, the epoch ended with the avant-garde in retreat.

A tentative return to narrative signalled the avant-garde's unease with its own reputation for obscurity. The charge was perhaps inevitable. Non-narrative styles (poetic, lyrical, abstract or structural) were never a popular genre, and groups from Cinema 16 to the Co-ops consequently sought new audiences outside the mainstream. But the tensions of this period produced some remarkable new artists, who combined the avant-garde's formal tradition with the autobiographical twist which Le Grice's trilogy also touched on but which was most successfully explored in Lis Rhodes's *Light Reading* (1979).

Among the film-makers who emerged in England in the later 1970s,[139] most had been students of Gidal (at the RCA) or Le Grice (at St Martin's): Steve Farrer, Panny Webb, Tim Bruce, Michael Maziere, Lucy Panteli, Rob Gawthrop, Joanna Millett, Nina Danino, Will Milne, Nicky Hamlyn. Taking up some aspects of Le Grice's films (domestic location, narrative glimpses), but not their structural implications for sound and action, they turned Gidal's negative critique of film into positive; interior space is subtly personalised and vision is explored as a celebration of light. This is most marked in the quiet and reflective films of Nicky Hamlyn, who continues to explore quasi-musical structure and the intricate edge between the still and the moving image. By contrast, Nina Danino moved towards a more explicit encounter between camera and iconic image, often invested with highly emotive and religious associations. Her recent long film *Temenos* (1997) turns to landscape and symbolism with a complex soundtrack of women's voices and song.

While some rejected the visibly handheld camera for the long-take and fixed tripod (Webb, Bruce), others such as Hamlyn, Maziere and Gawthrop explored new structures of shooting and editing which derive more directly from the formal side of structural film. The work corresponds to the prevailing ethos of minimalism, post-painterly abstraction, earth art, body art, performance and conceptualism. It was anti-object and anti-gallery, seeking an art of system and process rather than commodity and product.

An early minimalist work by the American artist Robert Morris, *Box with the Sound of its own Making* (1961) set the scene – a wooden box with a tape-recorder inside it which plays the sound of the box being constructed. Later, Morris – like other sculptors and performance artists of the period – made such films as *Gas Station* (1969) and *Mirror Displacement* (1970) which explore space and perception. But the English development of the ideas implied in *Box* quickly took the form of film, sometimes in the sculpture-based work of David Dye, David Hall and Tony Sinden but also in such younger Co-op film-makers such as Steve Farrer who showed performance and cameraless films from 1975. In *Ten Drawings* (1976) lines are drawn over large areas of film made up of 16mm strips laid out in rows. The strips were then joined together to form the film which is projected. When lines cross into the soundtrack area of the film, the graphic marks are heard as abstract noise so that the drawing itself produces 'the sound of its own making'.

Morris's ideas, and minimalism generally, were based on the logic of the signifier and on teasing out degrees of self-reference within the work and on its perception by spectators. The viewer is both outside the work but also completes it by participating in its production of meaning. Morris, who works in public and museum spaces, stoically accepts (in his later essays) that art is always complicit in the power relations that govern its context. Environmental art, for example, is bound up with the corporate and state ownership which permits and indeed commissions it. Gidal and others sought to move beyond the logic of the signifier to its politics. Part of this process is a severe reduction of imagery. Gidal's most severe interdiction is on the presence of the human figure in his films, especially images of women, which he argues always provoke ideological and fantasy relations between viewer and viewed, 'the mystery, the secret, the unknown'.

Consequently in Gidal's films images never resolve into fully fledged representations. This is achieved by extremes of close-up, camera movement and focus pulling. The aim is to confront the viewer with their assumptions about, and identification with conventional representation. Gidal objects to these norms because they 're-present', i.e. show again, the already known and familiar.[140] Therefore they reinforce and reinscribe basic and unquestioned social concepts and ideologies. The task of the film-maker is to make this difficult. It leads to a self-referential cinema which is not voyeuristic. At the same time these films are wholly – it might be 'purely' – aesthetic, as in the almost musical structures, the greenish film-stock and the grain of *Room Film 1973* (a fully descriptive title). Like the colour flashes and vivid movement of his later films, they recall Brakhage – a comparison Gidal opposes, since he rejects Brakhage as myth maker and image maker.

Gidal's films thus hover on the cusp of a contradiction which they also recognise. On the one hand they lead outside film itself to the rationising and cognitive world of political debate, as does Morris. But also like Morris (for whom 'the disorienting in Art is the as yet unperceived new structure'), the films are firmly aesthetic. Providing that viewers accept the basic challenge which they offer, there is every reason for Gidal's highly visual and abstract films – and the ideas they embody to deny those very attributes – to be shown and discussed more widely. Their main impact has so far been on partisan audiences of film-makers for whom, in one respect, they are probably intended. To this extent they are also 'internal documents' of the avant-garde and part of its critical history.

Apart from Le Grice, with whom Gidal shared 'a concern for the spectator', two other contemporaries drew very different conclusions from the common nexus of 'the politics of perception'. Another migrant from New York, Steve Dwoskin, has a particular concern for both image and voyeurism. A childhood polio victim, he is severely restricted in movement. As a disabled (if extraordinarily energetic) man, he is also a visible object of attention. Two major aspects of his films spring from these facts. The first is the restricted field of vision, shooting handheld or static from one position, often hovering in close-up. The second is the image which this voyeuristic eye depicts, usually a woman who – like the film-maker – is an object of the gaze, in this case of male desire. His films explore the registers of this mutual exchange of glances, a double-reflection in which gender, spectatorship and power (over the image) are all in play. As Gidal was expunging the image of woman as sign, Dwoskin was encoding it. In *Girl* (1974) a naked woman returns the camera's gaze to challenge the viewer. The shot enshrines the 'fourth look' elaborated by Paul Willemen from Laura Mulvey's theory of 'three looks in the cinema' – camera, subject and spectator.

A second film-maker (also sculptor, installation artist and seminal video-maker) in this period, David Hall, dissents from Gidal's refusal of the image and from Dwoskin's subjective eye. His work is resolutely 'time-based', a term partly transmitted through John Latham (with whom Hall had collaborated in the Artists' Placement Group, for 'no-strings' location of artists in industry).[141] In such films as *Phased Time* (1974) the limited space of a room (less purged of personal touches than Gidal's, and more objectively shot) records the passage of time cued to rhythmical and metric sound-beats. A series of films made with Tony Sinden open up film's realist surface by creating conceptual puzzles: repetitive actions never completed, visual paradoxes caused by the plane or angle of shooting, or figures who seem to approach each other but never meet.[142]

In 1971 Hall began his unique intervention into – and against – television as a dominant, broadcast medium. Invited to contribute to the opening of Scotland's first independent channel, STV, he shot a sequence of short films (on 16mm but for TV transmission) called *Seven TV Pieces*. Each explores and ultimately destroys a particular visual image, using mostly time-lapse shooting or a single shot. They include a 'rapid-eye' compression of people watching a TV monitor in a gallery over several hours, a sink (the screen) impossibly filling and emptying with water at an angle, a double-image of two independent figures in the same space and, most elaborately, a 'multi-camera' shoot of a busy city intersection.

Each film returns us to where we began, with the monitor and image, but only after it has revealed the process of making and breaking meaning which the image encodes. In one piece a television on fire in a field is shown (by time-lapse) against scudding clouds until it is burnt out and only the frame remains. The forward flow of the film is linear, but is also fragmented by stop-frame shooting. Elegantly, for all its rough-hewn style, the film ends when the action is completed, so linking the metrical act of time-lapse shooting with the irregular time of the event itself. The film is punctuated by occasional blank screen and a male voice announcing the word 'Interruption'. This both defines the film, as it breaks into the normal television flow, and instantiates a second moment of rupture and absence within the film itself. Such double-reflection is typical of Hall's rhetorical strategy, in which an event in one medium or time-frame will comment on its enactment in another. In form, content and structure it concisely prefigures the manner and the tone (often aggressive-ironic) of Hall's later installation work.

Video stirs

Contemporary with the Film Co-op, the first stirrings of video as an art medium in the UK during the 1960s had been inspired in part by news from abroad.[143] This began with Korean artist Nam June Paik's first experiments in New York with a new portable video camera in 1965, and his guerilla slogan 'Television has been attacking us all our lives, now we can attack it back'. Like Wolf Vostell in Germany, Paik had earlier used TV sets in his Fluxus-style 'happenings', but now artists moved towards making video directly just as the first film avant-garde in the 1920s had adapted 'amateur' 35mm cine-cameras to their own devices. As many artists saw from the beginning, however, the public and corporate world of television was a very different context from the museum and gallery.

From the early 1960s, British television had gained a reputation for new ideas through such directors as Ken Russell, John Schlesinger (*Monitor*) and Ken Loach (*Wednesday Play*), through the already innovative ads, Mike Hodges' *New Tempo* arts programme, and music shows like *Ready, Steady, Go!* which – at the height of Pop Art – had already picked up visual graphics and style from the experimental cinema. The music link, which was central to the burgeoning 'counter-culture', ran through Peter Whitehead's early Rolling Stones promos and the efforts of video activist John Hopkins (always known as 'Hoppy') in his pioneering rock-nightclub UFO. The video–rock fusion, which reappeared twenty years later in Manchester, London and Brighton, was seeded here.

Fired by the expanding video culture he saw in New York, Hopkins founded the first British TV workshop and research centre, TVX, based in London's second Arts Lab – the Institute for Research into Art and Technology – at its Robert Street venue from 1969. TVX proposed to 'operate in and through electronic media … to relate to TV rather like the Film Co-op relates to cinema in general'. Through David Curtis the Arts Lab showed full and famous programmes of avant-garde and experimental films. It now acquired some video equipment – passed on by the Beatles! – and an early video projector, sometimes used by artists like Mark Boyle who at the time was doing light-shows as low-budget and home-made synaesthesia.

Hopkins's vision was public access and community art. Among his umbrella organisations the Institute for Research into Art and Technology (IRAT) was close to the US-based Raindance group, whose influential journal *Radical Software* featured the mix of video, cybernetics and science fiction now called cyberspace from 1970. Beryl Korot, better known today for her video collages with composer Steve Reich (*The Cave*, 1995, *Hindenberg*, 1997), was a member of this group.

In 1975, and buttressed by a series of impressive research papers which bear a passing resemblance to the conceptualist writings of the Art-Language team, Hopkins with Sue Hall founded the Fantasy Factory as a post-production centre for community artists. Fantasy Factory survived for over thirty years. At first the group only had limited success in gaining direct access to TV, although a notable exception was their video footage of a fruitless drugs raid on the Arts Lab in 1970 which the BBC transmitted that night – on an arts programme aptly called *Late Night Line-Up*.

The BBC established its own Community Programmes Unit, much on the Hopkins model, in 1972. Twenty years later the unit produced *Video Nation* (1994) and *Video Diaries* (1990–5) in a direct line of descent from the TVX project of public access and programme-making. A similar impulse to escape the closed world of the art scene and the gallery, but with very different results, was seen in the Artists' Placement Group, founded in 1966 by John Latham and Barbara Steveni, whose members have included David Hall, Stuart Brisley, Barry Flanagan, Ian Breakwell and Garth Evans.

Latham's radical cosmology was a highly personal construct, but APG collaborators shared his vision of 'disturbances' to the prevailing power and information sources. APG predicted the end of traditional control hierarchies and looked to the empowerment of the individual. Far less 'New Age' than Raindance, and more sceptical of cybernetic salvation, APG's interventionist tactics look ahead to the

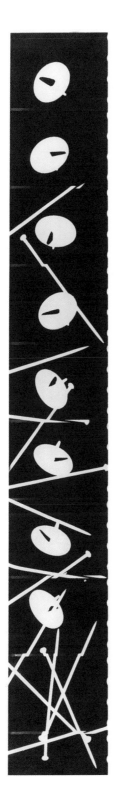

PLATE 1: *Return to Reason* (Man Ray, 1923)

PLATE 2: *Anémic cinéma* (Marcel Duchamp, 1926)

PLATE 4: *Rhythm 21* (Hans Richter, 1923)

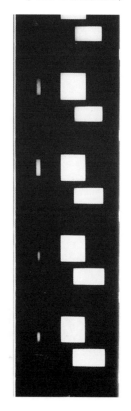

PLATE 3: *Diagonal Symphony* (Viking Eggeling, 1924)

PLATE 5: *Film Study* (Hans Richter, 1926)

PLATE 6 (ABOVE): *Allegretto* (Oskar Fischinger, 1936)

PLATE 7 (OPPOSITE): *Ballet mécanique* (Fernand Léger & Dudley Murphy, 1924)

PLATE 8 (LEFT): *Adventures of a Good Citizen* (Stefan & Franciszka Themerson, 1937)

4

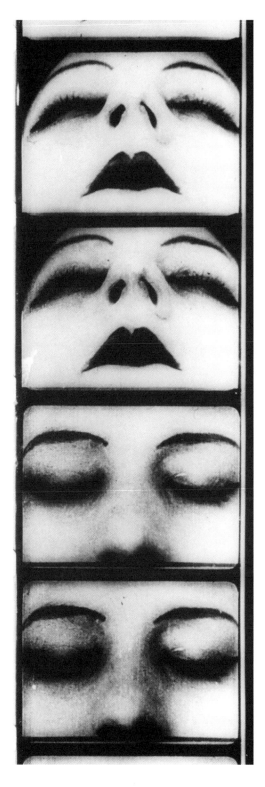

PLATE 9: *Blood of a Poet* (Jean Cocteau, 1930)

PLATE 10: *Midnight Party* (Joseph Cornell, 1940's)

PLATE 11: *Rainbow Dance* (Len Lye, 1936)

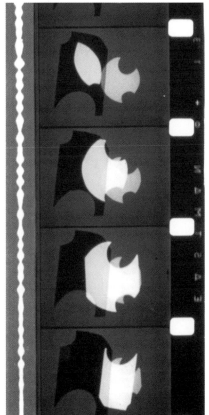

PLATE 12: *Abstract Film Exercises* (John & James Whitney, 1943–4)

PLATE 13: *Fireworks* (Kenneth Anger, 1947)

PLATE 14: *Meshes of the Afternoon* (Maya Deren & Alexander Hammid, 1943)

8

PLATE 15: *Mothlight* (Stan Brakhage, 1963)

PLATE 16 (OPPOSITE): *Thirteen Most Beautiful Women* (Andy Warhol, 1964)

PLATE 17 (ABOVE): *Flaming Creatures* (Jack Smith, 1963)

PLATE 18 (RIGHT): *The Dead* (Stan Brakhage, 1960)

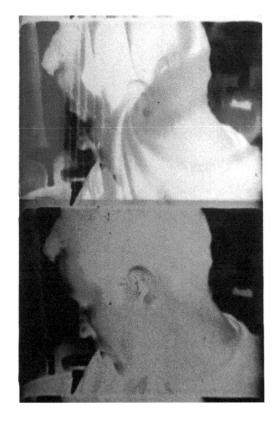

PLATE 19: *Sirius Remembered*
(Stan Brakhage, 1959)

PLATE 20: *Zorns Lemma* (Hollis Frampton, 1970)

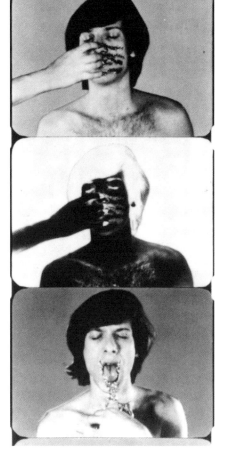

PLATE 21: *T,o,u,c,h,i,n,g* (Paul Sharits, 1968)

PLATE 22: *Runs Good* (Pat O'Neill, 1970)

PLATE 23: *Railroad Turnbridge* (Richard Serra, 1976)

PLATE 24: *Wavelength* (Michael Snow, 1967)

PLATE 25: *Lemon* (Hollis Frampton, 1969)

THIS IS A FILM ABOUT YOU

THIS IS A FILM ABOUT YOU

THIS IS A FILM ABOUT YOU

PLATE 26 (OPPOSITE): *Wind* (Joan Jonas, 1968)

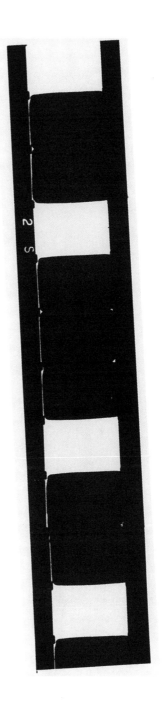

PLATE 27 (OPPOSITE): *Remedial Reading Comprehension* (George Landow, 1970)

PLATE 28 (RIGHT): *Arnulf Rainer* (Peter Kubelka, 1960)

PLATE 29: *TV* (Kurt Kren, 1967)

PLATE 30: *Rohfilm* (Birgit & Wilhelm Hein, 1968)

18

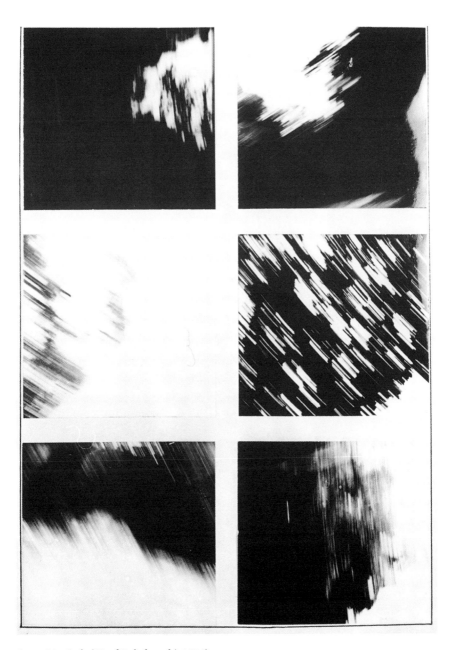

PLATE 31: *Cycle* (Józef Robakowski, 1976)

PLATE 32: *Reel Time* (Annabel Nicolson, 1973)

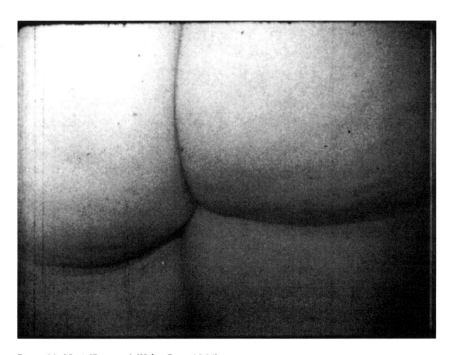

PLATE 33: *No.4 (Bottoms)* (Yoko Ono, 1966)

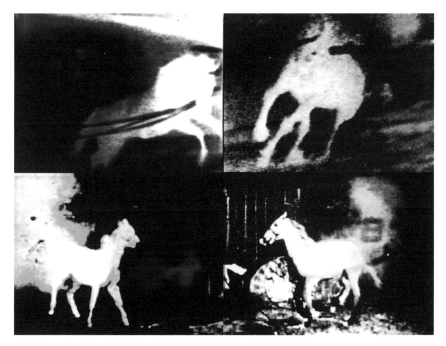

PLATE 34: *Berlin Horse* (Malcolm Le Grice, 1970)

PLATE 35: *Five Bar Gate* (David Parsons, 1976)

PLATE 36: William Raban
shooting *Thames Barrier*, 1977

PLATE 37: Rotating camera/
projector – Steve Farrer

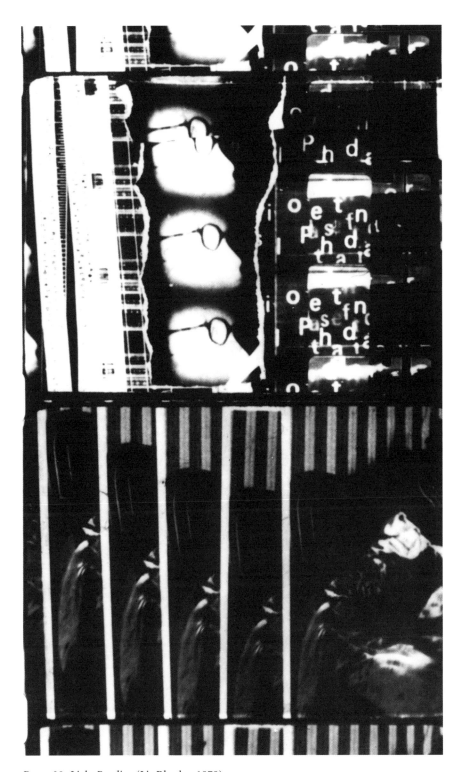

PLATE 38: *Light Reading* (Lis Rhodes, 1979)

PLATE 39: *Ghost Stories* (Nicky Hamlyn, 1983)

PLATE 40: *Short Film Series: Portrait with parents* (Guy Sherwin, 1976)

PLATE 41: *Close Up*
(Peter Gidal, 1983)

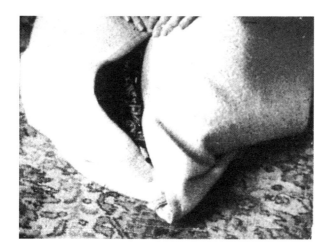

PLATE 42: *Fattendre*
(Will Milne, 1978)

PLATE 43: *Expanded Movie* (Tony Hill, 1990)

PLATE 44: *Chronos Fragmented* (Malcolm Le Grice, 1995)

PLATE 45: 'Salon of 1984' – new romantic invitation card

PLATE 46: From *7 TV Pieces* (David Hall, 1971)

PLATE 47: *Night Dances* (Sandra Lahire, 1995)

PLATE 48: *Temenos* (Nina Danino, 1998)

PLATE 49: *A13* (William Raban, 1994)

PLATE 50: *The Watershed* (Alia Syed, 1994)

PLATE 51: *Death Valley Days* (Gorilla Tapes, 1985)

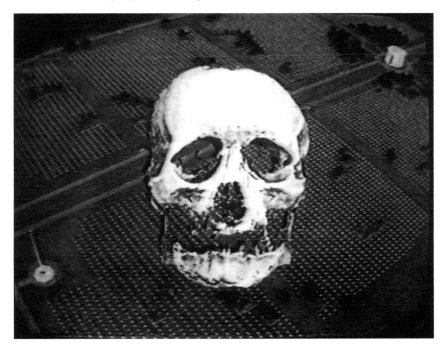

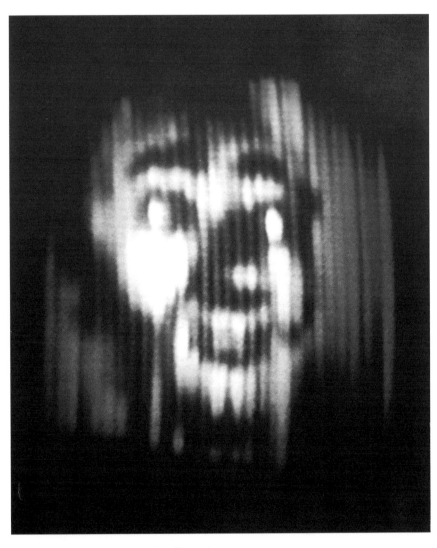

PLATE 52: *Stooky Bill TV* (David Hall, 1990)

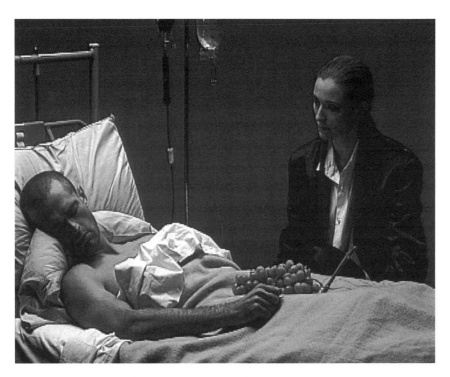

PLATE 53: *Remembrance of Things Fast* (John Maybury, 1993)

PLATE 54: *Crystal Aquarium* (Jayne Parker, 1995)

PLATE 55: *Garden of Earthly Delights: Hell* – right-hand screen of a video triptych (Judith Goddard, 1991)

PLATE 56: *Slow Glass* (John Smith, 1992)

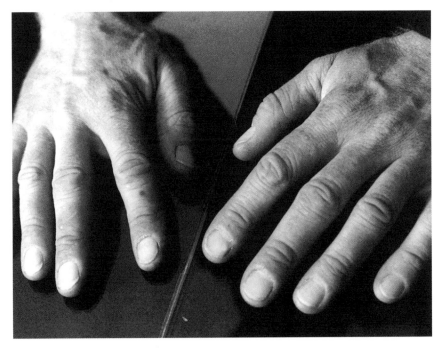

world of ambient and digital communication and to the ways its users can reshape it as artists.

The supposed 'formalism' of much early British video in the 1970s was attacked as such by Stuart Marshall for a lack of social content in a much-reprinted *Screen* article (1985).[144] But the context of the period is easily forgotten. The virtual impossibility of video editing at the time locked artists into long-takes and real-time shooting and playback. Warhol had already opened this avenue in film. 'A nice end to a piece of work was having the tape simply wind off the spool,' comments Steve Littman, a second-generation video artist. 'It seemed only logical.'

The wider scene in the 1970s included Joseph Kosuth and Dan Graham placing fake advertisements in newspapers and on billboards, Gustav Metzger's auto-destructive art events,[145] Latham's burning of his SKOOB book towers, Richard Long's slight alterations of landscape, APG's infiltrations. Daniel Buren pasted stripes on the hoardings of the Métro, Joseph Beuys swept streets as an art action and lectured on art to a dead hare, and Gerry Schum pioneered artists' video through German TV, with new work by Gilbert and George, Barry Flanagan, Hamish Fulton and Richard Long.

Although TV transmission seemed a ready extension of this anti-gallery and anti-high art movement, which in hindsight was proleptically post-modern, video artists in the UK were disadvantaged compared to those in the USA, with its network of non-commercial 'public TV' stations, and those in Germany, with its regional TV structure. The national BBC and the commercial ITV networks were harder nuts to crack, and artists' access relied on independently minded producers such as Mark Kidel, Anna Ridley and Tom Corcoran. The video movement soon fractured into three blocs, sometimes allied but often antagonistic, much as the early film avant-gardes had been, and the question of access was a particular bone of contention.

One branch were willing to be known as 'video artists', and concentrated on the conditions of video as a mode of perception and production. A second grouping includes those making 'artists' video', as David Hall dubbed it, and was inspired by such artists as Bruce Nauman (USA) and Martha Rosler (USA), using video as a rejection of traditional media rather than as an unexplored primary medium. A third set of video-makers took up the cause of community art, on the Hopkins model, in the name of content rather than form.

The absence of a developed theory of video – in contrast to film – can perhaps be traced back to these splits, in which only one of the factions, namely the video artists, was concerned to develop a conceptual apparatus for video and electronic media. But their 'formalism' was alien to the broader type of artist and to the community groups, and this brought with it the rejection of theory as well, in favour of supposedly direct art or action. The results of this disabling lack continue to hold back critical debate and analysis of video and its digital descendants.

Marshall, who did attempt to articulate the problem in the early 1980s, had begun in the milieu of video art and installation, but ultimately turned to more conventional social documentary, mainly about gay politics. His early death in 1993 deprived the community of an active and respected video-maker and polemicist. In his reply to Marshall's attack, David Hall denied that he and others accused of 'formalism' were uncritical and latter-day modernists. The context of early video art was shared with events-based and anti-object tendencies in the 1970s, and was at the time construed as an attack on high modernism and museum culture (just as the library book which Latham and his students chewed and bottled, and for which St Martin's Art School sacked him in 1966, was Greenberg's 'Art and Culture', no less).

Hall also dismisses the populist ideology of access and transparency, and the 'nebulous' notion of a broad 'moving-image culture'. Far from self-enclosed formalism, he claims that his early installations enlist the viewer's interaction 'with his/her image as collaborator rather than spectator'. He accepts that broadcast TV has already shaped or 'sited' the viewer's expectations of video art, but contests the process and language of that conditioning by exposing the specific properties of the medium. 'A conscious acknowledgement of the system's specificity here identified it as the producer of illusion which called to question dominant modes of representation.'

The recent spread of video installation into all spheres of art gallery exhibition contrasts with the 1970s when museums in the UK were less welcoming to video art, high modernist or not. An ambitious show at the Serpentine in 1975 was followed by a smaller one at the Tate in 1976, featuring Hall, Marshall and Tamara Krikorian. London Video Arts (later London Electronic Arts) was founded to promote the medium as an art form. That same year BBC's *Arena* devoted a programme to the new art, and *Studio International* – a then leading journal to which Hall and Le Grice regularly contributed – published a special video issue. These remain the peaks of British video art in its first stage, although the video debate was to re-emerge with a new set of issues at the start of the 1980s.

The questions passed on by this generation to younger film-makers in the later 1970s were therefore various and divided. Gidal proposed the most extreme position in rigorously excluding the iconic image as representation. The highly iconic films of Dwoskin (and David Larcher) blended neo-structural film with an underground tradition which expanded vision through an erotics of the eye. Le Grice further compounded elements of both, but with the erotic structure neither suppressed (as by Gidal) nor celebrated (as by Dwoskin and Larcher) but rather sublimated into the metaphors of 'family romance' which underpin his structural return to narrative. Hall steps outside of these internalised and subjective scenarios to affirm temporality as measure and the iconic image as undeniable but transient. Tellingly, and unlike the structuralist tendency which treats the 'spectator' as an individual in a cinema, Hall's notion of 'the spectator' increasingly embraced the greatest passive audience of all, who are watching TV rather than avant-garde films.

Art and politics

Broadly the structural tendency won out in those younger film-makers who showed their first films around 1977. It was their immediate legacy and context, although each distanced themselves from it. The underground visionary tradition (in Larcher and Dwoskin, partly in Jeff Keen and later in Derek Jarman) went further underground, and was only picked up again in the 1980s by new groups who definitively rejected structural film. These were not the only options. Political film-makers who had emerged in the wake of 1960s radicalism, and who were influenced by diverse movements from the avant-garde through to Godard and documentary cinema, were still active throughout the 70s.[146] They included Cinema Action, whose origins in agit-prop later produced *The Miners' Film* and the extraordinary working-class community portrait *Shirley*, the Poster/Film Collective and other grassroots campaign groups.

The Berwick Street Collective began *The Nightcleaners* (1975) as a straight documentary but it ended as a highly formal film which questioned its own mode of representation and tried to break established conventions of viewing. Peter Wollen and Laura Mulvey's *Riddles of the Sphinx* (1976), preceded by their more 'writerly' and formal film-essay *Penthesilea* (1974), traced the politicisation of a young woman through the themes of separation and childcare. It has a pyramidical structure with a central section of thirteen circular pans. The film attempts to construct feminist discourses in a triangulation of Marxism, semiotics and psychoanalysis. In this context, and by contrast, structural film did not produce the polysemous cinema which Wollen had earlier called for, a combination of word, image, drama and photography. It was therefore seen as essentialist, although judged by its own abstract criteria no more so than music, long regarded as the purest and most non-referential of the arts.

The wider context of the English avant-garde was bordered by the general idea of an independent cinema, the role of the journal *Screen* in disseminating the artistic and political theories of Russian Futurism and formalism, and its promotion of theory on the broader front, and – on the horizon – the changing and expanding world of 'cultural' television.

When the Independent Film Maker's Association was founded in 1975 (video was added to the title in the 1980s), it resembled the unions of artists, political cinema and intelligentsia which formed in Europe between the world wars. It was a timely move, but only just, to link the factions of the radical cinema between two moments of defeat. These were the visible dissolving of the political moment of the 60s, which had stimulated film-makers globally from Rocha to Godard, and the soon-to-be visible ascendancy of the right which under Thatcher and Reagan dominated the next decade.

The IFA fought on several fronts. The first was to secure funding, initially by pressure on the UK's cultural centre for cinema, the British Film Institute. Under Peter Sainsbury, co-editor with Simon Field of the then leading avant-garde journal *Afterimage*, the BFI's Production Board swung decisively to the IFA position. But with the exception of such films as *The Nightcleaners* and *Shirley*, and a clutch of experimental films by Gidal and others, the results were often disappointingly weighed down rather than liberated by the role-models of Godard, Straub and Duras. The post-Straubian costume-drama became a minor genre, usually used to revisit working-class history, and some procedural tropes – notably the long-take and an insistent screen flatness – were overvalued as direct purveyors of meaning. Brechtian dramaturgy was here taken too literally. Nonetheless, these modes were later transmuted into a more pliable moulding of television language (through the early experiments of Channel 4) while regional circulation by the BFI led to active film groups well beyond the London-based centres.

This regionalisation cracked open the metropolis-led BFI, and its Regional Film

Theatres were often test-beds for new film ideas. Like the other main funding agency, the Arts Council of Great Britain (now split into the substates of the UK), the BFI tried to spread the network of independent film screening and even production. This was the period of the IFA-inspired 'workshop movement', which pioneered community and local access to film-making. Few remain in their original shape, but the systems set up during this period by the BFI and the Arts Council have survived, enabling films to be made outside the commercial framework. Here, as notably in Germany and the USA, the need to cost and secure film as a cultural and artistic 'non-profit' medium was recognised. David Curtis made an early (1967) case for cultural subsidy, lambasting the then recalcitrant BFI in the pages of the underground magazine *The International Times*. A decade later, as a Film Officer at the Arts Council, he was able to set these principles in motion.

Along with Rodney Wilson, who revitalised the British art documentary and turned it into an innovative broadcast genre, he made the Arts Council into the lead funding agency for artists' film and video production and exhibition for over twenty-five years. Its selection panels, which comprise artists, critics and curators, reflect the changing and often volatile climate in which experimental work is made and shown. It has particularly promoted artists' work on television and in the art gallery, two distinct venues which in the earlier days of the Co-op were not on the agenda but which now are vital to its survival.

The IFA was a more fragile and temporary union, strung together by partisans for a 'free cinema' from many different and contradictory if overlapping directions: Cinema Action, the Co-op, disaffected media workers, parts of *Screen*, film students, documentarists and artists in loose alliance. Astonishingly its impact lingers on. Many of its members were to spread out into the wider mainstream, transmitting its key values into documentary television: John Ellis, Anne Cottringer, Simon Hartog, Keith Griffiths, Rod Stoneman.

Most notably it exerted pressure on the formation of the new 'cultural channel' C4, arguing for flexible crewing in production (an avant-garde model later ironically adapted by the industry to cut costs) and for innovative programme-making. When C4's own independent slot, very much of the IFA ilk, was set up by Alan Fountain and Rod Stoneman in the early 80s, they aptly called their weekly late-night programme *The Eleventh Hour*. It showed both historical work and new commissions. Again burdened by good intentions but flawed productions, its programme title ironises its own moment. Yet, even if its hour was almost over, the programme opened the TV airwaves to independent commissions and screenings where before, of course, there was nothing at all.

A final effect of the IFA period was on the intellectual climate in which film was understood, disseminated and discussed. While *Screen* was by no means unanimously in favour of the (existing) independent cinema or the avant-garde – which was sceptical both about popular culture and direct political statement – it was in part sympathetic to the theory and rhetoric of the structural avant-garde. Firstly, the journal's historical rediscoveries of the early to mid-1970s notably included Russian Futurism, a movement which coincides with the first film avant-garde and indeed is part of its own story. At the same time, structural film-makers – then at their zenith – were similarly refinding their partly constructivist ancestry. The coincidence of names – 'structure' appears in both – suggests as much.

Secondly, the radical reconstruction of viewing and understanding film which *Screen* undertook can obviously be related to the deconstruction of vision pursued by Gidal, Welsby and Le Grice. The journal thus made room for Stephen Heath, Peter Wollen, Deke Dusinberre and Gidal himself to explore the adjacence of avant-garde film theory to post-structural film critique. The role of the spectator was high on the agenda of both. Emblematically, the full ideological, historical and psychoanalytic apparatus of 'Screen-theory' was astutely deployed by Philip Drummond in 1977 to anatomise a key film of the avant-garde, *Un Chien andalou* (the same film, but compared to *Meshes of the Afternoon*, opens Sitney's *Visionary Film*).

Screen and the avant-garde could group together on certain historical revisions (both could contribute, for example, to the growth of a new film history grounded in theories of film space and archival research), and via the IFA they united on a more active programme of screening and debate. They divided more severely on the issues of narrative, realism and representation, which *Screen* analysed critically but which the avant-garde rejected as primary goals for film.

It was in this climate that Peter Wollen produced his essay 'The Two Avant-Gardes', which sought to draw together the political-art cinema of Godard and Straub with the artists' cinema of Snow, Landow and Brakhage.[147] It first appeared in a special 'avant-garde film' issue of the then leading British art journal *Studio International* in 1975, alongside David Curtis's lucid and anecdotal diary of the English avant-garde and Dusinberre's exposé of the landscape genre then emerging. A year later the essay was reprinted for the 'other', i.e. political, theoretical avant-garde assembled at the Edinburgh Film Festival (at that time a cultural-interventionist event rather than an industrial showcase).

In this essay, and in line with Peter Bürger's *Theory of the Avant-Garde*, modernism itself is seen to make up the cultural mainstream, and as such was now compromised by its own assimilation to past traditions through the long march of history – especially art history. The weight of cultural critique or rupture is therefore axially shifted from the mainstream to the marginal avant-gardes which haunt the fringes of conventional modernism. These include radical film movements, whether led by political or by cultural motivations. While Bürger focused on the failure of the historical avant-gardes and their latter-day revivals to achieve their aims, Wollen was (and remains) more optimistic about them. The IFA is now itself history – and barely remembered – but the dilemmas Wollen adduces still remain, adapted to new social pressures.

A cinema of small gestures[148]

Just as the new film theory was permeating the institutions of film culture in the UK (paralleled in the USA), so film-making emerged in art colleges as an addition to traditional media. Some younger structural film-makers (and many of the Godard–Straub drama documentarists) grouped at the RCA, where Gidal, Dwoskin and Ray Durgnat taught. Rob Gawthrop was especially prolific in the late 1970s in films about time structures, image degeneration and the physical manipulation of the filmstrip. *Distancing* (1979) pulls focus on a rainy window, throwing light and the shapes of objects into flux. Superimposition thickens the texture while dematerialising the image and object. The film is shot from a fixed position but no transcendental or cardinal viewpoint is implied. Lucy Panteli integrated images of women into the formal agenda, shooting time-exposures over long periods to show women knitting, making up and so on (*Photoplay*, 1982). The compression of time is extreme, but the film is at the edge of content that took it elsewhere, to a plane of expression where gesture becomes action.

A new cinema of small gestures emerged on two adjacent fronts. The first was an elaborated rhetoric of the handheld camera, purified – via Gidal – of its more Brakhagean excesses although similarly using focus-pulls, pans, tilts, superimposed zooms and staggered repeats (as with Michael Maziere) or close-up, transition, abstracted colour and 'serial' editing (in Nicky Hamlyn who, with Nick Collins, was linked to this group through the LFMC). Maziere, Hamlyn and others made 'room films' in which, space, window, exterior, camera and light are subjected to systems or processes which combine chance and predetermination. They were inspired by Gidal, but he had neutralised his rooms to become 'a dimly lit arena in which low-powered signifieds could not flood the workings of the signifier' (Hamlyn). The new films were more personal. In essence they were in the lyric tradition of the film poem and the art of vision.

Maziere's later work was to become even more autobiogaphically centred on the seeing eye (as in *Cézanne's Eye I and II*, 1987/8) while Hamlyn concentrates on the camera-eye to destabilise space and to reorder the visual flux. His most compressed abstract film, *Minutiae* (1990), a 1-minute commission for the *Late Show* (BBC TV) is comprised wholly of images (notably a chair) and sounds taken from the TV studio in which the film was made. The longer and episodic *White Light* (1996) explores rhythmic variations on objects and reflections in close-up, a lineage that goes back to Chomette and particularly to Léger/Murphy's *Ballet mécanique*. These films seek the viewers' active participation in film as process, to revise the codes of perception which structure the visible. They expand positively on Gidal's strategies of denial through the hallmarks of film grain, colour, light and focus.

Le Grice too had turned to domestic space, in his narrative trilogy. These are built on formal patterns of point of view around icons which enigmatically evoke, but in pared-down variant form, the psychodrama (as in *Emily*, 1979, in which the film-maker appears, a table is cleaned, a lamp is lit, a record is played, recalling the tropes of Maya Deren). The trilogy descends from such films as *After Lumière – L'arroseur arrosé* (1974) which both inscribes the primitive cinema (through Lumière) and the Dada epoch (Satie's music as soundtrack) within two further emblems – the film-maker's house and garden. The actors are family and friends, as in the trilogy. Le Grice has discussed these works in terms of the psychology of space-perception, and of narrative identification achieved and exposed in the cinematic shift of attention and viewpoint. These concerns are, not accidentally, shared with cubism (Le Grice was another former painter). He has not commented on the autobiographical aspects of these films, but some of their implications for visual narrative were influential towards the end of the structural era.

This comprised a second cinema of small gestures, closer to the narrative domain. It includes Tim Bruce's *Corrigan Having Remembered* (1979) which has a story and vestigial drama but is projected in fragments as a multi-screen instal-lation. Penny Webb's *Young Girl in Blue* (1977) stands for a number of cryptic and minimalist narrative films, notable for their use of silence and long-shots, partly modelled on Straub as well as structural film. The absence of activity is a strategy of eknosis, or 'emptying out'. Only a few were able to sustain and fill the founding 'negative moment' of this trend. Some did so by merging into the 'room film' sub-genre, with its small human actions, domestic locale and occasional glimpses of nudity.

In the films of Will Milne, one of the most talented of this circle (but who became disenchanted with film and gave up in 1987), the urge to visual poetry supersedes any impulse to fiction. Like the surrealists he called for 'films to get under your retina', a clear rejection both of straight drama and concept-art. *Parts* (1975) comprises two black and white shots, one of a close-up fingertip hovering over a surface, the other a quadruple exposure of a figure in a room. Both are abstracted, resisting interpretation and even visuality in the line of Man Ray, also a film-maker of absences.

By 1977 Milne was making elliptical narratives rhetorically anchored by a fixed time-frame, a predetermined number of words spoken in shot, and formal brack-eting between shots such as dissolves, focus and the like. Of such neo-Cagean pro-cedures, Milne said 'the idea was to void text, acting, montage, etc. of drama, to emphasise the drama of decision and technology meeting the given of objects, bodies, spaces'. The culmination of Milne's ideas in *Same* (1980), where space is subtly sexualised by body images, effectively but regrettably ended his career as a film-maker.

In the USA Sue Friedrich (*Gently Down the Stream*, 1981) and Leslie Thornton (*Adynata*, 1983) combined elements from the trance film (dream as source), structural film (handmade process), direct performance (via Yvonne Rainer) and feminist theory. In the UK structural rigour was inflected by personal vision and memory. John Smith rivals George Landow in humour and style, crafting in *Slow Glass* (1988–91) an engaging personal narrative which is slowly revealed as both a filmic construction and a metaphor of urban history. He draws attention to the ephemeral and paradoxical nature of the visual world and its structuring by lan-guage. Jayne Parker, by contrast, uses elliptical metaphor and photogenic clarity to directly convey emotional states, although her long videotape *Almost Out* (1986) is an analytic exploration of speech, confession, nakedness and duplicity. Like Smith, her most recent films have TV backing (for example, *Cold Jazz*, 1993), which begs the question of avant-garde obscurity.

Other art forms in this period also sought to explore the extremes of duration and perception: an eclectic list includes Peter Brook, Peter Stein and Robert Wilson (theatre), Morton Feldman, LaMonte Young and Steve Reich (music), Christo, Robert Smithson and Carl Andre (sculpture). The passage of time is treated as a material component of the work, and essential to the viewer's experi-ence of it. In film, partly to escape the fictive elision of time in narrative drama, some film-makers stressed 'decay, transience and destruction as positive features of the cinematic experience' (Le Grice). Peter Gidal underlines his uncompromis-ing attack on narrative in the 'negative' titles of his later and highly abstracted films: *Denials* (1986), *Guilt* (1988), *Flare Out* (1992).

Although the origins of structural film lay well outside the academy (in Kren, Warhol and Fluxus), by the 1970s it was largely based in the colleges where many practitioners taught – from Buffalo and San Francisco to London, Hamburg and Lodz. Initially a strength, as education expanded, by the end of the decade structural film was charged with pedantry and élitism. For some, Gidal and Le Grice's anti-cinema polemic 'could not constitute a self-sufficient artistic theory', as Hamlyn notes in reviewing the period, although it passed on lessons to film-makers who deal with perception, the eye, the relation of time to movement and the technology of film.

But at this point the context was altering. The conceptual base of structural film stressed non-identity (sound and image; word and object; screen and viewer). This message was out of favour by 1979, with mainstream cinema poised for the consumer revolution and younger film-makers urged by post-punk aesthetics to break free of the structural grid. Image saturation triumphed over the interdicted image of the previous era (when Le Grice condoned representation only if it was critical, for example). There was a loss in conceptual grip and a flood of gratuitous imaging, but a gain in imaginative vigour and renewal.

Rebel waves

The rebellion came in the early 1980s, with a wave of low-tech 8mm and fast-cut video. 'Scratch' (improvised) video-makers in the UK (George Barber, the Duvet Brothers, Guerilla Tapes) re-edited TV footage with Reagan, Thatcher and the 'military-industrial complex' as main targets, using montage to create parody in the style of Montagu's *Peace and Plenty* (quoted in the Duvets' *Blue Monday* to a New Order soundtrack) and the films of Bruce Conner.[149] Politically astute and sharply cut (often to rock soundtracks), its devices were swallowed up by TV advertising and promos with alarming speed, especially after Scratch video was showcased at the 1985 Edinburgh Television Festival and made an immediate impact on the astonished TV executives. So were the more rigorous montage stylistics of the Polish film-maker Zbigniew Rybzynski (*Tango, Steps*), openly imitated by a now-famous ad for Ariston washing-machines.

This direction – very much of its epoch – 'split the movement' and temporarily united the other parts of the avant-garde in opposition to it. This was a sure sign that something new was in the air. The structural film-makers were understandably the most hostile, given their profound antagonism to commercialism. Structural film had already undergone a major crisis in 1979, when feminist film-makers challenged what they saw as the male bias and general authoritarianism of the major retrospective of formal work, 'Film As Film', at the Hayward Gallery in 1979. Their withdrawal left empty spaces in the show itself (although historic figures such as Dulac and Deren were still represented) and precipitated a women's film collective and distribution centre Circles, under Felicity Sparrow.[150]

Now, however, there was a shared distaste for the after-effects as structural hegemony disintegrated. The political-narrative film-makers agreed, and the Co-op's journal *Undercut* (a major achievement for the times which ran to over eighteen issues between 1981–90) reflected a serious and sombre tone well after an even newer generation was running riot in the media. *Undercut* extended the range of thought about experimental film, and by attracting contributors from across the arts scene – especially for its exemplary 'Landscape' issue – it maintained very high standards. It therefore became a voice, sometimes a lonely one, against the commercialisation of art. At the same time this cut it off from some of the more open directions that were emerging. This even applied to those varieties of the new romantic trend which appeared within the Film Co-op itself, partly in the person of the then cinema organiser, Cordelia Swann.

Swann's 'New Romantics' similarly represented a return of the repressed in the form of the post-Cocteau baroque, even though it saw itself as an artists' group and had no direct commercial goals. The provocative epithet 'Romantic' suggests this, as does the persistence of avant-gardism in the term 'New'. But this was not a war of words, except in the sense that anti-structural film-makers rebelled against theory and language. They did not write critiques or manifestos as their predecessors did, especially not for *Undercut* let alone *Screen* (that came later, especially through the mediation of Isaac Julian and gay media politics). The debate in the earlier 1980s was largely tacit. It was, however, enacted and implied in the films of different factions.

In the UK 'New Romanticism' revived interest in Kenneth Anger, Jean Cocteau and Jean Genet as film-makers outside the structural canon. Genet's *Chant d'amour* (1950) become an emblem of the radical gay film culture. Clandestine love between warder and prisoner is evoked in high symbolism (hands pass a rose between barred windows) and grainy realism (men in cells). It inspired a new 'cinema of transgression', promoted by the charismatic Derek Jarman and seen notably in the early films of John Maybury and Cerith Wyn Evans. Tellingly, an early compilation film from this milieu was titled *The Dream Machine* (1984). They share something of the baroque 'new spirit in painting' of Cy Twombly, Sandro Chia and Francisco Clemente. As with them, the rough look is a crafted one, exploiting 8mm beyond its limits (Steve Chivers' technical skills were much in demand at the RCA and the Slade, before he turned to feature film and advertising cinematography). Film and video were pioneeringly fused in the edit-suite, an anti-purist gesture which was soon commercially exploited and is now standard practice.

The turn to 'low-tech' and often to Super-8 thus coincided with the rise of a commercial fringe, pioneering the eclectic rise of rock videos and promos in which this group took part. By the end of the 1980s the margins had spread to the core of the new commercial rock culture. Sophie Muller's *Savage* (1987), for The Eurythmics, blends avant-garde elliptical editing with comic pastiche (from Americana to Julie Andrews) and 80s urban paranoia. This new sub-cultural style drew heavily on the aesthetics of experimental film. Paradoxically, the residues of structural form (repetition, duration, flicker and blur) – never eradicated from New Romantic films – finally seeped into industrial film and video.

Three currents, only loosely connected at first, had fused by the end of the decade. The first was the 'scratch' movement, which revived political collage and pioneered low-band video, the then equivalent to the 16mm bolex camera. The second was the low-budget promo, revitalising an almost lost surrealism and moving from film to video and back again in a new form of hybrid editing. This group merged into the third category, the largely 8mm film-makers in the 'New

Romantics' camp. Together, they sparked off a decade in which younger experimental artists and film-makers blended into the commercial sector inspired by new TV outlets and popular culture.

While this shocked the traditional avant-garde by a wholesale adoption of once-tabooed imagery and style taken in part from Anger and Cocteau, the new avant-garde was a run-up to the explosion of 'Brit Art' over the next decade. Embracing another taboo, commercial culture, distanced it from its predecessors and drew it close to a growing distaste for high theory, partly expressed in the rise of media studies and its valorisation of popular style. It also invented new formats – the pop video was latent in Conner, Anger and Jarman but this group made it manifest – and were part of the new music culture represented by independent labels. It was to this volatile cultural economy that the avant-garde shifted its interests. The 'youth' link led it to directly participate in mainstream output, once the 80s led to a consumer boom in which music and youth cultures were market leaders.

At the same time, many of the film- and video-makers promoted other values besides the commercial; dedicated to low technologies as well as the most advanced, this was a cinema with its own politics of the dispossessed (gays, visionaries, cardboard city) and an iconography of the bizarre and the extreme which – however recuperated in the commercial work they undertook – kept a sharp edge to the work. A compact example is the opening of Jarman's *The Last of England* (the title an allusion to Ford Madox Brown's famous Victorian portrait of poor *émigrés* leaving Britain, here with an anti-Thatcher twist) in which handheld 8mm cameras move around derelict urban landscapes while young toughs shoot heroin, desecrate the Union Flag and roam the burning wasteland.

Art Cinema's odd couple: Derek Jarman and Peter Greenaway[152]

As structural film broke up as a coherent movement and a new wave of younger film-makers grew beyond its margins, roughly between the late 1970s and the late 1980s, two older film artists rose into public view. They were not alone in crossing from the avant-garde fringe to a more mainstream style of production in this period. Sally Potter, for example, moved swiftly through multi-screen projection and live-art to the much-debated feminist drama *Thriller* (1979) and ultimately to more expansive 35mm features such as *Orlando* (1992). But Derek Jarman and Peter Greenaway succeeded on a quite different scale, outside the ghetto of the Coop but inside the art world as film-makers on equal terms with other artists. By the end of the decade they were household names, with a clutch of feature-length films widely screened, broadcast and sold on video in mass outlets. In short, they made up – but with considerable differences between them – a fully fledged auteur-based art cinema for the first time in the history of British film-making. And like the international Art Cinema, their appeal was international, even though both of them embraced particularly British themes.

This unexpected rise of the dynamic duo, who were of course wholly at odds with each other in terms of film aesthetics, was all the more remarkable since they shared the same artisan-maker and art-school base as their contemporaries such as Le Grice and Larcher. Jarman, Curtis and Le Grice all went to the Slade School of Art in the 1960s, and Larcher was at the RCA. Also like Larcher and Tom Phillips (one of Greenaway's main collaborators), Jarman studied for a university first degree before he took up his main career as an artist. Both Jarman and Greenaway continued to work in other art forms, notably collage and painting, while they made their increasingly ambitious films. Greenaway is also a prolific designer of large-scale installations which expand his capacity for urban myth making, data catalogues and taxonomies of the body.

These backgrounds and activities, which correspond so closely to the general make-up of the Co-op structuralists, and to underground film as a whole, did not lead them to identify with the structural project or the Co-op movement itself. Mutual antagonism has, rather, characterised their relation to the avant-garde more strictly defined. Although both were of the 'first-Co-op' generation in age, their rise to public attention dates from the later 1970s. Jarman began with 8mm diary films in the 1970s, with much use of the single-frame and of slow-motion refilming from the screen. Greenaway, who also more normatively worked for many years as an editor at the Central Office of Information, a linear descendant of Grierson's documentary cinema, first came to prominence with such films as *Vertical Features Remake* (1978) – a parody of structural cinema, imbued with its style and obsessions but counter to its internalised ambitions. Both film-makers celebrated rather than denounced illusionist cinema, even as they gave it a unique and personal twist.

At no point in their careers, however, did their films adopt British mainstream realism. Jarman's films, although they were often heavily scripted and acted, are punctuated by the same formal features which appear in Greenaway's films, notably the slow pan and the lateral track. In his more recent films, Greenaway has turned to full multi-media production, weaving text, image and light in a digital collage which overtly alludes to high modernism and post-cubist space, as in *The Pillow Book* (1996). This parallels Jarman's enthusiasm, towards the end of his life, for breeding new cinematic cross-breeds between Super-8, 16mm and digital video editing. Such thoroughgoing anti-realism does not however bring these authors any closer to the Co-op orbit. And while it might be supposed that the high theoretical tone of Co-op debate in the late 1970s might have alienated any but the initiated, which was indeed the case, both Greenaway and Jarman were far from anti-intellectual artists. But the same is true of Larcher, Keen and Dwoskin, each of them highly literate and not at all 'structural-materialists', but who kept closer to their Co-op roots while avoiding the ambitious drama film – such as *Caravaggio* or *The Draughtsman's Contract* – with which Jarman and Greenaway made their names.

So it remains a question as to why, in the end, two film-makers from the same background as the 'classic' English avant-garde have broken so free of it as to appear, in the eyes of many of their supporters and audiences, to inhabit a different space from it and to be untinged by the traditional complaints about avant-garde obscurantism even as they remained defiantly 'arty' and anti-populist. Neither did they split this new audience into divided factions, however deep the differences between them – despite, for example, the relentless gay politics of the one and the heterosexual (if misanthropic) masculinity of the other. For much of the 1980s Jarman-and-Greenaway appeared to be two equal sides of the same new coin, British Art Cinema, as it spun in the air.

The reasons for this improbable alliance, which led to great individual success and achievements for the decidely odd couple of British cinema, are complex and various. First of all, their formidable personal energies were expressed in a prolific output of work, not just of films and television programmes but also of books, diaries, exhibitions and (as has been noted) visual work in other media such as painting and printmaking. The volume of their artistic production is impressive in itself. British film directors of comparable vigour – most of them also, incidentally, with art school training – headed to Hollywood in this generation as fast as they could go: Ridley Scott, Alan Parker and John Boorman, for example. By contrast, Jarman and Greenaway stood against the tide, and anti-Americanism was among their hallmarks. Rather than surrendering their visual talents to American commercialism, as did their peers, they stood up in favour of cinema as a fine art and gave high modernism an openly British flavour. There had been nothing like it since Ken Russell and Lindsay Anderson, older film-makers who similarly resisted the safer options and who were roundly attacked for their pains – as was Michael Powell in his time.

Secondly, they rose to fame when the social and political climate was dominated by Prime Minister Thatcher's resurgent capitalism and triumphalist heralding of free enterprise, which both of them clearly loathed. While Jarman set a new agenda for gay pride as an art form, Greenaway's arcane savagery undermined straight society in a different way. If Mrs Thatcher was the new Elizabeth, or even Bloody Mary, here were two Jacobeans ahead of the game. Each made proleptic and caustic attacks on the new order to come, Jarman with his nightmare vision of derelict London, *Jubilee* (1977), and Greenaway with his troubling morality tale of private enterprise, *The Draughtsman's Contract* (1978). In the long period of Tory rule from 1979 to the later 1990s, their films explored the extreme edges of the national psyche and irritated its sore spots: sexual psychosis, greed, nostalgia, corruption, madness and exploitation. This heady mixture had a ripe appeal for the disaffected liberal intellegentsia who had precious few images to identify with in the age of Essex Man. And so, in this sense, they spoke to – and against – the age, and found for themselves a ready and radical audience.

But were they an avant-garde?[153] Socially and culturally, yes – but artistically, less so. This was for two main reasons. In the first place, and in spite of their own protestations, both film-makers were driven towards the theatrical, the literary and the symbolic. Their films are highly text driven, and their visual impact was chained rather than liberated by the preordained shooting strategies which they adopted. While the long-take and the swooping camera were containers of focused vision in the hands of Snow, Brakhage, Le Grice and Gidal, the same procedures – once they were inflated to fully crewed 35mm production by Jarman and Greenaway – seemed to lose the direct authorial touch and acquired a bombastic, overblown weight. By the mid-1980s, when these two directors had achieved high profile and seemed ready with an opinion on everything, this seemed to hold them back from the artistic freedom they craved for their films. It is perhaps this limitation which by contrast gives their smaller scale and personal work its particular freshness and resonance: Jarman's *The Garden* (1990) and his film of terminal blindness and vision, *Blue* (1993), for example, or Greenaway's exemplary TV profiles of composers such as John Cage and Meredith Monk (C4, 1983) where his documentary concentration on these artists subdues the aggrandisement which often overpowers his creative work.

A second reason for questioning their role as an avant-garde is that they failed directly to influence the mainstream, either by questioning it to the point of aggravation (in the manner of Hall and Gidal) or by altering its visual grammar in a process of osmosis and transformation (as in the impact of structural film on the montage ad or TV sting, devices which now permeate 'normal' television). Both Jarman and Greenaway were pretty much *sui generis*. It is difficult to think of any mainstream or TV work which has been touched by their style or hand – other than the work they themselves have made for these media. Jarman's influence has indirectly been filtered through film-makers such as John Maybury and – in the early years – Cerith Wyn-Evans. Greenaway has no disciples through which to act. Patrick Keiller's films, notably *London* (1996), share his qualities of dry commentary and formal stasis (and have similarly found wide audiences for the avant-garde film), but seem to emerge independently from related roots, such as surrealism and the subversive side of the English baroque from Rochester to De Quincey.

With no school to follow them, they remain sacred monsters of the British cinema, independent but to that degree also isolated. And this isolation, paradoxically, is what undermines their effectiveness as an avant-garde. Classic avant-gardes either stand squarely on their own ground or they influence their surroundings – with any luck, they do both. Jarman and Greenaway are wild birds in the media jungle, part of the landscape rather than divergent from it. Their impact on cinema audiences has been greater than that of their artistic contemporaries – but this is not the point insofar as their continual influence is concerned. Jarman's canon is now sadly closed, while Greenaway's remains vigorously open, but it is difficult at this stage to see who will take up their cinematic options as film- and video-makers.

Ironically, their popular appeal may ultimately rest on what they share with the conventional British cinema, which they otherwise loathe and oppose as individual authors. Despite their anti-realism, both directors adopted the drama and acted script, with its narrative implication. Two early key works are in the 'costume-drama' mode, as in *The Draughtsman's Contract* and Jarman's first feature-length success *Sebastiane* (1977) – although this film subverts the genre by its spoken text in Latin and its wholesale nudity! But the construction of illusionist and narrative space through set design and drama, however destabilised or combined with image manipulation (frontality, digital abstraction and shooting speed) is a hallmark of their cinema films. This brings them closer to the picaresque British drama and history film than either perhaps could have wished. Perhaps nothing illustrates this more than their ambitious but very different versions of late Shakespeare, Jarman's film of *The Tempest* and Greenaway's *Prospero's Books*. In a sense, both projects seek to realise Michael Powell's long-cherished aim to film this particular and emblematic play. To do so, however, is to adapt to the overwhelming tradition of the English drama, in this case through its most visionary instance.

The films of Jarman and Greenaway raise cultural questions which exceed the scope of this book, but which can't be wholly avoided if the focused limits of the British post-war avant-gardes are to be made clear. And this is also the reason for perhaps unfairly yoking these directors together in this context. The key rationale is surely that both invoke the dissident Anglo-British tradition from the Elizabethans through Congreve and Gay to the dystopian satirists Wilde, Waugh and Orwell, down to Dennis Potter, Peter Reading and Iain Sinclair in our own time. This tradition, as is obvious, is based on words and not pictures.

It cannot be a coincidence that, as painters, Jarman and Greenaway are closer to the expressionist and illustrative veins in English art, respectively; and that the Co-op structural avant-garde emerged (from Le Grice to Hamlyn) through colour-field abstraction. Younger artists, including the generation of Jayne Parker, John Maybury, Cerith Wyn-Evans and Gillian Wearing, inherit an even more flexible climate in which the territorial borders between the art media have been relaxed. This was reflected in the art education which they would have received from the 1970s and 1980s, when they graduated and made their first films. But while this relaxation – which does not exclude rigour and defined purpose – can be traced back to 1960s Pop Art from which Jarman, Le Grice, Greenaway and Gidal all emerged, there are substantial differences which complicate the picture.

British Pop Art undertook the reverse task from its American version. For Warhol, Lichtenstein and Johns, Pop was an exit route from what they felt to be the narrow corridors of purist painting. What they experienced as oppressive – the high art regime of colour abstraction – was for the British a liberation, and so British Pop tended to merge abstract art with figuration in ways that at that point were blocked off to the Americans. From Bacon to Hockney and Hamilton, this gave the British a way out of *their* dilemma – the old choice between age-of-anxiety expressionist painting and its alternative in illustrative drawing, which dominated the post-war years through to the 1950s. The blurring between colour-field painting and mass-culture iconicity was thus a creative option for the British, even though it presented the Americans with a stark choice and no alternative at almost exactly the same time.

The result of this seemingly bizarre procedure was that, arguably for the first time since the 1930s (since Read, Moore, Nicolson and Hepworth soaked up surrealist and constructivist ideas from mainland Europe), but on a massively expanded scale, British art finally and belatedly entered the modernist mainstream around 1962 and has never looked back. The recidivist elements in Jarman and Greenaway, their reliance on text and emblem in their painting as well as their films, suggest that they never achieve full parturition from the 'native' English tradition, and never break free of English art's damning tendency to whimsy. The irony is that the native tradition wasn't all that English; like the best ideas in British art it was imported. Unlike the St Ives group in the 1930s, who embraced abstraction with righteous fervour, mainstream British 'modern art' down to the 1950s was the product of half-absorbed French influences, from Impressionism to cubism via the Euston Road school of realists, crossed with neo-gothic and celtic fringe mystery-art. Pop Art gave all this a good kicking, and not before time.

But arguably the jostling influences of Pop Art, Expressionism, naturalistic cinematography and hermetic art – difficult if not impossible integers – cause major weaknesses in Jarman–Greenaway avant-gardism. It perhaps explains why, ultimately, their films don't breathe: every inch of the screen has to be filled, like an academic canvas, but there is still too little work for the eye to do. The fantastic in this case is a form of disavowal.

Jarman's slow rise from the 1960s experimental fringe to virtual canonisation in the 1980s was partly due to his own engaging and polemical personality, his tireless support for young film-makers of all shades and his role in the campaign for AIDS awareness. He also contributed to climatic changes which led to a new wave of activity among younger artists, such as Damien Hirst's 1988 'Freeze' exhibition, the very name of which echoes the 'Fridge' video venue in Brixton which opened in 1984. By this time *Art Monthly* was running a regular video column (latterly by Michael O'Pray and then Catherine Elwes), although often extending it into coverage of live and performance art – genres which were to engulf the art scene in the next decade.

Dance and theatre also participated in the new world of 'expanded video' which started in the 1980s, with work by Jeremy Peynton-Jones, Rosemary Butcher and Siobhona Jeyasingh. Ideas which had originated in the desolate warehouses of East London, such as 2B Butler's Wharf (1975–9), temporarily taken over by artists before the developers moved in, now came to public fruition. The Bracknell Media Centre supported artists' and community video throughout the decade, and the BFI appointed Ben Gibson as its first video officer in 1987 to fund new work.

New pluralism[154]

This era was dubbed the 'New Pluralism' by O'Pray and Tina Keane for a seminal 1985 Tate Gallery exhibition. It indicated not only the breakdown of barriers in the film and video movement, but also the spread of new media into all contemporary art. The first of the National Review of Live Art shows in 1987 was another sign of the times, and London Video Arts became London Video Access – video was spreading more widely, as Julia Knight notes, 'at the cost of losing its own identity'. Similar 'hybrids' (a favourite buzzword in cyberculture) appeared in the 'Image and Sound' Festival at the Hague and the Media Arts Festival in Osnabruck. The 1990 Biennalle of the Moving Image in Madrid brought together video and installation from Godard to Scratch, Snow to Larcher, and an episode of David Lynch's *Twin Peaks*. More recent but historicising descendants of this wave include 'Spellbound' at the Hayward Gallery, London (by Ian Christie and Philip Dodd) and the Los Angeles 'Hall of Mirrors' (curated by Kerry Brougher), to celebrate film's 1996 centenary year.

In the same period Bracknell's *Independent Video* magazine started as a forum for video artists – the later switch of title to *Independent Media* took a step back from art. But artists' work was expansively packaged and toured by curators and critics from London Electronic Arts (formerly London Video Arts) and the Arts Council-funded 'Film and Video Umbrella', including O'Pray, Jez Welsh and Steven Bode. The 'Umbrella' began in 1983 under O'Pray, and quickly toured the new work then emerging from the fringe of the Co-op and beyond – Super-8 and

Scratch – as well as the classic avant-garde, Svankmajer, Jarman, the Kuchars and a clutch of then little-known film-makers such as Patrick Keiller, Andrew Kotting, Cerith Wyn-Evans, John Maybury and Jayne Parker. In 1988 Welsh expanded its video dimension. Eddie Berg of Moviola meanwhile prepared the first of the Video Positive Biennales in 1989, which featured new commissioned work and was importantly based in Liverpool – later extending to Manchester as well – rather than the metropolis. For this opening exhibition, with sites spread across the city, Steve Littman commissioned Video Wall installations at the Liverpool Tate by David Hall, Judith Goddard, Kate Meynell, Steve Partridge, Simon Robertshaw and other new and older talents.

Shortly afterwards, in a joint BBC and Arts Council venture, the popular arts programme *The Late Show* began the first of its '1-minute film' commissions, a series that lasted for four years and created over fifty new pieces of artists' work. Anna Ridley and Jane Rigby produced a new set of 'TV interventions' in Glasgow for Channel 4 in 1990, re-running David Hall's originals from 1971 and a clutch of new work by younger video-makers and groups. This expanded Ridley's *Dadarama* TV commissions of 1984, the title of which harks back to avant-garde roots in the 20s, with videos by David Cunningham, Rose Garrard, John Latham, Michael Nyman and Stephen Partridge. Partridge has produced an interesting and diverse body of video work beginning with *Monitor* (1975), a classic exploration of video logic, in which successive shots of the monitor are self-embedded within its original frame. *Dialogue For Two Players* (1984) reveals the process of manipulation in the context of a seemingly personal confessional drama, while the single monitor is expanded to videowall scale (a bank of thirty-four monitors) in *Interrun* (1989) to expose the technical construction of TV's 'window on the world'. In a series of works with composer David Cunningham, notably *Soundtapes* (1983) and *Sentences* (1988–93), the focus is stripped down to respectively concentrate on rhythmic image montage and on rapid manipulation of single statements (text without pictures). The potential of video remix is here given a structural twist, and taken further in CD-Rom format between 1994 and 1998 to open up the screensaver option as an artistic device, and as an expanded 'dialogue' for two or more players, including the viewer.

The David Hall (and Fluxus) idea of showing short work by artists on TV unannounced and uncredited had been revived before: Lis Rhodes and other women film-makers made a few for Channel 4 in the early 1980s. For the Glasgow Festival, however, in line with the smoother flow of TV air-time in the 1990s, the work was signposted and credited. Hall's new contribution to this event was *Stooky Bill TV*, in which a copy of Logie Baird's dummy, the source of the first suc-cesful TV image, argues with his off-screen master in a comic dialogue about audience expectations and the baleful shape of TV to come. The piece was shot on a reconstruction of the inventor's own system, using a 30-line vertical scan to render its hauntingly spectral image.

Under the impact of the media revolution in the 1980s and 1990s, which spanned the artist's film and video avant-garde as well as the free-market economy of 'indie' edit-suites and rock promos, TV producer and animateur John Wyver argued the meltdown factor. TV and video art were no longer separate, let alone opposed. It was necessary, he advised, to abandon the separation of the artist and accept the new media environment which made the old battles irrelevant. Even his opponents agreed that it was certainly difficult to fix the core of video art. In ten years, from 1975 to 1985, it had generated primal work with the video signal and process, low-key domestic narrative drama, the Scratch movement, a flood of special effects and edit-suite wizardry, and a shift from the single monitor to elaborate installations.

Video critic Sean Cubitt responded to this optimistic vision by pointing to the conflicting pressures on creative video, with its dual proximity to popular TV and to the demands of fine art. Artists still had a contestatory role in this environment. Also picking up the classic idea that art must be difficult and challenging, Michael O'Pray replied to Wyver by arguing that the personal stance of artists' work – especially when it uses the human body – questions the authenticity of representation. It deals with core art issues, not those of a moving-image culture. In a debate at the ICA, Jean-François Lyotard also made a succinct reply to Wyver's case: since TV culture doesn't deal with concepts and argument, the artist using it should aim to produce 'an effect of uncertainty and trouble, . . . in the hope that this disturbance will be followed by reflection'.

Film and video artists were not alone in resisting full assimilation to the digital universe promoted by Wyver in his punchy and pioneering TV seasons 'Ghosts in the Machine' (Channel 4, 1986, 1988) and 'White Noise' (BBC, 1990), but mostly showing American and European video. In 1986 London got its only brief round of guerilla television – a dream of the 1960s – with the short-lived pirate station Network 21. Its first transmission was silent footage from John Maybury's *Big Love* (1985).

As well as inspiring Janet Street-Porter's *Network 7* (Channel 4, 1987/8), the pirates stood for the kind of polymorphous new video wave which embraced Dora Birnbaum's feminist deconstruction of TV style but also the rapid montage and visual flair of Bruce Conner and Len Lye. Like Scratch videos, they were mostly shown in night-clubs rather than film clubs, such as the Video Café, Digital Nation, Heaven (with Marshall as a programmer) and Brighton's Zap Club. These were copied from New York, with its grand style Danceteria and low-scale Red Bar, but course UFO had been there long before too.

Black British[155]

The break-up of the structural mould coincided with the growth of militant minority cultures which succeeded the collapse of the broad political left in the USA and Europe. As well as 'gay' film-making, black and feminist artists also turned to forms of contestational cinema which both rebelled against 'formalist' structural film and (as with the pop promo) continued its iconoclasm. By turning from structural 'purism', the retro-garde of the 1980s paradoxically helped to spread the audio-visual language of experiment into a wider culture eager for self-renewal in the wake of a consumer boom and an expanding youth market as its visible core. In contrast – though with some connections too – the early films of Spike Lee (USA) and Isaac Julien and John Akomfrah (UK) shared this cultural milieu of the post-avant-garde, exploring fragmentation and sound montage to evoke black urban experience. The creative role of music in their work embedded the new film-video blend (achieved in the edit suite by mixing diverse kinds of footage) into fully audio-visual terms in which, as Godard and others envisaged, neither picture nor sound were privileged over their joint and dialectical engagement.

Of these, the best and most influential early examples were made collectively but also authorially. *Territories* (1984) is a two part film/video from St Martin's School of Art by Sankofa/Isaac Julien. It blends diverse sources into a new mixture of voices, from 8mm footage of the Notting Hill Carnival to historical news footage from the archives, to make a collage of black culture in Britain from the 1950s to the present day. In the spirit of *cinéma vérité*, but more abstractly, the source material is reworked in front of the viewer on an edit-suite, while a chorus of young women chant a series of questions, quotations and fragments which emphasise the title of the film. The second part is even more abstract, and more music-led than Godardian, notably in an image of a young white policeman which is overlaid in video by a fluidly turning shot of two young men embracing, one black and one white. A multitrack soundmix, which includes the voice of Joan Baez, links the film to the broad civil rights movement and underscores its complex political statement. For *Territories* is not one-dimensional or separatist in its message and scope. Its gay subtext challenges straight machismo, while its celebration of black culture is located fairly and squarely in the British context, 'here' rather than 'there', even as it draws on critical theory to articulate rather than to alienate the underclass and the dispossesed.

Handsworth Songs (1987) by Black Audio Visual – John Akomfrah, and focused on Midlands Birmingham rather than the metropolis, is in some respects similar – dynamic use of music, archive footage, shots of riots, montage structure – but with crucial differences. Its stance is more documentary, interspersed with interviews as well as extended footage from British documentaries which touch on class as well as race. Shots of riot police in the streets are returned to, re-commented on and reworked to evoke further layers of meaning. Some of the material is unflinching – a police car revs away backwards from an angry crowd, a young man is grabbed and beaten by police with shields and batons, and an elderly white woman memorably walks as if in a trance down a riot-littered street. The music soundtrack pulsates through, rather than overdramatises, these remarkable scenes. The direct interviews emphasise the spoken voice in a lineage that goes back to *Housing Problems*; some younger people speaking patois, an older black man outside his garden astonished by what he has seen, an Asian community group in conference, the eloquent and classically 'English' voice of a young Sikh man who simply asks for social equality.

Like *Territories*, but more objectively for all its densely packed textures and codes, the film crosses race and class lines to emphasise more than one message – less a 'campaign' film than a reflection on process and meaning, including its own construction as a statement. The word 'songs' in the title underlines this choric and abstract intent which runs alongside its vivid eye for social detail and the powerful sense of injustice which inspires and drives it. Both of these seminal films, by their stance and by their collective making, revitalise the social-political cinema to track the jagged lines that lead from Vertov through to *cinéma vérité*, and from Grierson's eclectic vision to the 1968 'cine-tracts' shot by the politicised French New Wave.

The more subjective mode of *Territories* was followed by Isaac Julien in a series of more stylised portrait films, notably *Looking For Langston* (1989), while John Akomfrah took up the objective and documentary option in his later films for television. A generation later, Alia Syed turned the theme of race and diaspora in a uniquely personal direction with *Fatima's Letter* (1992). In contrast to the films of the 1980s, it owes little if anything to the classic documentary mode but emerges directly from the tradition of the individual artist's film. The rhythms of passing trains evoke passing traces, shadows and abstract memories; London and Pakistan blur as a woman's voice reads a letter in Urdu. The film underscores its deliberate sense of uncertainty, forgetting and asynchrony: the letter is translated into English subtitles only much later, and set against white to enforce the difficulty of reading. Focused on difference and disconnection, it reflects its ethnic theme of conflict but eschews any simple notion of identity politics. Her more recent film *The Watershed* (1994) similarly employs overlapping voices against photogenic black and white shots of a woman in close-up, set on the borderline of pain, pleasure, touch and sight.

Electronic arts

Ideas sown a decade or more earlier flourished with curious twists in the Thatcher–Reagan years.[156] Artists based at the Slade School's Department of Experimental and Electronic Art during the 1970s – grounded at the time in conceptual and systems art led by Anthony Hill and Kenneth and Mary Martin – now emerged as market forces, notably Chris Briscoe and Paul Brown. Founding Digital Pictures in 1981, they made the first completely computer-generated TV ad in the UK for Michelin in 1983. From a similar background, ex-architect John Lansdown of the Systems Simulation Company designed computer graphics for Ridley Scott's *Alien* (1979). From the RCA, and in 1974 the first artist to have abstract computer art broadcast on TV, Peter Donebauer then founded Diverse Productions which in 1990–1 made the graphic documentary series *Small Objects of Desire* for the BBC.

Several younger artists such as William Latham (Computer Artworks) followed in their wake, although many ex-Slade and RCA graduates who deploy technology as artists (such as Darrel Viner) and more specifically as video artists (for example, Judith Goddard) resolutely did not engage in commercial production. Those who did so were crucial to the media revolution of the 1980s, the distant baseline for which was seen to be Jasia Reichardt's 1968 ICA exhibition and book, 'Cybernetic Serendipity'. Paik's work was included in this, for those who had not yet made the Portapak pilgrimage to New York. Coincidentally, Reichardt is the niece and archivist of Stefan and Franczziska Themerson, Polish avant-garde artists, publishers and film-makers.[157] Wartime refugees in the 1940s, their spirited Gaberbocchus (Latin for 'Jabberwocky') Press brought Dada-constructivist ideas under the rubric of 'Semantic Poetry' to grey literary London in the 1950s and 1960s.

Richard Wright, also from the Slade's experimental unit, has traced its demise in the underfunded college world during the 1980s and the rebirth of its ideas in the newly expanding commercial sector. While the eruption of glamorous computer graphics from a strictly constructivist tradition may seem wayward, even as it casts an interesting light on the rise of abstract art and film in the first avant-garde of the 1920s, Wright explains the logic. He links the cool, machined and plane surface of constructivism to the smooth non-texture and gloss of computer imaging. Both constructivism and computers call on mathematical and sequential operations. Both use abstraction to engage the real – the final computer image has little obvious relation to the algorithm which made it. The constructivist tradition, still vibrant in the 1970s with such figures as artist and AI expert Harold Cohen, was also concerned with ideal and 'virtual' universes, although its computer-oriented descendants have shifted their attention from the pure concept to the simulated image.

Constructivist radicalism, on the other hand, was ice-packed for the duration. The computer-led revolution was a key component of the new corporate culture. But it also opened new pathways for young artists and designers, signalled in the icon of Channel 4's famous 'ident' which drew on many talents. A mixture of goodwill, artistic sympathy and shrewd investment by the professional media industries also opened edit-suite access to inventive ex-Scratch makers such as Rik Lander of the Duvet Brothers and George Barber. Sony, Samuelsons, Samcon and other industrial companies became major sponsors of artists' video through loans and donations of professional equipment for projects and shows.

yBa

The thrusting new generation of the 'yBa' (Young British Artists), most of whom graduated in the 1990s, did not, however, follow this lead.[158] Instead they stuck resolutely to the handmade (and sewn and stitched and cut and stacked) object. The film-makers among them were divided into those who turned to low-grade media like Super-8 or VHS and those who took the digital option; but the latter – as with the slightly older John Maybury – turned for their example to David Larcher and the surviving underground ethos of image manipulation rather than to its straight commercial counterpart. Only the ubiquitous pop-promo (everyone seems to have made one at this period) provided common ground across the many factions, and an important source of income.

The yBa took to the galleries rather than the airwaves and satellites. Some made live or performance art, although this was largely the province of more 'serious' artists than they pretended to be.[159] Many more took to installation work, and by extension to video and projected images. Distant ancestors included the astonishingly prescient 1968 Arts Lab event 'Drama in a Wide Media Environment', in which structural film-makers Malcolm Le Grice, Mike Dunford and others presented 24-hour closed circuit video installations and performances, with audience participation.[160] In the USA in 1969 Frank Gillette and Ira Schneider showed the interactive *Wipe Cycle*, using CCTV, live broadcast TV and video loops playing variously on nine monitors. And in 1972 David Hall and Tony Sinden gathered 60 TV sets in Gallery

House, London (for the exhibition 'Survey of the Avant-Garde'), and systematically detuned the signals they received from all three of the channels then broadcasting.

These were long forgotten by the 1990s. Their principles were discovered independently or through more immediate, but American, examples; Bruce Nauman, Gary Hill, Bill Viola, Tony Oursler, Vera Frankel, Stan Douglas. On the whole, these artists were more interested in image and event than in perception and structure. The spectator is an observer of the work rather than an active participant. The difference is seen by comparing 1996 Turner Prize-Winner Douglas Gordon's *24-Hour Psycho*, a video copy of Hitchcock's appropriated film at slow speed on a transparent screen visible from both sides, with a distant and presumably unrecognised ancestor, Michael Snow's *Two Sides To Every Story* (1974). This work also employs both sides of the screen, in gallery installation. On one side the artist gives instructions to an actress and camera-operators, but the results of this can only be seen by walking round to the other side of the screen. The spectator cannot look at both events at the same time, and has to make active choices in this participatory object-lesson about narrative drama.

These are two distinct approaches to the phenomenology of viewing. Gordon's is arguably more deconstructive and iconic, in which the dramatic image (Hitchcock's film) is a 'given'. Snow is more constructivist and procedural, and his images enact a 'process'. Both works lead back to the concept of film as duration (exemplified differently in Warhol's films and Hall's *This Is a Television Receiver*, 1976) and as projection-event (the theme of much British structural film and of such American film-performance artists as Ken Jacobs). Both of them also show that viewing is a subjective 'psycho'-logical act which owes nothing to self-expression on the part of the artist.

Much recent British art is built on a myth of self-expression and personality – the documentary TV programme on Sarah Lucas, *Two Melons and a Stinking Fish* (1996) is a wild and witty account of the milieu – but the reality is more complex. Material is often 'appropriated', as by Gordon, without comment or remixing. Personal trauma is registered as a trace – damaged objects, broken shapes – rather than a presence. The latter tactic was also marked in the 70s and 80s, when mirror-images or reflections were motifs of a search for the elusive self.[161] In film and video this runs through Tamara Krikorian's *Vanitas* (1978), Lis Rhodes's *Light Reading* (1979), Tina Keane's *Shadow of a Journey* (1980), Judith Goddard's *Lyrical Doubt* (1984), Kate Meynell's *Hannah's Song* (1987), Mona Hatoum's installation *Hidden From Prying Eyes* (1987), Breda Beban and Hvorje Horvatic's *All Her Secrets Revealed in an Image* (1987), Jeremy Welsh's installation *Immemorial* (1989) and Catherine Elwes' *(Wishing) Well* (1991). The influence of Mary Kelly and Susan Hiller, and hence of Lacan's formative notion of the mirror-phrase, is seen in some of this tellingly titled work, which often focuses on feminine identity and parent–child relations.

By contrast, much 1990s work is up-front in both senses: flat on the screen and confrontational. Sam Taylor-Wood[162] and Gillian Wearing[163] have each made films in which a performer dances frontally to the camera, in *16mm* (1993) (with Frances McGreal) and *Dancing in Peckham* (1994), respectively. As this suggests, both artists began in the Warhol-inspired and low-tech end of film and video. Their context is gallery installation space rather than cinema (although both have had their work broadcast on TV). Taylor-Wood is more self- or inner-directed, even when like Wearing she elicits performances from others, such as people miming to opera in their living rooms for the 1994 installation *Killing Time*. Here the artist sits in front of the video-taped results, complete with Warholian pauses and empty moments.

Wearing won the 1997 Turner Prize with her humorous and revealing 1-hour static-take of uniformed police in a row facing the camera (*One Hour's Silence*) – more shades of Warhol. Other recent works, notably *10–16* (1996) engage with fundamental and even classic aspects of experimental film. Here adult actors in a variety of streets and interiors mimic in lip-synch the words of children whose voices are heard on the soundtrack. The results are illuminating and sometimes disturbing, and not only by their confessional intimacy or the contrast of speech and performance. In this aspect, it reconnects to the underground tradition which elicits the bizarre from the everyday. But it is also an intensely linguistic and even structural piece, built on the concept of delayed time. It directly recalls the vexed issue of 'non-synchronous sound' which has preoccupied Soviet, surrealist and avant-garde film since the late 1920s.

The apparant populism of yBa film and video is to a degree a misleading spin-off from its immediate context. For the first time since Pop Art a group of ambitious and demanding UK artists have forced themselves on the public mind – but with little concession to public taste – and made national and international headlines. For many of them, video is simply absorbed as 'another medium', updating 'artists' video' as Hall defined it. Here, Damien Hirst has set a weak example – unlike his other activities as an artist and activist – since his only foray into filmmaking has been *Hanging Around* (1996); a fully-crewed imitation of a soap-opera which is wholly conventional, fiercely misogynistic and oddly sentimental.[164] By contrast, installation art rather than the single-screen drama is still the major genre for many of the artists who constellate around Hirst.

But the attempt to capture the popular voice – as in the 'vox-pop' material of Taylor-Wood and Wearing – also extends an old ambition of experimental film to tap into dailiness and preserve the human scale, as Jonas Mekas does in his high-speed diary films of street, family and the passing scene. It appears more mutedly in British structural film, in the street and domestic locales of John Smith, William Raban, Nicky Hamlyn and Guy Sherwin, as well as in political film and video makers from the 1970s (for example, Cinema Action) to the present day (from John Akomfrah's TV documentary on mixed-race families, *A Touch of the Tarbrush*, to the 'underground' Exploding Cinema group).

The confessional mode, another return of the repressed in the 1990s, reasserts the individual and social voice against consumer-led values and assumed norms. This path runs through Warhol's *The Chelsea Girls* and Shirley Clarke's *Portrait of Jason* in the USA, and the rawly confrontational videos of Ian Breakwell, Ian Bourn, David Critchley and Mick Hartney from 1975–9 in the UK. At that point it passed more obliquely into 'identity politics' and into feminist film and video, where the mother–daughter theme was paramount, as in Jayne Parker's *Almost Out* (1984) and Mona Hatoum's *Measures of Distance* (1988) (the first confronting the presence of the mother, the second meditating on her absence and memory). The new direct confessional mode included not just the street-wise video but also

Lucy Gunning's *Climbing Round My Room* (1994) (the title echoes the 'direct' early videos of Vito Acconci or William Wegman) and such gay psycho-fantasies as Sadie Benning's *It Wasn't Love* (1992) and Michael Curran's *Amami se vuoi* (1994), the latter notorious for its unsafe shots of a young man spitting repeatedly into another's mouth.

Most yBa artists use video to expand their bank of images, but as recording or playback devices the media they employ are not often the specific core of their practice. Others have taken up the classic issues of the historic film avant-gardes, such as duration, camera-vision and sound-image montage. In such work the systems by which meanings are produced become central to the spectator's apprehension of the work. The making of images is only one aspect of the whole. Sean Cubitt recently recalled this context in the example of the Russian formalists (shades of *Screen*?), for whom art emphasises the object as vision-in-process rather than the subject of simple recognition. Duration, for example, reveals perception as an act of 'becoming' rather than as the presentation of what has already 'become'.

Wearing takes one route to this goal by subverting video's supposed immediacy. Steve McQueen uses highly iconic images in the spirit of Maya Deren, Jayne Parker and Isaac Julien to question the gendered and racialised gaze by repeated, alternated shots (as in *Stage*, 1996). Tacita Dean turns to expanded cinema in using film loops and emblematic images of light and landscape.[165] Her 1996 Tate Gallery installation was based on the work of 'Foley' artists, who make complex sound effects for the movies by an engagingly inventive use of simple, household materials. In this documentary cross-section of sound-image relations, Dean employs sound and video tapes, objects, interviews and graphic charts to investigate the hidden backbone of film realism. In contrast, Douglas Gordon, among many others, recycles narrative cinema as a given iconic fact to question relations of consumption but not of production.

'Where are we now?'

(*The Cut-Ups,* Balch/Burroughs, 1966)

For some, the digital revolution and the convergence of technologies put into question not just the old divisions between media but the survival of art as a separate sphere. They see TV, fibre-optics and the global satellite system as the key to the future of art – if it has one. Others resist the consumer ideology which is latent or blatant in the digital vision. They reject technological determinism to defend the critical function of art and culture in advanced and advancing societies.

But to pit the mega-media culture against the lone artist is misleading. Without jumping into futorology – how late is late capitalism and how post is postmodernism? – the question requires greater nuancing where the arts are concerned.

For example, it is a mistake to crudely polarise the 'handmade' ethic of the formal-structural avant-garde, which argued that film or video are art media with specific properties, as simply the opposite of currently converging multi-media technologies. The polarity is more subtle.

These new technologies were, in the first place, partly shaped by the avant-gardes. As so often the USA gives the first examples, as in the Whitney brothers. Their abstract electronic experiments in the 1940s, based on Duchampian chance operations, eventually led to the rebirth of lyrical and mythic abstraction and to their own later role in the corporate culture of industrial computer research. Gene Youngblood, whose seminal *Expanded Cinema* (1970) analysed this approach, has had a similar career.[166] His very terminology in this book bridges the thirty-year gap between past and the present: 'Paleocybernetics', 'The Intermedia Network', 'Popular Culture and the Noosphere', 'The Artist as Design Scientist', 'Oceanic Consciousness', 'Global Closed Circuit', 'Synaesthetics and Synergy', 'Image-Exchange', and even, proleptically, 'The New Nostalgia'. Lenny Lipton, who wrote the instructively libertarian *Independent Film-Making* (and the song 'Puff the Magic Dragon'!) became a leading figure in the computer industries. Perhaps more surprisingly, Maya Deren was a consultant for computer program research in the later 1950s before her untimely death in 1961.

While some of this interchange between art and technology recalls such UK events as the spin-off into media-land by Slade School and RCA artists during the 1980s, other British perspectives show less direct but illuminating links over a similar period. Le Grice – the very image of the 'hard-line' structural film-maker by most accounts – made his first experiments in computer-based art in the 1960s, picking up the medium again in his most recent work over the last decade (when he also led the expansion of film and media at Harrow College / University of Westminster before returning to St Martin's as head of media-based research in 1997).[167] Likewise, but totally outside the academic frame, Gustav Metzger, the avatar of 'auto-destructive art' in the 1960s, was at the same time a pioneer of computer-generated art. As with the machine-style art of Eduardo Paolozzi in his early printmaking series (for example, 'As Is When', 1965), it was the 'post-modernity' of these media, and their insistently automatic processes which sidestep the artist's personal signature, which were the central lures of electronic image-making.

The 1970s disputes between experimental film-makers and the then new video-art movement have long abated for most artists. These former antagonisms were in part the result of different generations pursuing different ideas. But this is only a partial reason; David Hall, former sculptor and former film-maker, stolidly defended the video-making faction against the prior claims of the film avant-garde who were, in the main, his own contemporaries or younger. He argued that there were major differences between the two media. These were institutional – the relation of video to television rather than the cinema, for example – as well as 'formal'. The real-time aspect of video, its directness as a medium and its basis in electronic signals rather than (as with film) photo-chemical images, were among these formal characteristics which made up the distinctive character of video as an art practice.

Within two decades, from the 1960s to the 1980s, video expanded massively as a medium in the wider culture. The cumbersome Portapak – the first portable camera which so inspired Paik, Hopkins and Hall himself – was replaced by the lightweight camcorder. The format of video changed from spooled tape, of variable gauges for the TV and the non-broadcast sectors, to the compact cassette. As George Barber describes, the rise of Scratch video depended on new and flexible editing systems devised by Sony in the early 1980s, which made rapid video cutting possible for the first time. The avant-garde, notably in Jarman's circle, thought nothing of shooting on 8mm or 16mm film, editing on tape and printing back to film again. This is now a 'normal' industry procedure, and artistically is seen in such films by Greenaway as *Prospero's Books* (1989) and *The Pillow Book* (1995). Here source material which ranges from film to drawing is combined on high-definition video and scanned back onto 35mm negative film for cinema release – and then to domestic VHS tape for home distribution.

Points of resistance

Film-maker (and video-digital promoter) Michael Maziere argues against the media meltdown theory to show that the new digital environment is able to expand the options for artists without reducing them to one megamix culture indiscriminately shared with TV and popular culture. It is the opposite of John Wyver's position, although it should be added that Maziere's own personal work is firmly film-based (8mm and 16mm) in the tradition of lyrical structuralism.

Many film-makers of the first underground and structural avant-garde, far from rejecting video and digital media *per se*, have embraced them. The majority still work – in 'the tradition' – as artisans rather than directors. Post-film media give them a greater degree of control over the final product than the labour- and time-intensive procedures associated with film-making. Video gives the artist direct access to image manipulation and production. It is also cheaper, an important consideration for those who are self-funded with the aid of limited grants and commissions. They are less anxious about video and digital media as such than about the social, cultural and economic applications of high technology. The desire not to be swamped by mass media culture is a principled and not a reactionary objection. In this sense, the post-film media provide points of resistance for artists to the bland new world of 'infotainment'.

Among the film-makers whose careers go back to the 1960s and 1970s but who now use video and digital media for all or part of their work are Malcolm Le Grice, Lis Rhodes, Jeff Keen, David Larcher, Nicky Hamlyn, George Saxon, Tony Sinden. At the same time most of these are probably still better described as film-makers than given any other label. Others whose first work dates from the 1970s and 1980s have made videos and other work specifically for television, but are still essentially film-makers: John Smith, Jayne Parker, Phil Mulloy, John Maybury, Chris Newby. In a class of his own is hard-line video spokesman David Hall who, surprisingly (?), made a number of short and pungent pieces for MTV in 1993 (MTV shows avant-garde work from all sources, a move pioneered by producer Peter Dougherty).[168] At the same time, a smaller number of artists – notably Peter Gidal and Guy Sherwin – have followed none of these routes, and argue the aesthetic or philosophical primacy of the film medium as a vital element of their practice.

For the first time in its long and intermittent history the experimental film and video movement in the UK has four active generations at work.[169] At the older end of the spectrum are Jeff Keen and Margaret Tait, now in their seventies. Behind them are such film-makers as Le Grice, Larcher, Gidal and Hall, and a younger middle generation of film-makers now in their forties. The largest but most various grouping is made up of young artists in their twenties.

The middle generation is partly associated with the rise of British art in the 1980s, which included film and video exhibition in such touring exhibitions of new work as 'The British Art Show'. In some ways these mixed exhibitions foreshadowed the later 'Goldsmiths' generation by seeding the roots of a new approach to art: less formal, more allusive, oblique, and strangely blending concept-art with symbolism. Among artists who began to reach a new gallery rather than cinema or film theatre audience for film and video at this time were Mona Hatoum, Jayne Parker, John Smith, Kate Elwes, Kate Meynell and Judith Goddard.

This new work included both single screen and installation film or video. Film-makers in the 1960s and 1970s, with some older experiments going back to the Bauhaus, had sought an 'expanded cinema'. Some wanted just that, an art of expanded vision beyond the single image. Jeff Keen's performances and Stan VanDerBeek's multi-screen films are part of this celebratory wave. A closely related strategy expands the film by sheer duration, so that time rather than space is unpacked, as in the 5-hour *Art of Vision* by Brakhage or Michael Snow's 4-hour *La Région centrale*. British structural film had downplayed the elements of grand myth in this form of visionary cinema, but reworked the idea to focus on perception, landscape and duration, as in multi-screen films by Le Grice, Raban and Welsby.

David Larcher had merged both the underground and the structural film in his performance-based installations. For the Channel 4 late-night broadcast of *EETC* in 1986 he played out-takes and variants on an assembly of monitors in a mock-domestic setting at the LFMC, together with 'live' transmission on a central screen. A maker of such early extra-long travel and diary underground films as *Mare's Tale* (1969), Larcher has explored digital and multi-layered imaging since *EETC* and *Granny's Is* (1990). The first centres on his sister, the second on his grandmother; each is highly visual, personal and challenging. 'From the trace produced by a single drop-out [says Larcher] is created a series of digital landscapes that provide the backgrounds for the flight of the Zenoian arrow towards void.' The transition from film to electronic media taken by Larcher was aided by TV commissions such as the 'Experimenta' series backed by Channel 4 and the Arts Council. Similar schemes in Europe encouraged video work by 'the other avant-garde' – Godard, Ruiz, Marker – and by artists-in–transit like Bill Viola and Derek Jarman (in his final work, *Blue,* 1993, the pure film colour of the title is crafted electronically).

John Maybury, of a younger generation, is close to Larcher in spirit. His *Remembrance of Things Fast* is, like *Videovoid*, a TV commission of 1993. Like Larcher, his films seek an interface between the maker and the medium. The work is free, indirect autobiography which focuses on the film-maker's clubworld milieu. Maybury's first world was grainy, hand-printed and gestural with rock-and-voice-over intonation in the manner of William Burroughs. His iconography of hunched figures, mirror-play and thwarted narcissism was part of the revival of an image-making avant-garde film in the post-structural era. Maybury's films are closer to bricolage than collage; they eschew formal unity and stress fragmentation. *Remembrance* includes camp sequences, sex-scenes, cut-up news programmes, re-edited confessions, hospital sequences, fast graphics, imaginary creatures from 'TV-Land' and a battery of visual stylistics which evoke a post-television sense of broken flow. Larcher, by contrast, uses fluid collage and repeated tropes to loosely draw together the large structures which have characterised his films since the 1960s.

While none of Larcher's films use actors, Maybury has explored drama and text since *Big Love* (1984). In this respect his films link back to Steve Dwoskin's explorations of acting and personae and also the breaking of sexual taboo, in Maybury's case the prohibition on showing homosexual sado-masochism. His most recent film, a feature-length production about Francis Bacon, takes him for the first time into the fully narrative drama cinema. His career to date has led him from 8mm club, loft and college screenings through to pop promos with Boy George and Sinead O'Conor and latterly to high-grade electronic imaging whose main themes are visual, optical and physical 'breakdown'. Self, persona and myth are overlaid in complex structures. Between his early work and his latest attempt at shooting a literal 'art film', with Bacon as its emblematic core, Maybury's prolific output scans the field of options which make up the contemporary artists' cinema.

At another extreme Jayne Parker explores personal and sexual imagery but in a classical and stark style which contrasts to the electronic flux of Maybury and Larcher. A contemporary of Maybury whose first films date from the early 1980s, Parker takes the human figure as her main subject, as in *Crystal Acquarium* (1995). Here she links up with contemporary performance art and its photographic documentation, as when her films depict, in fine-grained and stark detail, the human body swimming, dancing, eating and – in *K.* (1989) – even knitting a garment from a tangle of animal guts. In these films, a protagonist's inner crisis is shown and controlled by an underlying sense of visual order.

Parker's early films, some made while she was a sculpture student in the 1970s, inhabit the hinterland between animation and performance; stark moral tales with women, cats, fish and blood. *I Dish* (1982) explores narrative space through an oblique narrative in which an alienated young man and woman enact rites of washing and cooking, but in a direct naturalistic style which carries through to the final sequence of change as the woman sifts stones by the sea at the edge of the frame. Dramatic space is implied but also subtly disrupted by montage. Her direct and confrontational video *Almost Out* (1984) slowly reveals its manipulation of the image as film-maker and mother – both naked – face the camera.

She then abandoned speech and language in film to make fully pictorial works. They centre on the act of making and the search for source, and explore evocative icons (like fish, flesh or water) which recur from film to film. Her themes – the naked body, personal space, sexual identity – link her to the contemporary visual arts as much as her eye for oblique but sharp-edged connections. At the same time her language of gesture, her concept of the artist as performer and her use of metaphor also evoke the cinema of Cocteau and the later surrealists. But in some ways she goes further: her icons are never pre-existing symbols, and meaning only emanates from the relation of shot to shot, image to image, to bypass verbal translation. If the result is indeed metaphor, which is arguable, it is in the way her flowing imagery – the metonymic chain of assocation – is punctuated by a poetics of emblem, alterity and montage, for the viewer to intuit and interpret.

The rhythm in *Crystal Acquarium* is set by a female percussionist, seen in impassive, photogenic close-up (the film is in black and white). Her drumming is intercut with a series of performers, whose actions (the montage implies) are interconnected. Parker herself 'impossibly' eats and drinks underwater, as in a circus act, while a second woman performs underwater gymnastics and a third dances on ice into which – in breathtaking close shots – she digs with her skates. These actions are cut against a fragmented scenario, in which a young woman ritually burns the bed on which she finally lies.

Parker's films emphasise the idea of the interior in at least three ways. The interiority of the performers is made objective in the form of gesture. All action takes place inside rooms, pools and – in some recent short works made for TV – stage and concert room. Finally, the films are shaped to their necessary conditions of viewing, in the dark of cinemas or galleries. Her films are structured around this taut control of the medium and its viewing space, to evoke a sense of contemporary classicism. This is especially evident in her *Thinking Twice* (1997). In this 10-minute film the pianist Katharina Wolpe plays short pieces by her father, the composer Stefan Wolpe (innovator and mentor of the New York School). The film concentrates on the pianist and the piano itself, weaving a text of light, sound and movement from these sparse elements. The rapid flow of hands in close-up, in a blur of vertical motion, recalls the strict but rich tradition of the German abstract film, just as the film itself attains the goal of 'pure cinema' to which that tradition aspired.

Among film-makers of the structural cinema who have expanded their work in new directions is William Raban. Unlike Welsby, Le Grice and Gidal – who have refined their work more or less in line with their first base – Raban has blended the structural film with the documentary. *Island Race* (1995) was partly shot in east London, with racist scrawls on streets and walls. The rise of ultra-nationalism (shot outside a polling station) contrasts with the everyday scenes of daily life in street and market. Public events such as a marathon run, a navy flotilla, the Kray funeral, and a Victory Day street party are scanned and silently questioned (there is no commentary). Montage and rhythm govern the film. Blurs of traffic flatten the screen, light on the Thames is seen in time-lapse. The soundtrack comprises ambient sound, radio clips and David Cunningham's vivid score for the framing device which opens and closes the film, a speeded-up cross-Channel car journey.

Raban's recent films revive the spirit of lyric documentary associated with Humphrey Jennings and Free Cinema, but his background was in early structural film. In the 1970s he used film to 'record changes in the landscape' and to document the passage of time. Raban was then one of a group of young artists at St Martin's and the London Film Makers' Co-operative, for whom film was not a narrative medium but one which extended 'process' and 'systems' painting and music to explore perception, time and chance procedures. Landscape was Raban's main subject, so that the English realist tradition, and its eye for detail and place, seeped into this advanced outpost of conceptual art. At the time, however, the new movement was better known for its minimalist and quasi-scientific approach to art, notoriously rejecting lyric abstraction and Romanticism in the US underground cinema.

Raban's single and multi-screen films of the 1970s investigate natural light and movement, using time-lapse and variable speeds or lenses to explore the paradoxes of camera vision, with the viewer as a participant observer. After the 3-screen *Thames Barrier* (1977) Raban took up some themes which the landscape film had neglected up to that point. Scenes of urban decay and blight begin to appear in his work. This reflected a growing politicisation of the structural filmmakers. Chris Welsby too was troubled by the seemingly pure landscape genre he had earlier explored; the soundtrack of *Skylight* (1988) is accordingly made up of Geiger counter readings.

A late formal film by Raban shows this new concern in the urban dereliction of *Autumn Scenes* (1979). With Marilyn Halford he then made his only narrative drama, the lyrical *Black and Silver* (1981). A stylish play on painterly and cinematic illusionism, it heralded the 'New Romanticism' of the early 80s, although Raban himself rejected this in favour of documentaries about London's rivers. This direction bore new results with the one-minute *Sundial* (1992) which briefly sums up his London documentaries such as *Thames Film* (1986) and *A13* (1994). Centred in the frame, but seen from many different viewpoints, the giant Canary Wharf Tower becomes a gnomon to mark the hours of the day. Raban's innate eye for formal shape and the passing scenes of daily life have led him to mastery of the city-based film poem; a lyric mode underpinned by structural shape, colour and light. At the same time, the urban subject-matter echoes the social aspiration which runs through the historic avant-gardes.

Among the image-based (as opposed to 'process'-centred) film-makers currently active, John Smith stands between Parker's personal stance and Raban's social focus. Structural film was at its peak in the mid-70s when he made his first films. His generation of 'second-wave' structuralists already saw the movement with a more distant and critical eye, although *Leading Light* (1975) and *Blue Bathroom* (1979) are classic explorations of colour and space to reveal perceptual change. But Smith's most original hallmark is the use of humour to evoke but also to question film narrative.

In *The Girl Chewing Gum* (1976) the commanding voice-over of a film director appears to control the traffic and people in a busy London street as if they were actors in a movie. But they are not: in fact the commentator is describing, not prescribing, a scene of daily life. A second and final sequence ambiguously locates the commentator in a distant field. By reversing the logical order of the drama film – where the script and not the shot comes first – Smith deconstructs its truth claims by exposing its fantasies of control and its illusionist bias. Later Smith embraced the 'spectre of narrative' (suppressed by structural film), to play word against picture and chance against order. This early work anticipates the more elaborate scenarios to come, and like them is ghosted by the narrative impulse which drives the film medium.

Shepherd's Delight (1984) is a quasi-narrative film of language games in which shaggy-dog stories scan the dark side of humour to deliberately confuse deception with confession. The narrator of *The Black Tower* (1987) becomes obsessed with a mysterious building which he sees wherever he looks – an illusion created by *tour de force* editing. The brooding 'dark tower' of the British poets is here sited in the flow of daily life, while the changing face of street and skyline is charted by time-lapse. The final pan (in a film made largely of still shots) evokes continuity even as a new narrating voice, that of a woman, subtly disrupts it.

The rich visual surface and engaging voice-over of *Slow Glass* (1991) convey an extended metaphor which links light, glass and lens. The film is framed by an 'opening' shot (a smashed windowpane) and a 'closing' one (the window bricked up). As it slowly reveals its own artifice, the realist surface is interrupted, as when a car mirror shows reflections of a different journey than the one visible through the windscreen. These constructed 'mistakes' which break the flow are so crafted as to invade the image and unsettle the word. Direct evocation of the past – a 1950s childhood – allows the film to question its depiction of the present. Unlike *The Girl Chewing Gum*, which turns casual passers-by into screen stars, the participants in this film mainly act or reconstruct the scenes in which they appear, a factor masked by an apparent surface realism. Smith brings formidable skill to bear in a film which scrutinises the very 'speculations' it incites.

These films offer the pleasures of camera-eye vision, often fooling the eye when distinct time-sequences are 'matted' to make up complex illusions within the frame (as in the changing seasons seen in the two halves of a single window in *The Black Tower*). They can be enjoyed as stories; films for everyone, especially in their humour. They comprise a personal topography of East London, blighted but alive. Echoes of British documentary in *Slow Glass* allude to (and perhaps mourn) the passage of time which all films encode. Smith's recent film *Blight* (1996) was a TV commission with the composer Jocelyn Pook. A stunning montage depicts the destruction of a London street to make way for new roads. The rhythmic, emotive soundtrack is partly musical and partly a collage of the resident's voices. Shots and sounds echo and cross-link in the film's 14 minutes to (like Raban) reinvent a radical documentary tradition which goes back to *Housing Problems* and *Coalface*, both made in 1935.

Smith, Raban and Parker are among artist film-makers now reaching new audiences, as TV takes such films beyond traditional venues (which continue to thrive) like clubs, co-ops, film workshops and artists' galleries or studios. This trend began with such schemes as the '1-minute film' series for the BBC's *Late Show*, 1991–4, the 'Midnight Underground' series and other direct commissions by TV companies, the Arts Council and the BFI. Ideas like these have brought avant-garde film into the TV schedule, although in very different ways from the 'interventionist' strategy which is also occasionally revived and which inserts artist's work between programmes without scheduling, commentary or introduction. At the same time both these systems avoid the 'arts ghetto' of specific cable or satellite channels for new art, a tactic explored in continental Europe and the USA. The presence of artists' film and video within the 'normal' TV broadcast flow is almost an emblem of the avant-garde's double-edged relation to the mass media, to question the semi-narrative sequencing in which it participates.

Art gallery exhibition was also transformed during this period by a media explosion impelling artists of all kinds to use installation and video projection, much of which drew – albeit often unawares – on avant-garde predecessors dating back to the Bauhaus. But some important gallery shows focused specifically on artists for whom film, video and digital media were not primarily ways to expand painting and sculpture, but made a practice in its own right. Simon Field inaugurated a polemical Bienalle of artists' film at the ICA, which provoked very mixed selections indeed – from structural film to TV ads – by curators Tilda Swinton (1990), Peter Wollen (1993), John Wyver (1995) and Ruby Rich (1997).[170] The '*Spellbound*' exhibition curated by Ian Christie and Philip Dodd at the Hayward Gallery in film's centenary year of 1996 celebrated a constellation of artists and film-makers from mainstream to margin (including Ridley Scott, Peter Greenaway, Eduardo Paolozzi and Terry Gilliam), but also newer artists associated with the yBa such as Fiona Banner and Steve McQueen. At the same time, other younger film and video artists were to be seen *en masse* at the 'Pandaemonium' ICA festival. But for some, programmes such as these, however diverse, are limited by jury selection and official imprimatur. In response, groups like the Exploding Cinema and festivals such as 'Volcano' in London continue to promote the classic underground principles of non-selected, open screenings and avoid the more high-profile venues. The current organ of this movement, *Filmwaves* (1997), is dedicated simply to 'low-budget film-makers and audiences'.

Middle-generation artists such as Paul Bush, Patrick Keiller, Lis Rhodes, Chris Newby, Nina Danino, Jayne Parker, Malcolm Le Grice, John Smith and Guy Sherwin continue to question the boundaries of fiction, documentary and the artistic film. In a sense they make up one half of a new British Art Cinema, the other half consisting of narrative, drama-documentary films by young directors, such as *Trainspotting*, in which overheated subculture themes meet up with a social realist tradition going back to the 1950s. Unlike other periods in the history of experimental and innovative cinema, however, these two halves do not connect. They are radically divided by aesthetic doctrine and by production methods. It is not likely that the underworld genre and the underground film will, in this instance, fuse.

The current state of experimental film (and now video) defies summary. While it lacks the clear profile which the classic avant-gardes attained in their various heydays, from cubism to structural film, those privileged moments are themselves the products of historical hindsight as well as of unique conjunctions between artists' film and wider cultural tendencies. Commercial media culture – rarely able to generate new ideas – still draws from the reservoir of experimental art. Rock videos, which at the end of the century need continual transfusions of new ideas, have turned back to structural film as a graphic source. At the same time a generation of film-and video-makers disaffected by endless rock-blatz are also looking to structural film for traces of resistance. Consequently, the hybrid and voracious nature of the mass media impel reactions that – among the older generation – range from 'ultra' rejection (Gidal), calls for intervention (Hall) and almost full participation (Greenaway, Wyver).

While the avant-garde is often declared dead, most of the living artists mentioned here (and many more unlisted) continue to make films and videos regardless, as do large numbers of younger film-makers. The European scene is scattered (most avant-gardes anywhere are loose collections of individuals), but the USA sustains such important journals as *Millenium*, *Cinematograph*, *Motion Picture* and *October*, often devoted to the contemporary 'iconology of the body' pioneered by film-makers from Menken to Dwoskin. Even *Film Culture*, long dormant, has produced a number of special issues, notable for reminiscences of a now disappearing generation (Jack Smith and Harry Smith among them) and for an analysis of pasta by former film-maker and present cook Peter Kubelka. As the electronic media fill the gap between the mega-budget feature film and the low-budget experimental film, it may be that these two extremes of cinema will be the sole survivors of the film era. If so, they will continue to confront each other in newly heightened ways, across the cultural divisions which the next century of film will necessarily inherit from its past.

Film and video have also permeated the gallery-based arts, carving space for site-specific installations and for regular screenings by film and video artists. No single tendency characterises the work of the last decade, which has been organised around clusters of activity rather than by a single or even dominant movement. Some artists have pursued complex imaging with digital technologies, such as Judith Goddard's *Garden of Earthly Delights* (1991), a densely collaged triptych which plays on the symbolic codes of femininity and visuality. A more occult digital vision is pursued by Simon Biggs in videos such as *Alchemy* (1990), whose symbolist impulse is shared by a broad span of artists from Paul Bush and Kathleen Rogers to the Brothers Quay. Film as an electronic art is dfferently pursued in Graham Wood's *Cowgirl* (1994) with text and image loops (and sound by Underworld) and a hand-made style to imitate digital forms. By contrast David Larcher's *Ich Tank* (1998), made for TV, constructs illusionistic but impossible spaces which warp and twist within the moving frame to create Larcher's 'video metaphors'. But during the same period Chris Newby's *Stromboli* (1997) has stunningly rediscovered the visual power of the 16mm film lyric, cutting from colour to black and white (its underlying matrix) to evoke fusion and separation, while Matt Hulse's *Take Me Home* (1997, edited by Greg Allen), rediscovers the structural tropes of flicker and repetition in the context of an early avant-garde context, the comic-burlesque mode. This random cross-section of the period shows no unity but a great deal of vitality.

As for the digital media themselves, where the possibility of new fusions of text and image carry the promise of new concepts too, the media-specific arts are far from rendered redundant by them. Because the digital state is a hybrid, constructed on a notional and virtual space-time code which relies entirely on electronics and not on any medium of material support as traditionally conceived, it has no choice but to engage with the media – including film and video – which comprise its output forms and modes. Here the experimental arts are in a good position, since the critique of drama, visuality, identification and non-linear thought have been its hallmarks across its wayward and contradictory history. And these will be the way forward for digital innovation too. The same combinations of art and technology which made up the activity of the first decades of artists' films are at work today – even down to the very images which are explored in digital forms as we have them now, in their primitive state (images of the body, dance, abstraction, rolling text, multi-space, non-naturalistic sound, dissolves and superimpositions, even the windows which echo on screen the early films of the abstract avant-garde). It might even be said that the role of media artists in this environment is, at last, to be an avant-garde.

Notes

General   This short history draws from many previous studies which are acknowledged, where possible, in the notes. Most of the books and articles on experimental film mentioned here are to be found in the British Film Institute Library. Journals and other material from the Dada, surrealist and constructivist period can be consulted in the Victoria and Albert Museum Library. Many of the films and videos mentioned in the book can be hired from LUX, which houses the former London Film-Makers' Cooperative and London Electronic Arts collections, and which also shows and distributes new moving-image art (www.lux.org.uk). Some key historical films, from early abstract films to the 1950s, are available from the BFI. Revoir/Light Cone in Paris issue many avant-garde films on VHS, and others are now issued on DVD by foundations like the Center for Visual Music (USA) and many other sources, including museums. BFI Southbank, Tate Modern, Tate Britain and the ICA in London regularly show film, video and digital art, as do galleries across the UK. The former LFMC film printing and processing equipment is now housed at the artists' workshop *no.where*, which offers courses and forums for new film-makers (www.nowhere-lab.org). Luxonline (www.luxonline.org.uk) in the UK and the Video Data Bank (www.vdb.org) in the USA contain copious clips, extracts, articles and information on film and media art. Large collections are also found on UBUWEB (www.ubu.org), and many artists have individual websites where their work can be studied and sampled. The Oasis archive initiated by Woody Vasulka offers 'video analysis tools' (www.oasis-archive.org). The Vasulkas' extensive archive of work and texts by artists is hosted by the Daniel Langlois Foundation (www.vasulka.org). In the UK, the British Artists' Film and Video Study Collection, based at Central St. Martins College of Art and Design, is an invaluable research resource that can be consulted online (www. studycollection.co.uk). Rewind is a major archival project about UK video artists in the 1970s and 1980s, based at the University of Dundee, with restored work, documentation and interviews (www.rewind.ac.uk). Frameworks, founded by Pip Chodorov of Light Cone in Paris, is 'an international forum on experimental film, avant-garde film, film as art, film as film, or film as visual poem…', with regular bulletins of discussion, information and screenings (subscription details from www.hi-beam.net/fw.html or PipChod@aol.com).

References   The Notes try to guide the viewer to the sources quoted or referred to in the main text, supplemented by further reading in or around the key topic. The text is mainly based on secondary sources, and this is reflected in the notes which refer to them for ease of access (for example, by citing recent or more easily found editions). References to primary materials are kept to a minimum in the main text, but not in the Notes. Many of the principal books cited contain good bibliographies on their subject. Most of the major books and articles referred to are available in film and university libraries and many are in print.

Texts cited are mostly listed in the Bibliography, with publishing details. A few such details are given in the Notes themselves, where appropriate. In general, the Bibliography contains books and other material with direct film references; other texts (social, philosophical, etc.) are cited in the Notes only. Journals, pamphlets and ephemera (all categories) are mainly listed with publication details in the Notes rather than in the Bibliography.

Selected list of books published since 1999

Curtis, David *A History of Artists' Film and Video in Britain* (London: BFI, 2008).

Elwes, Catherine *Video Art: a guided tour* (London: I.B.Tauris, 2005).

Hamlyn, Nicky *Film Art Phenomena* (London: BFI, 2003).

Hatfield, Jackie (ed.) *Experimental Film and Video* (Eastleigh: John Libbey, 2006).

Le Grice, Malcolm *Experimental Cinema in the Digital Age* (London: BFI, 2001).

Meigh-Andrews, Chris *A History of Video Art* (Oxford: Berg, 2006).

Michalka, Matthias (ed.) *X-Screen: Film Installations and Actions in the 1960s and 1970s* (Cologne: Walther König, 2004).

O'Pray, Michael *Avant-Garde Film: forms, themes and passions* (London: Wallflower, 2003).

Sitney, P. Adams *Eyes Upside Down: Visionary Filmmakers and the Heritage of Emerson* (New York: OUP, 2008).

Spielmann, Yvonne *Video: the Reflexive Medium* (Cambridge, Mass.: MIT Press, 2008).

Preface

Interview with Clement Greenberg by Edward Lucie-Smith (originally published in *Studio International*, January 1968) from *The Collected Essays of Clement Greenberg vol. IV; Modernism with a Vengeance, 1957–1969*, ed. John O'Brian (Chicago: University of Chicago Press, 1993), p. 281. For further comment, see pp. 11–12 above.

1 **Arnheim**   Rudolf Arnheim, *Film As Art* (London: Faber & Faber, 1958). The 'distinguished predecessors' (and some contemporaries) include Vachel Lindsay, *The Art of the Moving Picture* (1915, revised 1922); Hugo Munsterberg, *The Film – A Psychological Study* (1917); Roman Jakobson, 'Is the Cinema in Decline?' (1933); Erwin Panofsky, 'Style and Medium in the Motion Pictures' (1936, revised 1947); Maurice Merleau-Ponty, 'The Film and the New Psychology' (1947); Béla Balászs, *Theory of the Film; the Character and Growth of a New Art* (1952); Siegfried Kracauer, *Nature of Film – the Redemption of Physical Reality* (1961); Andre Bazin, *What is Cinema?*, (2 vols, 1967/1971). These books and essays make up one half of the serious tradition of film writing in the cinema's first half-century, the other half comprising texts by film-makers such as Dreyer, Eisenstein, Vertov, Epstein, Dulac and others. See Preface to P. Adams Sitney, *Visionary Film* (pp. viii and ix).

2 **non-linear aspect**   See Manuel DeLanda, *A Thousand Years of Non-linear History*, Swerve Edition (series editor, Jonathan Crary; New York: Zone Books, 1997). Manuel DeLanda is a former avant-garde film-maker who now writes about digital systems, war and society; see interview with Scott MacDonald, *A Critical Cinema*, 1988.

3 **after Le Grice**   'London Film Co-op After Le Grice', Monthly Film Bulletin, vol. 51, no. 609, October 1984. Contains feature article on the LFMC by Michael O'Pray, and reviews of recent film releases. One of a series of MFB avant-garde film profiles published between 1983 and 1987, edited by Richard Combs.

4 **the international perspective**   Probably the most serious omission is any detailed discussion of the continental European avant-garde during and after the structural era. France, Germany, Holland, Yugoslavia, Poland and even (in its latter days) Soviet Russia all produced substantial experimental film-makers in the 1970s and down to the present day, as has Japan. In the context of this book, reference to Klaus Wyborny, Birgit and Wilhelm Hein, Karl-Heinz Emigholz, Margaret Raspé, Dore O., Werner Nekes, Valie Export (in Germany) or to Guy Fihman, Claudine Eizykman, Rose Lowder, Yann Beauvais, Jean-Michel Bouhours, Maria Klonaris and Katerina Thomadeki (in France) or to Ryszard Wasko, Jozef Robakowski, Zbigniew Rybczynski, Wojciech Bruszewski (in Poland) – and many others in these and other countries – would have been intolerably superficial. The reader is referred to earlier books which mention these film-makers' works between 1967 and 1979 (Curtis, Dwoskin, Le Grice and *Film as Film*) and to later documentation. For Germany, see catalogues including *The German Experimental Film of the Seventies*, ed. Ulrich Gregor (in English, Munich: Goethe Institute, 1980); *Videokunst in Deutschland 1963–83* ed. Wulf Herzogenrath (Stuttgart, 1982); and *Video-Art in the Federal Republic of Germany since 1976* curated by Wolfgang Preikschat (in English; Munich: Goethe Institute, 1986). For France, see the copious catalogues and screenings organised through the Beaubourg Centre and Light Cone, Paris, together with the critical research and curating of Dominique Noguez and Alain Sudre. See Dominique Noguez, *Eloge du cinéma experimentale: définitions, jalons, perspectives* (Paris: Centre d'art et culture Georges Pompidou, 1979); for historical and new work in sound, see *Musique Film*, eds/curated Yann Beauvais and Deke Dusinberre (Centre d'art et culture Georges Pompidou; Paris: Scratch/Cinématheque Française, 1986); for video, see *Video et aprés: la collection video du Musée Nationale d'art Moderne* ed. Christine Vassche (Paris: Centre Georges Pompidou, 1992); and for a fully comprehensive film catalogue, see *L'Art du Mouvement: la collection cinématographique du Musée Nationale d'Art Moderne 1919–1996*, ed. Jean-Michel Bouhours (Paris: Centre Georges Pompidou, 1996). For contemporary works and events on the international front, see:

Dfilm at www.dfilm.com; Onedotzero at www.onedotzero.com; and the two Flicker sites at www.chapel-hill.nc.us/flicker/index.html; and www.sirius.com/~sstark/

5 **John Cage**   Peter Greenaway's hour-long TV documentaries on Cage, Meredith Monk, Philip Glass and Robert Ashley were produced by Channel 4 in 1987.

6 **define the terms**   For a concise and contentious summary of major terms and book titles on the avant-garde, see Anne Friedberg, *Window Shopping* (1993), notes 15–17 (pp. 268–9).

Introduction

Siting the avant-garde

7 **innovative film-makers**   For the general relation between the pre-Second World War avant-garde and the mainstream, see David Curtis, *Experimental Cinema* (1971) and for the post-war period *Art and Film Since 1945: Hall of Mirrors* ed. Kerry Brougher (1996). Passing remarks on the underground film are made by *Scorsese on Scorsese* (1989), *Cronenberg on Cronenberg* (1992) and *Lynch on Lynch* (1997) (London: Faber & Faber). The influence of the avant-garde on the 'movie brat' generation is a topic in itself. Scorsese's early *The Big Shave* (1967), an anti-Vietnam War statement, is also an exercise in montage, with imagistic shades of Cocteau–Eisenstein in its editing as well as its young male actor, and has a Bunny Berrigan soundtrack in a direct line of descent from Bruce Baillie's 1966 *All My Life* (song by Ella Fitzgerald). *Mean Streets* (1975) opens with a brief reduction of the classic psychodrama shot in blue tones – a young man wakes, restlessly moves round the room in front of a window and a mirror (tropes found in Deren's *Choreography* and Anger's *Fireworks*) and returns to his bed where his head hits the pillow in a three-shot montage which is cut to a rock soundtrack. The next sequence opens with a projector beam and 8mm footage. This was to be his most radical film formally until *The Last Temptation of Christ* (1988) and even more so *The Age of Innocence* which takes his film rhetoric in new semiotic directions. See the early 'dinner-party sequence' with its multiple shooting-angles, and inventive bounce-back relation between voice-over sound, pictorial image and written word as hero and heroine prepare to meet. For Oliver Stone, see *JFK* – especially the scenes where Kennedy's assassination is analysed in scenes that blur documentary and fiction through abrupt montage of diverse kinds of footage, recapped in the courtroom scene with its similar sequence. Despite the ponderous naturalism of the acting in this and other films by Stone (and indeed Scorsese), this is a very different approach to narrative than in the classic Hollywood film, where non-realist sequences are confined to special-effects, dream scenes and inter-syntagmatic montage (superimposed clocks, newspaper headlines and the like) to depict the passage of time or changes of space. For the later generation, avant-garde style enters into the full body of the film drama and is not restricted to its margins. David Lynch, the most independent in this direction, is also the most thorough in his surrealist displacement of the normal film codes, as in the opening of *Blue Velvet* (which quotes the fence and roses of Baillie–Deren, the firetruck and colour of George Landow and of course the 'missing dog' from *Un Chien andalou* by way of Lumière's comic *The Hoser Hosed*). *Lost Highway* goes far beyond this, signalled in the house and curved pathway which are quoted from Deren's *Meshes of the Afternoon*, to hint at Lynch's reworking of that film's spiralling and reprised structure, as well as of its complex eroticism. Stone, Scorsese and Lynch have each attested to their early viewing of experimental work. See *Scorsese on Scorsese*, pp. 21–2, while Lynch's 1986 *Arena* BBC2 TV presentation focuses exclusively on surrealist and abstract film of the 1920s to the 1940s, presumably the films he saw at art school. Cronenberg's first films were underground dramas, Paul Verhoeven (initially an underground-style documentarist) and Paul Schrader studied art history, Susan Seidelman and Lizzie Borden have an experimental film

school background, Kathleen Bigelow is another art school graduate ... The list could go on.

8 **ways of seeing**   The title of a well-known Granada TV series and book by John Berger (1972), but here taken from p. 58 of the 'cubism' section in his 1965 book on Picasso (see Bibliography).

9 **formalist tricks**   See S. M. Eisenstein, *Film Form* (New York: Publisher, 1949) pp. 43–4. An account of the Eisenstein–Vertov dispute is in Jay Leyda's *Kino*, and Annette Michelson's introduction to *Kino-Eye: Writings of Dziga Vertov* (Berkeley: University of California, 1984). Eisenstein's grumbles at the avant-garde are in his biographical notes *Immoral Memories* trans. H. Marshall, re-translated and expanded in the BFI *Selected Works (vol. 4); Beyond the Stars – the Memoirs of Sergei Eisenstein* ed. Richard Taylor (London: BFI, 1995).

10 **conjunctions**   These issues, and a political reading of the underground and avant-garde film, are taken up by David James in his *Allegories of Cinema* and *Power Misses*. Also see Dana Polan, *Politics and the Avant-Garde Film*. For a recent essay on documentary and the avant-garde (which opens with a comparison between Bazin and Greenberg on aesthetic autonomy), see Paul Arthur, 'On the Virtues and Limitations of Collage', *Documentary Box* #11, 1997, published by the biennial Yamagata International Documentary Film Festival, Tokyo (see 'Film Literature Index' or <http://www.city.yamagata.yamagata.jp/yidff/en/home.html>)

11 **negative element**   Sitney, *Avant-Garde Film: A Reader of Theory and Criticism*, p. vii, quoted in Friedberg, *Window Shopping*, p. 269. The theme is developed by Peter Gidal – but in a different sense – in *Materialist Cinema*.

12 **deconstructed**   Bürger's *Theory of the Avant-Garde* and its aftermath are discussed in Friedberg's *Window Shopping*, pp. 163–4, in relation to the avant-garde film.

13 **outrage**   Carl Andre's *Equivalent VIII*, but dubbed 'the bricks' by the mass media, was purchased by the Tate Gallery in 1972. A major show of 'young British Art' (from the Saatchi collection) was held at the Royal Academy, London, in 1997, and titled *Sensation*. Also see Peter Wollen's review in *London Review of Books* **30**, Oct. 1997, 'Thatcher's Artists' and (from the hard right) by George Walden in *TLS* no. 4930, 26 September 1997.

14 **Baudelairian**   The phrase was used by Jonas Mekas about Jack Smith, suggesting a cinema of excess and self-willed decadence – and perhaps camp irony too. The 1980s mode can be traced – in Smith's wake – through US post-punk films, influenced by film-makers like Beth and Scott B., and journals such as *Semiotext*(e) which drew from Bataille and Nietzsche. Also see, for example, *Cinematograph – A Journal of Film and Media Art*, vol. 3, 1987–88 (includes 'The Body Lost and Found', John Muse, pp. 9–23). The 'body theme' grew in this period for a further decade, also looking further back to (non-Baudelairian) European artists like the Vienna Direct Action Group in the 1950s (Nitsch, Muehl) and ahead to yet more different and diverse artists such as Helen Chadwick, Orlan, Mona Hatoum and Judith Goddard.

Vision machine

15 **continuum**   For Greenaway's vision of 'expanded cinema' see, for example, 'Beyond Cinema' in 'The Art of Cinema' supplement to *Sight and Sound*, July 1994; and the essay on Greenaway by Thomas Elsaesser in the *Spellbound* catalogue (1996). Paul Virilio's views of film are in *The Vision Machine* and the *Aesthetics of Disappearance*.

16 **In the Dark**   See *Spellbound* catalogue for description of this work. It is also discussed in David Pascoe, *Peter Greenaway – Museums and Moving Images* (London: Reaction Books, 1997).

17 **Bergson**   Visual and cinematographic analogies recur in Bergson's writings. See *Matter and Memory* (London: George Allen and Unwin, 1896). His best-known film metaphors are in *Creative Evolution* (London: Macmillan, 1907). Also, see M. Antliff's *Inventing Bergson: Cultural Politics and the Parisian Avant-Garde* (Princeton, NJ:

Princeton University Press, 1993), for the impact of his thought on the artistic avant-garde and cubism. Bertrand Russell's influential and widely translated *Our Knowledge of the External World* (Chicago: Open Court, 1914), which helped to spread the 'new physics' to the Russian Futurists, among others, was written to refute Bergson's subjectivism (as the title implies). Also see Russell's *The Philosophy of Bergson* (Cambridge: Cambridge University Press, 1914). In the event, Bergson's philosophical psychology and the new physics of Einstein expounded by Russell were seen at the time as parallel pathways to understanding the 'modern age'. Both of them stressed the dynamic qualities of 'flow', the interaction of time and space (which they judged differently) and a new sense of relativist values. Also see Stephen Kern, *The Culture of Time and Space, 1880–1918* (London: Weidenfeld & Nicolson, 1983). For an excellent analysis of these issues, including Bergsonianism and cubist painting – and hence relevant to the whole of the first half of this book – see 'Time in the Visual Arts: Lessing and Modern Criticism', Jeoraldean McLain, *Journal of Aesthetics and Art Criticism*, vol. 44, Fall 1985, pp. 41–58.

Time base

18 **time** From a 'structural film' or 'abstract avant-garde' perspective, Malcolm Le Grice writes that

> the language or discourse of cinema is fundamentally altered – philosophically and in the socio/cultural arena – by emerging forms which first establish the screen as surface then reverse the symbolic space from behind to before the screen. Even more fundamentally, the relationship of the spectator to the work is transformed when the time of the action is reversed from being the 'once-upon-a-time' of the mythic past to the critical arena of the present. This becomes the time in which the spectators individually live – it is their time, their present based on a material experience of the presentation event. The conditions for this, like establishing the screen as surface, must be achieved in the FORM of the work, not . . . reinvested in the narrative, if the work is to change the experiential relationship with the spectator away from the that of the passive, surreptitious viewer.
> (Le Grice, 'Mapping in Multi-Space', p. 261 (see Note 144 below)).

19 **moment of cubism** See John Berger's collection *The Moment of Cubism and Other Essays* (London: Weidenfeld & Nicolson, 1969). The title essay is reprinted in his collection *The Look of Things* (New York: Viking Press, 1971). For a related and extended account, see his *Success and Failure of Picasso* (Harmondsworth: Penguin, 1965).

Point of view

20 **Benjamin** This essay is collected in *Illuminations* (London: Jonathan Cape, 1970). Many of his most important ideas about film are in the notes to the main text.

21 **regime of vision** See Krauss, Bryson, Bois, Mitchell, Rose, Mulvey. The quotations from Bois are in his catalogue essay for *Piet Mondrian: 1872–1944* (London: Little, Brown, 1994). Also see his *Painting as Model* (London: MIT Press, 1990). The issues are discussed at length in W. Rubin and K. Varnedoe, *Picasso and Braque: A Symposium* (New York: MOMA, 1992). Also see *Vision and Visuality* (1988), ed. Hal Foster, with contributions by Krauss, Jacqueline Rose and Jonathan Crary. A full historical survey is Martin Jay's excellent *Downcast Eyes* supplemented by *Modernity and the Hegemony of Vision* ed. Michael L. Levin.

22 **misrecognition** See Jacqueline Rose, *Sexuality in the Field of Vision*; Laura Mulvey, *Fetishism and Curiosity*; and the prolific Slavoj Žižek.

23 **modernity** Key founding texts of the contemporary debate include Fredric Jameson, *Postmodernism* (London: Verso, 1991); A. Huyssen, *Beyond the Great Divide* and D. Harvey, *Conditions of Postmodernity*. Also, see Peter Wollen, *Raiding the Ice-Box*. For a sociological and political perspective see Anthony Woodiwiss, *Post-Modernity USA: the Crisis of Social Modernism in Postwar America* (London: Sage Publications, 1993) (with extensive bibliography).

24 **'How to Read'** This essay (1927/8) is in *Literary Essays of Ezra Pound* ed. T. S. Eliot (London: Faber & Faber, 1954).

25 **quotation** Benjamin is quoted from Friedberg, *Window Shopping*, p. 50. For a full account of the Arcades Project see Susan Buck-Morss, *The Dialectics of Seeing* (London: MIT Press, 1989).

26 **'otherwise involved . . .'** Friedberg, *Window Shopping*, p. 162.

27 **Richard Abel** See his *French Cinema 1915–1929*, supplemented by the two volumes of selected and edited contemporary writings, *French Film Theory and Criticism 1907–1929* (with full bibliographies). Abel's argument is concisely prefigured by Ian Christie, 'French Avant-Garde Film in the Twenties; From "Specificity" to Surrealism', in *Film As Film* (1979).

28 **Barbara Rose** *How to Murder an Avant Garde* was published in *Artforum*, November 1965. This quotation is extracted from Janet Malcolm's 'A Girl of the Zeitgeist' (1986), p. 29, in *The Purloined Clinic* (London: Macmillan, 1992). For her later views and selected writings, see the aptly titled *Autocritique: Essays on Art and Anti-art, 1963–1987* (New York: Weidenfeld & Nicolson, 1988).

29 **Clement Greenberg** The essays 'Where is the Avant-Garde?' (1967) and 'Avant-Garde Attitudes' (1969) are reprinted in *Collected Essays vol. 4; Modernism with a Vengeance*.

30 **J. Hoberman** 'After Avant-Garde Film' in *Art After Modernism* ed. B. Wallis, pp. 59–73.

31 **Hal Foster** *The Return of the Real*, p. 54

32 **Robert Morris** *Continuous Project Altered Daily*, Chapter 13, 'Three Folds in the Fabric and Four Autobiographical Asides as Allegories (or Interruptions)'.

33 **Rosalind Krauss** See 'Grids' in *The Originality of the Avant-Garde and Other Modernist Myths* (1985). For Krauss's semi-autobiographical revisionist account, see *The Optical Unconscious* (1993). For her most recent development of the 'matrix', see *Formless: A User's Guide* (with Y-A. Bois, 1997).

34 **theorists of art** For the major earlier views, see Michael Podro, *The Critical Historians of Art* (London: Yale University Press, 1982), and Moshe Barasch, *Modern Theories of Art vol. 1: from Winkelmann to Baudelaire* (London: New York University Press, 1990). For later revisions of classical art theory, see *Visual Theory* eds Bryson, Holly and Moxey, which includes essays by Podro, Krauss, Nochlin, Bryson and others; and *Visual Culture* ed. Chris Jenks (1995).

35 **little lozenges** Dali in *Art in Cinema* eds Richter and Stauffacher (San Francisco: San Francisco Museum of Art, 1947).

36 **Kuleshov** The 'experiment' was to cut in the same shot (such as a close-up of a face) to different sequences, and to observe that the interpretation of the shot, i.e. the facial expression, was apparently modified by the surrounding montage. See *Kuleshov on Film* ed. R. Levaco (London: University of California Press, 1974); Jay Leyda, *Kino; The Film Factory* eds Ian Christie and Richard Taylor.

37 **a new concept** See Noel Burch, *In and Out of Synch*, on Eisenstein and 'intellectual montage', p. 49: 'This concept derives from the dialectical intuition – also felt to differing degrees by Pudovkin, Kuleshov and Vertov – that the juxtaposition of two *heteroclite* images (drawn, in other words, from two distinct spatial-temporal continuums) produces "a third image": inherent, mental, but pre-eminent. An intuition of cardinal importance.'

38 **triadic** See Annette Michelson, 'Reading Eisenstein Reading *Capital*', *October*, no. 1, Summer 1976:

Throughout his working life . . . Eisenstein was at pains to ground his conceptions of montage in the dynamics of the dialectic and, further, to specify the manner in which the former is the concrete film form of the latter. Although he will ultimately declare that 'montage thinking is inseparable from the general content of thinking as a whole,' he works, in the 1920s, towards an articulation of montage as the formal instantiation of cinema's triadic rehearsal of the dialectic.

For formal analysis of Eisenstein's montage methods, see Kristin Thompson, *Eisenstein's 'Ivan the Terrible': a Neoformalist Analysis* (Princeton, NJ: Princeton University Press); David Bordwell, *The Cinema of Eisenstein* (London: Harvard University Press, 1993); and J. Aumont, *Montage Eisenstein* (London: BFI, 1987). Aumont's *The Image* (London: BFI, 1997), expands this theme into wider questions of film art and style. For musical structures, see M. Nyman, *Experimental Music* (London: Studi Vista, 1971) and Kyle Gann, *The Music of Conlan Nancarrow* (Cambridge: Cambridge University Press, 1995). The most sustained development of the idea in recent times is by Morton Feldman; see (and hear) *Triadic Melodies* (1981) and T. diLio, *The Music of Morton Feldman* (London: Greenwood Press, 1996).

39 **forms . . . planes**   These terms are loosely adapted from the Danish linguist Louis Hjelmslev.

40 **Warhol**   For a recent analysis of Warhol's screenprints by Peter Gidal, see 'Different and the Same', *ACT*, **3** (Art, Criticism and Theory Journal), 1997, pp.11–21.

Part One: The canonical avant-garde

Origins of the moving image

This and the next section – on **photography** – are indebted to Martin Kemp's compendious study *The Science of Art: Optical Themes in Western Art from Brunelleschi to Seurat* (London: Yale University Press, 1990), which summarises the relations between art, perspective and colour systems from the Renaissance to modern times. It has a full bibliography. Useful studies of pre-cinema and primitive or early cinema include C. W. Ceram, *The Archaeology of the Cinema* (London: Thames & Hudson, 1965); *A Technological History of Motion Pictures and Television* ed. Raymond Fielding (1976/1983); Barry Salt, *Film Style and Film Technology* (1983); and Steve Neale, *Cinema and Technology: Image, Sound, Colour* (1985). Further references to the theory of early film and the avant-garde are found below.

41 **Debussy**   Quoted in Edward Lockspeiser, *Music and Painting – A Study in Comparative Ideas from Turner to Schoenberg* (London: Cassell, 1973), p. 30.

42 **Cézanne**   'We have to develop an optics, by which I mean a logical vision . . . Art is a personal apperception, which I embody in sensations and which I ask the under-standing to embody in a painting.' Reported in E. Bernard, *Souvenirs sur Paul Cézanne* (Paris: Michel,1912), as quoted in 'Cézanne's Doubt', M. Merleau-Ponty, *Sense and Non-Sense* (Evanston, Ill.: Northwestern University Press, 1964), p.13.

43 **triangulation**   For this and the next section, see Aaron Scharf's pioneering *Art and Photography* (Harmondsworth: Penguin, 1974) and Arnold Gassan's *A Chronology of Photography* (Athens, Oh: Handbook Company, 1972). Contemporary debates on the role of photography include Ron Burnett, *Cultures of Vision*; *Fugitive Images* ed. Patrice Pedro; and *Deconstruction and the Visual Arts* eds P. Brunette and D. Wills.

44 **Chevreul**   See William Innes Homer, *Seurat and the Science of Painting* (Cambridge, Mass.: MIT Press, 1964/1978), supplemented by 'Seurat and Colour Theory' in John Leighton and Richard Thomson, *Seurat and the Bathers* (London: National Gallery, 1997) and John Gage, *Colour and Culture: Practice and Meaning from Antiquity to Abstraction* (London: Thames & Hudson, 1993).

45 **clouds**   In addition to Kemp *et al.*, see – on meteorology and the structural film –

Peter Wollen's essay for *Chris Welsby Films* (London: Arts Council of Great Britain, n.d. [*c.* 1980]).

46 **roped together** Speaking of his major period of collaboration with Picasso (1909–14), Braque said in 1954 that

> it was as if we were two mountaineers roped together. We worked a great deal the two of us . . . museums did not interest us any more. We went to exhibitions, but not as much as people have said. We were above all very concentrated . . . We lived in Montmartre, we saw one another every day, we talked. During those years Picasso and I discussed things which nobody will ever discuss again, which nobody else would know how to discuss, which nobody else would know how to understand . . . things which have given us so much joy . . . all that will end with us.
> (Quoted (with ellipses as given) in John Richardson, *Georges Braque* (Harmondsworth: Penguin, 1954)).

47 **climbing** see Picasso as quoted in Françoise Gilot and Carlton Lake, *Life with Picasso* (Harmondsworth: Penguin, 1966), pp. 69–71:

> We were trying to move in a direction opposite to Impressionism. That was the reason we abandoned colour, emotion, sensation, and everything that had been introduced into painting by the Impressionists, to search again for an architectonic basis in the composition, trying to make an order of it . . . At that time our work was a kind of laboratory research from which every pretension or individual vanity was excluded . . . [The] canvas is made to be a painting, not an optical illusion . . . You see, one of the fundamental points about Cubism is this: not only did we try to displace reality; reality was no longer in the object. Reality was in the painting.

Also see *Picasso Anthology: Documents, Criticism, Reminiscences* ed. Maureen McCully (London: Thames & Hudson, 1981).

Photography

48 **Jonathan Crary** *The Techniques of the Observer* has sparked a lively debate which can be traced through Foster, *Vision and Visuality*, Jay, *Downcast Eyes* and Friedberg, *Window Shopping*.

49 **fluid-panning** See Charles Musser, *History of the American Cinema, Vol 1: The Emergence of Cinema – The American Screen to 1907* (New York: Charles Scribner's Sons, 1990), and Friedberg, *Window Shopping*.

50 **Tom Gunning** See 'The Cinema of Attractions – Early Film, its Spectator and the Avant-Garde' in *Early Cinema – Space, Frame, Narrative* ed. Thomas Elsaesser (1990).

51 **'avant-garde'** This outline of early uses of the term is taken from Linda Nochlin, *The Politics of Vision*, Chapter 1, 'The Invention of the Avant-Garde' (London: Thames & Hudson, 1990), as is the idea of removing the quotation marks (p. 12). Also see her *Realism* (Harmondsworth: Penguin, 1971).

52 **Cézanne** For classic texts on his theory of art, see his *Letters* ed. John Rewald (New York: Da Capo, 1976/1995); *Joachim Gasquet's Cézanne: a Memoir with Conversations* (London: Thames & Hudson, 1991); K. Badt, *The Art of Cézanne* (London: Faber & Faber, 1965); essays by Gowing and others in *Cézanne: The Late Work* ed. William Rubin (London: Thames & Hudson, 1977). For more recent debate, see *Picasso and Braque: A Symposium* ed. William Rubin (New York: MOMA, 1992), and bibliographies in the Tate Gallery Exhibition Catalogue, *Cézanne* (London: Tate Gallery, 1997).

53 **enthusiasts** See Berger on cubism and cinema for a concise view of this, e.g. his *Picasso* book of 1965, p. 70 ('The cinema is *the* art form of the first half of our century'). For specific references to films made by artists, see Standish Lawdor, *The Cubist Cinema*.

54 **artists**   Virginia Spate's *Orphism: the Evolution of Non-figurative Painting in Paris 1910–1914* (Oxford: Oxford University Press, 1979) is a comprehensive study of the many groups which made up the cubist movement at its broadest. Also see Christopher Green, *Cubism and its Enemies: Modern Movements and Reactions in French Art 1916–1928* (London: Yale University Press, 1987).

55 **1890-1914**   See Kern, 'The Culture of Space and Time' and 'Klee I and II' in David Sylvester, *About Modern Art* (London: Chatto & Windus, 1996), pp. 36–47.

56 **'paintings in motion'**   The most comprehensive selection of Apollinaire's criticism in English is *Apollinaire on Art* ed. L. C. Breunig (New York: Da Capo, 1972/1988). Texts by Aragon, Raynal and others in their Dada or early surrealist phase are published in Abel, *French Film Theory* and the equally invaluable anthology of surrealist film criticism, *The Shadow and its Shadow* ed. Paul Hammond. Quotations are from these sources.

57 **Survage**   See *Film as Film* and *The Cubist Cinema* by Standish Lawder.

58 **Aragon**   The quotations from Aragon, Raynal and others in the next pages are from Richard Abel, *French Film Theory* and from Paul Hammond, *The Shadow and its Shadow* (see Bibliography). The argument which follows can also be traced through the early Soviet cinema, which was much influenced by cubism and by the visual arts. For an early example, see L. Kuleshov: 'The whole point of cinema lies in its great degree of cinematic specificity.' Rejecting the idea that film must 'overcome' its 'non-stereoscopic quality, its contraction of depth into a flat and colourless screen', he says: 'It seems to me that we must make use of the non-stereoscopic quality of cinema and make the flatness of the image into a method of communicating the artistic impression . . . We must think of the individual frames of a film as if they were images akin to the flat and primitive painting on classical vases'. (From 'The Art of Cinema' (1918), in *The Film Factory*, p. 45.) For the contemporary impact of Western art (and relativity theory) on Russian formalism see 'Futurism' (1919) and 'Dada' (1921) by Roman Jakobson in the collection *Language in Literature* (see below, Note 89).

59 **Marinetti**   See under 'Futurists', p. 26.

60 **Kantian**   See Kahnweiler, *The Rise of Cubism* (New York: Wittenborn, 1949, originally 1916–20), and Yves-Alain Bois, 'Kahnweiler's Lesson', in *Painting as Model*, pp. 65–100.

61 **visual culture**   For a less formal account of proto- and early cinema, see Stefan Themerson, *The Urge to Create Visions* (1983).

The cubists

62   **Braque and Picasso**   See *Picasso and Braque: A Symposium* for a full analysis (from different viewpoints) and a chronology.

63   **Norman Bryson**   Quoted from a review, 'The Commonplace Look', subtitled 'objects and culture: still life from Cubism to the conference room' in *TLS*, no. 4933, 17 October 1997, p. 20.

64   **'retinal art'**   Duchamp discusses his ideas of 'retinal art' – i.e. art which appeals to the eye only – in Pierre Cabanne, *Dialogues with Marcel Duchamp* (London: Thames & Hudson, 1971). Pontus Hulton, *Marcel Duchamp* (London: Thames and Hudson, 1993), is a compendious catalogue with a day-to-day account of Duchamp's life (including many references to film). Krauss analyses his optical theory in her books *The Originality of the Avant-Garde, The Optical Unconscious* and *Formless*. Also see *Discussions in Contemporary Culture* ed. Hal Foster (Seattle: DIA/Bay Press, 1987). For an extended discussion of art and language, see P. Adams Sitney's 'Image and Title in Surrealist Cinema' in *Modernist Montage*.

65   **Gertrude Stein**   David Lodge discusses Stein and early modernism in *The Modes of*

Modern Writing: Metaphor, Metonymy and the Typology of Modern Literature (London: Edward Arnold, 1977). The Stein quotation on cinema (used by Lodge) is from 'Lectures in America' (1935), in *Look At Me Now and Here I Am* (Harmondsworth: Penguin, 1971), pp. 103–6. The statements by Bergson and James are also found in Lodge, pp. 145. The same Stein quotation is discussed in Marjorie Perloff, *The Poetics of Indeterminancy* (Princeton, NJ: Princeton University Press, 1981) p. 69.

66 **Cage gave it extra spin** See the techniques of writing and composition used in his books from *Silence* (Cambridge, Mass.: MIT Press, 1967), through to *Lectures I–VI* (Cambridge, Mass.: Harvard University Press, 1990), which develop the methods of Stein.

67 **Stan Brakhage** See his lecture 'Gertrude Stein: Meditative Literature and Film', Council on Research and Creative Work, The Graduate School, University of Colorado at Boulder, Fall 1990. The film *Anticipation of the Night* (1958) is discussed in *Visionary Film*, Sitney.

68 **vortex** See Ezra Pound's 'cinematographic' *Gaudier-Brzeszka* (1916; New York: New Directions, 1970), his *Literary Essays* ed. T. S. Eliot and *Guide to Kulchur* (London: Faber, 1938).

Primitives and pioneers (1880–1915)

69 **was it art?** Méliès' lecture and writings by Gance and Canudo are in *French Film Theory* by Abel, who discusses them in *French Cinema*.

70 **primitive stage** Elsaesser, Fell, Brewster, Burch, Hanson and Salt are among the key writers on early film form.

71 **Elie Fauré** His 1922 book was translated (by Walter Pach) as *The Art of Cineplastics* (Boston: Four Seasons, 1923).

72 **Maxim Gorky** This much-quoted description can be consulted in Noel Burch's *Life to these Shadows*, p. 23.

73 **philosophers** For Bergson, see Note 17. Moore discusses time, motion and the film in his *Commonplace Book* ed. by Casimir Lewy (London: Routledge, 1962; repr. Bristol: Thoemmes Press, 1993), sections 14, 15 and 16 (pp. 139–43). These date from the late 1930s to 1940. Wittgenstein refers to film throughout his works, including *Philosophical Investigations*, *Culture and Value* and *Philosophical Occasions*. For example, see *Philosophical Grammar*, item 28, p. 171, a remark from *c.* 1933:

> when we intend, we are surrounded by our intention's pictures and we are inside them. But when we step outside intention, they are mere patches on a canvas, without life and of no interest to us. When we intend, we exist among the pictures (shadows) of intention, as well as with real things. Let us imagine we are sitting in a darkened cinema and entering into the events on the screen. Now the lights are turned on, though the film continues on the screen. But suddenly we see it 'from outside' as movements of light and dark patches on the screen.

This note could be compared to Le Grice's *Castle 1 – the lightbulb film*, where this is precisely what happens when a light suspended in front of the screen flashes on and off.

74 **flipbook** Cubist animation is only hinted at in Kahnweiler's *Juan Gris: His Life and Work* (London: Lund Humphries, 1947), p. 88, where he mentions Picasso's ideas for sculpture 'which would be set in motion mechanically', around 1912, and 'the idea of pictures which would begin to "move" like targets at a fair when a switch was pressed'. These rather Pop Art notions are perhaps quite close to the more purist 'audio-visual' art envisaged by Mondrian and Moholy-Nagy a dozen or more years later, which are also on the verge of cinema (in which all these artists were interested). Picasso would certainly have known of his friend Survage's abstract film designs, around 1913/14 (see *Film as*

130

Film). In the same note, Kahnweiler is sceptical of the Futurists and Duchamp's painting of motion. In the *Nude Descending a Staircase* he sees simultaneous and hence static images, in distinct stages – literally, the nude is depicted in three steps; by contrast, 'in the case of the Stroboscope and the cinema the illusion is created by the fact that the images are presented *successively*; hence, all subsequent images are seen in relation to the original image, which thereby begins to "move"'. Whether or not this is correct, or represents Duchamp's intention, this is the same problem which vexed Moore, Wittgenstein and later Merleau-Ponty. 'A film is not a sum total of images but a temporal gestalt', he wrote in 1947 (*Sense and Non-Sense*, p. 54), just as Moore a few years earlier was pondering the same issue with the Gestalt psychologist Koffka as his own starting point. Similar issues are implied in Krauss's notion of the 'pulse' in motion art – including the rotor-reliefs of Duchamp – and for her analysis in this context of Picasso's late 'flipbooks', based on motifs from Manet drawings, see her contribution 'The im/pulse to see' in *Vision and Visuality* ed. Foster, pp. 70–4. Eggeling's first experiments in motion-art apparently also took a flipbook form.

75 **David Sylvester** The essay quoted dates from 1952 and is reprinted in his collection *On Modern Art* (1995).

76 **Bergson . . . influence** Munsterberg's 'psychological study' *The Film* is published by Dover, New York, 1970 (originally 1916). Panofsky's 1936 essay is in the collection *Three Essays on Style* ed. Irving Lavin (London: MIT Press, 1997). For Bazin, see *What is Cinema vol. 1* (Berkeley: University of California, 1967). Deleuze's *Cinema 1: the Movement-image* and *Cinema 2: The Time-image* were published by the Athlone Press, London in 1986 and 1989 respectively. Baudry's influential essay on 'The Apparatus' is in *Camera Obscura 1*, 1976. It is reprinted – along with texts by Barthes, Metz, Vertov, Straub-Huillet and Deren (her 'Anagram of Ideas on Art, Form and Film') – in the exceptional anthology *Apparatus* edited by Theresa Hak Kyung Cha (New York: Tanam Press, 1980). It is more easily available, with many other related essays, in *Narrative, Apparatus, Ideology: a Film Theory Reader* ed. Philip Rosen (New York: Columbia University Press, 1986). Metz's main work in this sphere is in *Psychoanalysis and Cinema* (London: Macmillan, 1982). Also, see *The Cinematic Apparatus* eds Teresa De Lauretis and Stephen Heath (London: Macmillan, 1980). The topic of 'the apparatus' is discussed in Friedberg, *Window Shopping*.

Futurists

77 **Futurists** Futurist film, performance and writing is detailed in such source-books as *Futurist Performance* ed. Michael Kirby (1971) and *Futurist Manifestos* ed. Umbro Apollonio (1973). Birgit Hein succinctly summarises Futurist cinema in *Film As Film*.

Abstract film

78 **handpainted film** See *Experimental Cinema* by David Curtis and entries in *Film As Film* (on Lye, Survage and the Futurists) for more detail. Survage's 'Colored Rhythm' is also in Abel, *French Film Theory*. Len Lye's writings and recollections are published as *Figures of Motion* eds W. Curnow and R. Horrocks (Auckland: Auckland University Press/OUP, 1984). More techniques are explained in Stan Brakhage, 'The Moving Picture Giving and Taking Book' (reprinted in Brakhage, *Scrapbook*).

79 **McLaren** See David Curtis's catalogue (Bibliography) and Deke Dusinberre in *Traditions of Independence*, ed. D. Macpherson.

80 **Canudo** For this essay, see Abel, *French Film Theory*.

81 **Art Cinema** This *ur*-version of the 'two avant-gardes' argument is detailed in Abel, *French Cinema*. Also see *The Cubist Cinema*, Standish Lawdor; and Ian Christie in *Film As Film* (note above).

82 *Close-Up* For more detail, see Roland Cosandey, 'On Borderline', in *Afterimage*, no. 12, Autumn 1985, reprinted (with bibliography) in *The British Avant-Garde Film* ed. M. O'Pray. The French journals are discussed in Abel, *French Cinema*. The novelist Dorothy Richardson also wrote for *Close-Up* from 1927 to 1932.

Reviewing Kristin Bluemel's study of *Pilgrimage* (1915–38), *Experimenting on the Border of Modernism* (Athens: University of Georgia Press, 1998), Jean Radford notes that this novel's 'narrative technique – the use of close-ups, montage, segmentation (where a blank space separates one scene from another), flashbacks and dissolves – can be likened to the techniques of experimental film. Cinema seems to have provided Richardson with an image of what she tried to achieve in language'. (*TLS*, 27 March 1998)

83 **La Sarraz** Full documentation of these important congresses is in *Travelling*, no. 55, but they are discussed in many books about the period, partly because Eisenstein was present at the first congress. See 'Introduction' by A. L. Rees to Hans Richter, *The Struggle for the Film*.

84 **The New Photography** For W. Graeff's book, see the translation in *Germany – The New Photography 1927–33* ed. David Mellor (London: Arts Council of Great Britain, 1978).

85 **collaboration** On Léger–Murphy's *Ballet mécanique*, see *Cubist Cinema*, Standish Lawdor. For contemporary writing by Ezra Pound on the composer of the film's musical score, George Antheil, see *Ezra Pound on Music* ed. R. Murray Schafer (London: Faber & Faber, 1978). For archival information, see *Tribute to Anthology Film Archives' Avant-Garde Film Preservation Program*, dedicated to Frederick Kiesler, and including material on Léger, Murphy, Ruttmann, Cornell, Deren and Leslie, MOMA/AFI (New York: Anthology Film Archives, 1977). Judy Freeman, 'Léger's *Ballet mécanique*', in *Dada and Surrealist Film* ed. R. Kuenzli is a detailed account of the film's making. For a recent and provocative study of the issues, which contends Léger's authorship of the film, see William Moritz, 'Americans in Paris: Man Ray and Dudley Murphy' in *Lovers of Cinema – The First American Avant-Garde 1919–1945* ed. Jan-Christopher Horak (1994).

86 *Manhatta* See essay in *Lovers of Cinema – The First American Avant-Garde 1919–1945* ed. Jan-Christopher Hurock (1994).

87 *Borderline* See Note 82 concerning *Close-Up*, above.

88 *Enthusiasm* See 'Dziga Vertov – A Russian [Soviet] Film-maker and his Legacy', Anthology Film Archives programme documents, Collective For Living Cinema, eds F. Canosa, S. Field and A. Michelson, April–May 1984; and Lucy Fischer '*Enthusiasm*; From Kino-Eye to Radio-Eye', in *Theory and Practice of Film Sound* eds Elisabeth Weis and John Belton (New York: Columbia University Press, 1985), pp. 36–8.

Cine-poems and lyric abstraction

89 **Jakobson's** See Roman Jakobson (with Morris Halle), 'Two Aspects of Language' (1956), in *Language and Literature* ed. K Pomorska and S. Rudy (London: Harvard University Press, 1987), pp. 111–12.

A salient example from the history of painting is the manifestly metonymical orientation of Cubism, where the object is transformed into a set of synecdoches [i.e. in which a part or fragment implies – 'stands in for' – the whole]; the Surrealist painters responded with a patently metaphorical attitude ... Ever since the productions of D. W. Griffith, the art of the cinema, with its highly developed capacity for changing the angle, perspective and focus of shots, has broken with the tradition of the theatre and ranged an unprecedented variety of synecdochic close-ups and metonymic set-ups in general. In such motion pictures as those of Charlie Chaplin and Eisenstein, these devices in turn were overlayed with a novel metaphoric montage with its lap dissolves – the filmic similes.

Also, see his essay 'Is the Cinema in Decline?' (1933), reproduced in the same collection and also in *Semiotics of Art* ed. L. Mtejka and I. R. Titunik (Cambridge, Mass.: MIT Press, 1976/1984). For some later views on film, see the 1980 'Dialogue on Time in Language and Literature', *Verbal Art, Verbal Sign, Verbal Time*, eds Krystyna Pomorska and Stephen Rudy (Minneapolis: University of Minnesota Press, 1985). See Lodge, *The Modes of Modern Writing*, for further explanation of metaphor and metonymy, and Roland Barthes, *Elements of Semiology* (London: Jonathan Cape, 1967), which is probably the main source for the spread of the metaphor–metonym idea (pp. 60–1). Jakobson's binary concept is widely discussed in many contexts: see, for a further application to film, Linda Williams, *Figures of Desire*. The *Shklovsky* essay is translated in *Russian Poetics in Translation vol. 9* (see R. Taylor, Bibliography), but the quotation here is taken from, Maya Turokovskaya, *Tarkovsky – Cinema as Poetry* (London: Faber & Faber, 1989), p. 10.

90 **Henri Chomette**   See Abel, *French Cinema* and *Film As Film* for more detail on these films.

Origins of abstract film

91 **abstract film**   See S. Lawdor, *The Cubist Cinema*; *Film As Film*; D. Curtis, *Experimental Cinema*; S. Dwoskin, *Film Is*; M. Le Grice, *Abstract Film and Beyond*. Also, see *Der Deutsche Avant-Garde Film Der 20er Jahre/The German Avant-Garde Film of the 1920s* (Eng/Ger), eds Angelika Leitner and Uwe Nitschke (Munich: Goethe-Institut, 1989).

The absolute film

92 **Viking Eggeling**   See the monograph *Viking Eggeling* by Louise O'Konor. For a recent assessment, see Peter Wollen, 'Lund celebrates Dada child', *PIX*, **2** (London: BFI, 1997).

93 **music**   See Peter Wollen, 'Tales of Total Art and Dreams of the Total Museum', in *Visual Display – Culture Beyond Appearances* eds L. Cooke and P. Wollen (Seattle: Bay Press, 1995).

94 **abstract film-makers**   In addition to the above accounts of the European abstract film, see the special issue on 'The films of Oskar Fischinger' by William Moritz, *Film Culture*, nos 58/59/60, 1974.

95 **Richter**   In addition to the historical studies of the abstract film in Lawdor and Sitney, Richter's two English-language books – *Dada, Art and Anti-Art* and *The Struggle for the Film* – should be consulted along with the monograph by Cleve Gray. The rolling dispute on Richter's reliability as historian and archivist can be traced through O'Konor (on Eggeling) and the entries under 'Hans Richter' and 'Werner Graeff' in *Film As Film*. Also, see 'Introduction' to *The Struggle for the Film*.

96 **shorn of sound**   For details of Edmund Meisel, who composed the music for the German version of *The Battleship Potemkin* (broadcast on BBC TV with sound, 1988) and for Ruttmann's later documentary film *Berlin – Symphony of a Great City* (still distributed in a silent version), see *Der Stummfilmmusiker Edmund Meisels* ed. Werner Sudendorf, *Kinematograph*, no. 1 (Frankfurt am main: Deutsches Filmmuseum, 1984).

Dada and surrealist film

97 **Surrealism** In addition to Abel's *French Cinema* and the source material in his *French Film Theory* and in Hammond's *The Shadow and its Shadow*, see *Dada and Surrealist Film* ed. R. Kuenzli for later critical studies. The work of Dulac is analysed in *To Desire Differently* by Sandy Flitterman-Lewis.

98 **Dada** Major source material is collected in *The Dada Painters and Poets* ed. R. Motherwell, with full bibliography. Also see *Dada*, another early collection edited by W. Verkauf, and *Dada and Surrealist Performance* Annabelle Melzer (1980/1994).

99 **Ball** This diary is published as *Flight Out of Time* (New York: Viking Press, 1974/1996).

100 **Eurhythmics** For more detail on this aspect of Dada and modern art, see Melzer and Peter Wollen's essay on Eggeling in *PIX* (see Note 92) and his essay in *Visual Display – Culture Beyond Appearances* (see Note 93). Taylor Downing's BFI Film Classic on Riefenstahl's *Olympia* (London: BFI, 1992) is also recommended for further details on dance and culture in the Third Reich.

101 **Man Ray** The films of Man Ray are discussed, with new historical research in the catalogue *Man Ray* ed. J-M. Bouhours (Paris: Centre Georges Pompidou, 1997). It contains essays by Bouhours, Deke Dusinberre and others, with a selection of documents spanning Man Ray's career.

The French avant-garde 1924–32

102 **major French films** The films discussed here are analysed in Lawdor, *Cubist Cinema*. For two contrasting views of *Un Chien andalou*, see Linda Williams, *Figures of Desire* and Philip Drummond 'Textual Space in *Un Chien andalou*', *Screen*, vol. 18, no. 3, Autumn 1977. Drummond's argument is summarised in his introduction to the accompanying screenplay and notes for the VHS reissue of the film (BFI, 1995). For *L'Age d'or*, see the vivid and detailed BFI Film Classic by Paul Hammond (London: BFI, 1997).

Voice and vision in the pre-war avant-garde

103 **legendary conflict** For the Artaud–Dulac debate, see *Antonin Artaud Selected Works vol. III: On Cinema* (London: Calder and Boyars, 1972); and Abel, *French Cinema*. The issue is fully aired by S. Flitterman-Lewis in her article for Kuenzli's *Dada and Surrealist Film*, and – slightly toned down and focused on Dulac – in her *To Desire Differently*.

104 **conscious hallucination** Quotations from the texts by Goudal and Dali from *The Shadow and its Shadow* ed. Paul Hammond.

105 **optics** For Benjamin, see 'The Work of Art' in *Illuminations*, including the footnotes which carry much of the argument. For Artaud, see his writings on film, but most of the quotations here are from Flitterman-Lewis's annotated article in Kuenzli's collection. For the broadest and most thorough account of the question of visuality (including the surrealist film) see Martin Jay, *Downcast Eyes*.

106 **parataxis** For Richter on the role of editing, see his *The Struggle for the Film*, written in the late 1930s but not published until the 1960s. Adorno's authoritative (1963) essay on parataxis is in his *Notes to Literature*, vol. 2, trans. Sherry Weber Nicholson (New York: Columbia University Press, 1992), esp. pp. 109–49. Compare Adorno's definition (in relation to Hölderlin) to Richter's: 'artificial disturbances that evade the logical hierachy of a subordinating syntax' (p. 131). It is possible that Benjamin – who was, like Richter, aligned to the Brecht circle – may be the link between the different

kinds of montage theory current in these cultural and artistic avant-gardes. Benjamin had made some translations for one of Richter's journals, *G*, as far back as 1922, perhaps through his former neighbour in wartime Switzerland, Hugo Ball. As an extension to the topic of parataxis, see Peter Quartermain, *Disjunctive Poetics* (Cambridge: Cambridge University Press, 1992), which discusses the Poundian model, and his more specialist study 'Parataxis in Basil Bunting and Louis Zukovsky', *Durham University Journal*, Special Basil Bunting Supplement, 1995.

Transition: into the 1930s and documentary

107 **problems**   For an early overview of the Soviet cinema, see *Kino* by Jay Leyda. The British debate over Grierson is unending. For early source materials, see E. Sussex, *The Rise and Fall of British Documentary* (Berkeley: University of California Press, 1975) and the BFI collection *Traditions of Independence* ed. D. Macpherson. More recently, see Ian Aitken, *Film and Reform: John Grierson and the Documentary Film Movement* (London: Routledge, 1990). The copious literature on Jennings includes *The Humphrey Jennings Reader* ed. Kevin Jackson (Manchester: Carcanet, 1993) and the curiously titled *Humphrey Jennings – More than a Maker of Films* eds Hodgkinson and Sheratsky. Also see his montage-book of the Industrial Revolution, *Pandaemonium*, compiled in the same period and with a similar method to Benjamin's 'The Arcades Project'. On Joris Ivens, see R. Delmar, *Joris Ivens*. For Germany, see *Germany: The New Photography 1927–33* ed. David Mellor. For the USA, see William Stott, *Documentary Expression and Thirties America* (London: University of Chicago Press, 1986); and William Alexander, *Film on the Left: American Documentary Film 1931–1942* (Princeton, NJ: Princeton University Press, 1981).

Reviewing the first avant-garde

108 **European borderlands**   For a concise overview, see Deke Dusinberre's article on 'the other avant-gardes' in *Film As Film*. The Polish avant-garde, which was far more extensive than indicated here (although almost all the films it produced are lost, except for the Themersons') are given more detail in A. L. Rees, 'The Themersons and the Polish Avant Garde' in *PIX*, **1**, London, 1994.

109 **Jonas Mekas**   Quoted in a recent book of essays on Hans Richter, Mekas remembered Richter's generosity: 'like a father standing on the side . . . an inspiration to all of us'. *Hans Richter; Activism, Modernism and the Avant-garde*, ed. Stephen C. Foster, (1998), p. 178, Note 1.

Origins of the post-war avant-garde

110 **in the 1950s**   For the Lettristes and situationists, Jean-Paul Curtay, *Letterism and Hypergraphics: the Unknown Avant-Garde 1945–1985* (exhibition catalogue; New York: Franklin Furnace, 1985), and *Situationist International Anthology* ed. Ken Knabb (Berkeley, CA: Bureau of Public Secrets, 1981). A full, annotated bibliography (1972–92) is Simon Ford, *The Realization and Suppression of the Situationist International* (Edinburgh: AK Press, 1995). For film, see the exhibition catalogue *On the Passage of a few people through a rather brief moment in time: the Situationist International 1957–1972* ed. E. Sussman (Boston: MIT and Institute of Contemporary Art, 1989), esp. T. Y. Levin on the films of Debord, pp. 148–53. Also see the filmscripts

of Guy Debord (Bibliography). *Lipstick Traces* by Greil Marcus is a 'wild' account of the period which seeks to link it to the punk era, but contains much factual and atmospheric detail.

111 **new waves**   The American avant-garde in the 1940s and 1950s is given extensive detailed treatment in Sitney's *Visionary Film*, with chapters on Anger, Brakhage, Deren and many other key artists. There is a concise overview in Curtis, *Experimental Cinema*. Parker Tyler's *The Three Faces of the Film* (1960) gives a contemporary view of films by Deren, Anger, Markopoulos and others at a key moment for avant-garde cinema. Among the many memoirs of the period by film-makers, Sidney Peterson's *The Dark Side of the Screen* is highly recommended, and the lively *Coming Unbuttoned* by James Broughton (San Francisco: City Lights, 1993) is exactly what its title says it is. Quotations from the writings of Maya Deren are found at length in Sitney, but her earlier work up to 1947 is thoroughly documented (in two volumes) in the uncompleted group project *The Legend of Maya Deren*. Jonas Mekas's film reviews are collected as his *Movie Journal*, and are put in context in *To Free the Cinema* (on Mekas) ed. by D. James. *The Underground Film* by S. Renan is still a good introduction to the period and beyond, and Steve Dwoskin's *Film Is* remains an illuminating guide to the avant-garde into the 1960s. Also see (in German) Birgit Hein, *Film im Underground* (Frankfurt: Verlag Ullstein, 1971). The later career of Fischinger is detailed in Moritz, *Film Culture*. Early writings by Brakhage are conveniently reprinted in *The Film Culture Reader* ed. P. Adams Sitney, which contains other important sources about the avant-garde and the New American Cinema. Nearly all the material in this part of the book is taken from these publications.

112 **abstract animation**   In addition to Sitney, *Visionary Film* (Chapter 10) and Curtis, *Experimental Cinema*, see *Articulated Light – the Emergence of Abstract Film in America* (with filmography), exhibition document, eds Gerald O'Grady and Bruce Posner (Cambridge, Mass.: Harvard Film Archive/Anthology Film Archives, 1996).

113 **Zukovsky . . . scenario**   For the Zukovsky *Ulysses* scenario, prepared with Jerry Reisman, see 'The Reisman–Zukovsky Screenplay' in *Joyce at Texas*, eds D. Oliphant and T. Zigal (Austin: Austin Humanities Research Center, 1983), pp. 69–77. This is discussed in Peter Quartermain, *Disjunctive Poetics* (Cambridge: Cambridge University Press, 1992), p. 67, p. 104 and *passim*. Joyce seems to have approved of the script, and suggested that John Ford direct it. Compare 'Notes for a Film of *Capital*', S. M. Eisenstein, *October,* no. 2, 1976, and contextual essay by Annette Michelson. Eisenstein's 'Notes' (but not Michelson) are reprinted in *October – The First Decade, 1976–1986* (Cambridge, Mass.: MIT, 1987).

Underground

114 **outside the museum**   Critical and other writing from and about this period, roughly the 1960s, dovetails with the preceding section: so Sitney, Curtis, Renan and Dwoskin are as useful for this era as for the last. In addition, Gene Youngblood's *Expanded Cinema* gives an early vision of cyber-culture (and is referred to later in relation to digital technologies).

115 **bomb culture**   From the British perspective, Jeff Nuttall's *Bomb Culture* (London: Jonathan Cape, 1968) is a breathless but richly detailed 'I was there' history of the UK underground in its heyday. For further detail on the situationists in this period, also see Note 110 above. Barry Miles's biography *William Burroughs: El Hombre Invisible* (London: Virgin Books, 1992) – who looms large for Nuttall, as for the whole era – adds detail to the information about this milieu, as does Jack Sargeant's informative book of interviews and investigation, *Naked Lens*.

116 **in Vienna**   An excellent – but purely formal – account of the Vienna Group films by film-maker Peter Weibel is in *Film As Film*. Kren's films are analysed in M. Le Grice, *Abstract Film and Beyond* and in Dwoskin's *Film Is*. Kubelka's films are given detailed

description and readings in *Visionary Film* by Sitney. Kubelka's powerful interview with Jonas Mekas is in *The Film Culture Reader* ed. Sitney. His film *Arnulf Rainer* is composed entirely of black and white frames which also generate the soundtrack; in principle, anyone can remake the film from Weibel's description of the mathematical system which generated it (in English translation, *Film As Film*, p. 112) and from the diagram reproduced in the original German-language catalogue, *Film als Film*, p. 217. The same is true of some diagrammed films by Kurt Kren (*Film als Film*, p. 211), installations by Taka Iimura (*Film als Film*, p. 209) and – using the photo-diagram on the front and back covers of *Film As Film* which reproduce a complete work – of Paul Sharits.

117 **Beat**   For the most recent account of Beat generation films, see Sargeant, *Naked Lens*, which includes Harry Smith, Jack Smith, Robert Frank, Taylor Mead, Jonas Mekas, Anthony Balch, Genesis P. Orridge and beyond.

118 **Warhol**   Steven Koch's study of Warhol's films, *Stargazer*, is still unique and invaluable. Peter Gidal's *Andy Warhol* is similarly a good introduction to both film-makers, and contains the roots of later ideas about film time. These early studies should be supplemented by *Andy Warhol – The Film Factory* ed. Michael O'Pray, which contains much historical and critical material from a wide range of contributors; and the likewise broad anthology (which covers fashion and style as well as films), *Who Is Andy Warhol?*, eds C. MacCabe, M. Francis and P. Wollen.

119 **Warhol's tactics**   Sitney's *Visionary Film* deals with these in detail; its final chapters (especially the 1978 2nd edition) are devoted to the structural film and its makers, including Frampton, Snow, Gehr, Sharits and Landow.

Two avant-gardes (mark 1)?

120 **Other artists**   For the Judson Church events (from the point of view of dance and choreography) see Sally Banes, *Writing Dancing in the Age of Post-Modernism* (Hanover, NH: Wesleyan University Press, 1994), which also traces the term 'postmodernism' from the early 1960s, as used by Yvonne Rainer to distinguish the new work from its predecessor, 'modern dance' (although today this direction would probably be called 'late-modernist'). 'Moteur!' by Rosalind Krauss in *Formless: A User's Guide* (pp. 133–7) discusses Serra's film-viewing and his own early films: the remark about 'the projector gate' on p. 73 above is taken from this entry. Also see *Films by American Artists*, the catalogue to a touring show by Regina Cornwell with essays and notes (London: Arts Council of Great Britain, 1981). The major monographs on Nauman, Morris, Serra *et al.* also discuss their films and videos.

121 **'art and objecthood'**   Michael Fried's seminal essay, originally published in *Artforum*, **5**, 1967, is anthologised in *Minimal Art* ed. Gregory Battcock (New York: Dutton, 1968). It is reprinted with his other art criticism of the period, and a memorable new introduction, in Michael Fried, *Art and Objecthood – Essays and Reviews* (Chicago: University of Chicago Press, 1998). Also, see notes to Peter Gidal, Note 122, below.

Structural

122 **high ground**   This era generated some key books, largely by film-makers, but sadly few are in print so they will have to be consulted in libraries. Luckily, some important articles are reprinted in Michael O'Pray's anthology, *The British Avant-Garde Film*. The final chapter of Sitney's *Visionary Film*, which happily is also still available, started the 'structural' ball rolling. Some reactions to his first version of the structural tendency, in the late 60s, can be traced in *The Film Culture Reader* and the equally invaluable reader (also edited by Sitney), *The Avant-Garde Film*. As for the British structural

film, the later sections of Curtis and Dwoskin give early insights into this 'new wave', which was in formation while their books were being written. The thorough *Structural Film Anthology* edited by Peter Gidal, and which went into two editions (1976, 1978), should be consulted for its introduction, reviews, interviews and articles by key film-makers. Similarly, Le Grice's *Abstract Film and Beyond*, which has the additional virtue of being illustrated (Gidal's anthology was tellingly not), has succinct analyses of films by the British and European avant-gardes. Further material is in *Film As Film*, the cat-alogue to a major Hayward Gallery exhibition which coincided with the close of this era in 1979.

123 **Frampton . . . Snow**   Frampton gave excellent interviews (see Scott MacDonald, *A Critical Cinema*, vol. 1) and his own writings – many appeared first in 'Art Forum' under Annette Michaelson's editorship – are collected as *Circles of Confusion*. An early insight is given in the *12 Dialogues 1962–1963* between Frampton and Carl Andre, ed. Benjamin Buchloh (Halifax and New York: Press of the Nova Scotia College of Art and Design/New York University Press, 1980). Snow is one of the few film-makers of this era to have received full documentation: *Snow Seen* by Regina Cornwell is especially recommended. Snow's own photo-books such as *Cover to Cover* are worth looking at in specialist art libraries. Brakhage's later writings, which cover this period, are col-lected in *Scrapbook* (ed. R. Haller).

124 **'tight nexus'**   This formulation is in Gidal, *Structural Film*.

125 **viewing as reading**   Apart from the earlier books noted above, the US film avant-garde of the 1960s–70s has been well-served by an increasing number of studies, which include William Wees' *Light Moving in Time*, Scott MacDonald's *Avant-Garde Film* and James Peterson's post-Bordwellian *Dreams of Chaos, Visions of Order*. MacDonald has also published three volumes of interviews with American (and some European) film-makers and a further collection of texts and documents which give valuable insight into their working methods and ideas. Wheeler Winston Dixon's *The Exploding Eye: a Re-Visionary History of 1960s American Experimental Cinema* records 'the work of lesser-known experimental film-makers whose work has been excluded from the dominant film canon'. All of these relatively recent 'area studies' should there-fore be consulted for US and some international experimental cinema from the 1960s to the 1980s.

126 **I said to Sitney**   Letter from Frampton to Peter Gidal (August 1972), *Structural Film Anthology*, p. 77. He also makes the remark quoted later about leaving structuralism 'to confound all Gaul'. This anthology also contains an interview with Gidal. A longer version is printed in the Hollis Frampton Memorial Issue of *October*, no. 35, Spring 1985.

Part Two: Britain, 1966–98

English structuralists

127 **creative misreadings**   Le Grice quotations are from the *Structural Film Anthology*, pp. 22–7. This article is extracted from Le Grice's *Abstract Film and Beyond*.

128 **London Co-op**   David Curtis's witty and lucid diary of the English avant-garde first appeared in a special issue of *Studio International*, Nov./Dec. 1975, devoted to 'Avant-Garde Film in England and Europe' with key articles by Wollen ('Two Avant-Gardes'), Gidal ('Structural/Materialist Film'), Deke Dusinberre, Ron Haseldon, Birgit Hein, Malcolm Le Grice, Barbara Meter, Annabel Nicolson, Alan Sheridan and Peter Weibel. The diary has since been reprinted, with new comments, most recently in *The British Avant-Garde Film* ed. M. O'Pray. This is supplemented by Duncan Reekie's concise and thought-provoking account of the Co-op in *Filmwaves*, 1, Summer 1997, though without his polemical conclusions. Issue 1 of Tony Rayns's short-lived but vivid

Cinema Rising, April 1972 (title after Kenneth Anger) contains photographs and a checklist of underground film-makers in the UK. Also see David Parson's memoir of the LFMC in *Filmwaves*, **2**, Nov. 1997. For a more critical theoretical account of the period, see David Bordwell, *Making Meaning*, 'Picture Planes' section, esp. pp. 53–60 (US structural film) and 60–4 (UK structural film).

129 **it almost happened**   In addition to Nuttall, *Bomb Culture*, and Sargeant, *Beat Cinema*, and for a different perspective on this period, see Peter Wollen on *Performance* (1970) ('Possessed', *Sight and Sound*, vol. 5, no. 9, September 1995) and, in the same issue, the recollections of the film's designer, Christopher Gibbs ('Tuning into Wonders').

130 **landscape tradition**   The most thorough and illuminating account of this tendency in LFMC film-making is by Deke Dusinberre, who wrote many articles and screening notes on this issue. Interested readers should consult Dusinberre's 'On British Avant-Garde Landscape Film', *Undercut*, no. 7/8, Landscape Issue, Spring 1983, which contextualises these notes (originally written for a series of Tate Gallery screenings, March 1975). Excerpts from this and other essays are in *A Perspective on English Avant-Garde Film*, the catalogue to a touring exhibition by Curtis and Dusinberre and an important source-book of the period with critical writings and film-makers' essays (London: Arts Council of Great Britain, 1978). Also, see his 'St George in the Forest: the English Avant-Garde' in *Afterimage,* no. 6, 1976, and his brilliant 'swansong' to the British Avant-Garde, 'See Real Images', *Afterimage*, nos **8/9**, 1981. Landscape and avant-garde film are also discussed by P. Adams Sitney in 'Landscape in the Cinema: the Rhythms of the World and the Camera', in *Landscape, Natural Beauty and the Arts* eds Salim Kemal and Ivan Gaskell (Cambridge: Cambridge University Press, 1993).

131 **explored in a different way**   These notes are indebted to Le Grice's descriptions in *Abstract Film and Beyond*, where much more detail can be obtained on these and related works.

132 **scientific writing**   For Caillois, see *October*, and for the influence of scientific film on early Buñuel, see Hammond, *L'Age d'or*.

133 **extreme opponent**   More detail on Peter Gidal's films is in Nicky Hamlyn's article for *The British Avant-Garde Film* anthology (ed. M. O'Pray), based on an earlier essay for *Undercut*, **19**, 1990 – 'From Structuralism to Minimalism: Peter Gidal and his influence in the 1980s' – which should also be consulted. An early photostat collection of essays on Gidal appeared as *Independent Cinema Documentation File No 1: Peter Gidal*, compiled by Paul Willemen (London: BFI, 1979).

134 **polemical introduction**   Peter Gidal's introduction to the *Structural Film Anthology* is also reprinted in the *British Avant Garde Film Reader*.

135 **Michael Fried**   See above, Note 121. The issues are complex, and – insofar as they to relate to cinema – so far untraced. Fried's (negative) references to the sculptor Tony Smith's emblematic car-ride on the New Jersey Turnpike (where Smith experienced 'a reality there that had not had any expression in art') looks ahead to the rise of the road movie and via Robert Smithson and Richard Long, back into art. At the same time (and just shortly before 'Art and Objecthood' was published), even Fried's main exemplar of pure painting was not immune from technology: 'The seminal Nine Evenings of Art and Technology in the USA in 1966, a collaboration between a number of visual artists and research technologists mainly from Bell Laboratories, even saw austere abstract painters like Frank Stella flirting with electronics' (Malcolm Le Grice, 'Mapping in Multi-Space' – for reference, see Note 167). The saga works its way back into film theory, despite Fried's strictures, by way of his intellectual association with the philosopher and cineaste Stanley Cavell: see Chapter 11, 'Excursus: Some Modernist Painting', of his *The World Viewed – Reflections on the Ontology of Film* (Cambridge, Mass.: Harvard University Press, 1979).

136 **'The Anti-Narrative'**   Peter Gidal's essay of this title is in *Screen,* vol. 20, no. 2, Summer 1979, with an afterword by Stephen Heath. In the same issue, also see 'Notes on Reading of Avant-Garde Films' by Felix Thompson.

137 **primitive era**   Books and articles by Burch, Gunning, Fell and others document the link between the avant-garde film and the early film. Of these, Gunning ('An Unseen Energy Swallows Space') takes a positive view that early film is 'inspirational' on the avant-garde, while Burch ('Primitivism and the Avant-Garde Film') is more sceptical of attempts to 'conscript [early] film into the modernist logic'; these essays are anthologised in Fell (ed.) *Film Before Griffith* (Berkeley: University of California Press, 1983) and in Rosen, *Narrative, Apparatus, Ideology* respectively. However, it is important that such seminal historians of early film as Noel Burch, Ben Brewster, Tom Gunning, Barry Salt and David Bordwell shared a more than passing interest in the experimental cinema, although their thoughts on this are very diverse. Among the film-makers who took up historical issues in this period – preceded by such independent books as Stefan Themerson's 'imaginary' film history *The Urge to Create Visions* – were (most idiosyncratically) Brakhage's *Film Biographies*, in which he reinvents Griffith and Eisenstein, among others; Klaus Wyborny's 'Random Notes on the Conventional Narrative Film', *Afterimage*, nos 8/9, Spring 1981, pp. 112–33; Frampton's essay 'Towards a Meta-History of Film' in *Circles of Confusion – Film, Photography, Video Texts 1968–80* (Rochester, NY: Visual Studies Workshop Press, 1983); P. Adams Sitney's short monograph on Ernie Gehr, *Ernie Gehr* (Minneapolis: Walker Arts Centre, 1980); Ernie Gehr's 'Notes' (obliquely) in *Films of Ernie Gehr*, retrospective catalogue p. 30 (San Francisco: San Francisco Cinematheque, 1993); Malcolm Le Grice's essay 'The History We Need', in *Film As Film* (reprinted in O'Pray's *The British Avant-Garde Film*). A more recent and full account is Bart Testa, *Back and Forth – Early Cinema and the Avant-Garde* (Ontario: Art Gallery of Ontario, 1992).

138 **innovative TV**   For an account and analysis of UK broadcasting, see John Ellis, *Visible Fictions* (London: Routledge, 1992).

139 **later 1970s**   This section, and many of the later remarks on the British avant-garde film from 1975 onwards, is indebted to Nicky Hamlyn's careful analysis of the 'late-structural' film, which is gratefully acknowledged. Many of his ideas and phrases are incorporated directly. His views can easily be found in their own right in an article for *The British Avant-Garde Film* ed. M. O'Pray. Similarly important to discussion of the period is Peter Gidal's *Materialist Film*, which covers the 'structural-materialist' idea. Worth consulting too is the compendious 20th Anniversary issue of *Millennium Film Journal*, nos 16/17/18, Fall/Winter 1986–7, which reprints Wollen's 'Landscape, Meteorology and Chris Welsby' and has a transcript of Sitney and Le Grice debating 'Narrative Illusion *vs.* Structural Realism'.

140 **the already known**   'It all boils down to the question of *un*recognition, of *dis*allowing the viewer the recognition of the known. The viewer must be placed as unknowing. If an artwork *re*presents the already known it voids its own necessity.' This variant of Gidal's position is taken from the 1991 Preface to the original text of his *Andy Warhol*. Readers vexed by Gidal's prose style are advised to read this lucid, short and autobiographical account as a summary. For Gidal's prose style, see Deke Dusinberre, 'Consistent Oxymoron – Peter Gidal's Rhetorical Strategy', *Screen*, vol. 18, no. 2, Summer 1977.

141 **APG**   For the Artists' Placement Group, see John A. Walker, *John Latham* (London: Middlesex University Press, 1995) which gives a rich and detailed account of Latham's career (with Barbara Steveni) as artist and art activist.

142 **David Hall**   Sean Cubitt gives a valuable analysis of Hall's work in his excellent *Videography*.

Video stirs

143 **first stirrings**   For the history and theory of British video art, see Cubitt, *Videography* and especially Julia Knight's full and aptly titled *Diverse Practices*, a collection of key

source texts and new articles – with bibliography and chronology – on British video. This and the later sections on digital art are indebted to Julia Knight's invaluable anthology. Also, see the special 'Video Art' issue of *Studio International* ed. David Hall, May–June 1976.

144 **'formalism'**   The Marshall–Hall debate, and its aftermath down to John Wyver's revisionist polemic in the 1990s, can be traced through Knight, *Diverse Practices*, which contains the key texts.

145 **Gustav Metzger**   Essays by Metzger on 'auto-destructive art' and other matters are in his *damaged nature, auto-destructive art* (London: coracle/workfortheeyetodo, 1996).

Art and politics

146 **diverse movements**   The history of political cinema in the late 1970s to the early 1980s can be traced most accessibly through the 'independent cinema' issues of *Screen* and in Ellis, *Visible Fictions*. The BFI Production Board Catalogues for the whole period are a further source, since they contain 'contextualising' essays and aspirations for the films which were funded. Colin MacCabe's introduction to his *Theoretical Essays: Film, Linguistics, Literature*, reviews the growth of 'independent cinema' more critically, and sets out a different political agenda for radical film culture.

147 **'The Two Avant-Gardes'**   Peter Wollen's essay, first published in 1975 can be found most easily in his collection *Readings and Writings*. It might be compared to Paul Willemen's 'An Avant-Garde for the 80s' (*Framework*, 24, Spring 1984), which similarly looked to an anti-purist rejection of film as ontology or investigation, in favour of 'semantic expansion' into heterogeneity, mixed media, and a montage of codes, signs and registers. Semiotic reductionism is allied here to an attack on Greenberg's ideas, seen as a search for essence and high art. For an update of Willemen's ideas, see 'An Avant-Garde for the 90s' in his *Looks and Frictions*.

A cinema of small gestures

148 **small gestures**   The phrase is from Derek Jarman, but it applies especially well to the domestic scale of much late-structural UK film and video in the 1970s and 1980s. This section draws gratefully and liberally on Nicky Hamlyn's 'Structural Traces' in O'Pray (ed.), *British Avant-Garde Film* and on his other writings about this period. Several of the films discussed in this section are also analysed in Peter Gidal, *Materialist Film*.

Rebel waves

Documentation for this period is sparse. In reacting against the structural avant-garde, younger film- and video-makers also rejected the theory-laden context of structural work. This is not to impugn anyone's motives, intelligence or reading habits – younger film- and video-makers in this period probably saw as much and talked as much as any other group of artists, but they were more reluctant to write about it than their elders (who were often also their tutors, giving them a double reason for steering clear of the written word). Not coincidentally, there was a move away from linguistics and hard (i.e. Freudian) psycho-analysis as theoretical models in this period, and a shift towards the more subjective and personal writing of Kristeva, Baudrillard and Blanchot. This swung the balance more towards literature than classical theory as understood to that point. The joint result is a dearth of essay writing by film-makers in the 1980s and a move towards ephemera from handbills and postcards to posters, just as venues shifted to clubs, warehouses, squats and a few galleries. A few more formal and hence available catalogues are noted in this and the following sections. For more detailed reference on films and screenings, the reader is advised to consult back issues of *Performance* magazine (edited at this time by Rob Le Fresnais) and *Art Monthly* (reviews by Michael O'Pray and others) from around 1983/4. This too tells its own story of what occured at this time in terms of the avant-garde ambience.

149 **Scratch**   See George Barber's essay 'Scratch and After' in *Culture, Technology and Creativity* ed. Philip Hayward. See Hayward's own essay in the same volume for the impact of video art on music videos.

150 **empty spaces**   'Film As Film' was based on an exhibition, 'Film als Film – 1910 bis heute' organised by Birgit Hein and Wulf Herzogenrath in 1977. The withdrawal of the women and Peter Gidal from 'Film As Film' is documented in the catalogue, and the women's statement is also reprinted in *The British Avant-Garde Film* ed. M. O'Pray.

151 **commercial fringe**   In retrospect, the 1980s blurring of rock videos and avant-garde style – which so antagonised the structural film-makers – might have come as less of a shock had local conditions been different. The downplaying of the underground mode for a decade in the 1970s was partly responsible for the return of the rock-based repressed ten years later. In the wider perspective, this mode can be traced back to the late 1940s, when Harry Smith synchronised his *Abstraction #2* to Dizzy Gillespie and then reissued all his *Early Abstractions* in the 1960s accompanied by Beatles songs. Bruce Conner cut Ray Charles to *Cosmic Ray* in 1961 and Kenneth Anger expanded the genre with *Scorpio Rising* in 1963. Warhol's *Vinyl* of 1965 cuts in rock music, and later he filmed Nico and the Velvet Underground. His clubland events, 'The Exploding Plastic Inevitable', featured lightshows and mixed media with live music. The 1967 structural film *Wavelength* by Michael Snow incorporates a Beatles song (played from a radio) and a rising sine wave on its soundtrack. David James in *Power Misses* updates the story through the artist Robert Longo's contribution to a mid-1980s New Order video, *Substance*, while Robert Breer and William Wegman imaged the same band's song 'Blue Monday' for a promotional video (compare the Duvet Brother's UK video of the same title and date, available on *Scratch Video – Greatest Hits volume 2*). Conner later used soundtracks composed by David Byrne and Brian Eno for *America is Waiting*. Eno had much earlier composed the soundloop for Le Grice's 1970 *Berlin Horse* and later produced sound for many films, including Derek Jarman's 1977 *Jubilee*. The 1970s–80s gap in this aspect of experimental film was not just the product of structuralist puritanism: the US punk film, exemplified by Beth and Scott B., was likewise not a music-based form, strangely enough. When music re-entered the frame, with the rock video, it brought with it vestiges of the old war between synchronised sound (i.e. realism) and contrapuntal sound (Eisenstein's concept of sound 'against' picture). The general rule was that the less lip-synch was used, the more radical the video became. Richard Heslop's videos are a good example, as is Jarman's video for The Smiths' *The Queen is Dead* (1986), which shows no footage of the band at all. The current position is much more complex and sophisticated – and now incorporates the structural style itself as another component of the visual mix. Film-makers such as Matt Hulse in the UK have taken post-pop-video montage back into the domain of the personal artists' film, as in the aptly titled *Take Me Home* (1998).

Art Cinema's odd couple: Derek Jarman and Peter Greenaway

152 **Jarman and Greenaway**   These film-makers have attracted much more critical writing than any other British film- and video-makers discussed or mentioned in this book. For key examples, see Michael O'Pray, *Derek Jarman* (London: BFI, 1996), *Derek Jarman: a Portrait* ed. Roger Wollen (London: Thames & Hudson, 1996), and Pascoe, *Peter Greenaway – Museums and Moving Images*. The bibliographies in these books should be used for further reference. Ian Shipley Books of London publish lists of books in print about both directors.

153 **avant-garde?**   Independently of the negative judgements about Greenaway in this section, the artist and critic Julian Bell reviewed Pascoe's book and Amy Lawrence's *The Films of Peter Greenaway* (Cambridge: Cambridge University Press, 1997) in the *TLS* (no. 4952, 27 February 1998, p. 36). Sympathetic but firmly independent, Bell's review is also troubled by the films. Admitting Greenaway's 'craft' and 'brilliance', Bell writes that 'far-ranging external allusions and intricate internal cross-references can induce the viewer to abandon the sequential expectations of naturalistic cinema. In their sheer ingenuity, Greenaway's pictorial contraptions have given avant-garde cinematic practice a new popular viability.' Impressed by Greenaway's use of actors, he notes that 'the formal discipline imposed by his regimented décor and long static shots seems to stimulate rather than constrain his cast' – the reverse view to the one taken here. But then Bell turns to the 'stridently banal' premises of the films, rooted in the propositions that 'humans are bodies, driven by biology' and (especially in the early works) that representations (such as maps) are inadequate to their referents. Bell calls these truisms or half-truths:

> Clearly, we have to exist as something other than 'bodies' to be able to conceive of 'biology', and clearly we can't criticize our representations of reality without reaching for further representations – such as films. Yet Greenaway has very little to assert, in his non-naturalistic cinema, apart from this cod-Darwinism and this dissatisfaction with fiction; and so he tries to invest these factors with an emotional weight they won't carry. This is where the films become stupid.

Bell explains Greenaway's rise as a European auteur to both his 'formal resourcefulness' and his 'vogueishness'. These he links to Greenaway's origins, so that he 'belongs with an intellectual culture that has staked out its discursive base on the Western tradition of painting'. Hence, Bell says that the model for Greenaway's major films from *The Draughtsman's Contract* to *The Baby of Macon* is Foucault's discussion of Velazquez's *Las Meniñas*. But like Foucault, as they 'stride their way into the imaginative interiors bequeathed by the Old Masters', the films hover between subverting that tradition and fascination with it; which 'makes Greenaway's films monuments to a kind of contemporary double standard: crudely essentialist about nature, evasively relativist about culture'. Bell alludes to the early extremism of *The Falls* ('an uncirculated, three-hour pseudo-documentary') as preferable to Greenaway's most recent 'lapse into bathos', but inventively concludes that the glittering surface rather than the evaporating sense makes the films most rewarding – rather like the critical writing which Greenaway attracts from his admirers. Greenaway is finally 'a showman, a crowd-puller for the institutionalized avant-garde; but a resourceful one, always worth turning to watch'. As a locus of Greenaway's current and very contemporary role, Bell's essay is also worth turning to read, and not just because its terms of reference – from outside the avant-garde – overlap with but differ from those adopted here.

New pluralism

154 **New Pluralism**   This was the title for an important exhibition of new and diverse work selected by Tina Keane and Michael O'Pray. See catalogue with this title, *British Film and Video 1980–1985: The New Pluralism* (London: Tate Gallery, 1985). For a related but more historical exhibition and catalogue, see *The Elusive Sign: British Avant-Garde Film and Video 1977–1987* (London: Arts Council of Great Britain, 1987), selected by Michael O'Pray, Tamara Krikorian and Catherine Lacey and organised by David Curtis. The video aspect of this era is also discussed in *Diverse Practices* ed. Knight.

Black British

155 **Black British**   See 'Aesthetics and Politics; Working on two Fronts' (Martine Attille, Reece Auguiste, Peter Gidal and Isaac Julien) in *The British Avant-Garde Film* for a debate which conveys the flavour of this period.

Electronic arts

156 **curious twists**   This section draws especially on Richard Wright's informative essay *Diverse Practices* ed. Knight, together with other contributions by Peter Donebauer and Michael Maziere.

157 **the Themersons**   See pp. 54–5 above.

yBa

158 **thrusting**   Matthew Collings's *Blimey!* (Cambridge: 21 Publishing, 1997), is an excellent and more critical review of young (and older) British art than it is reputed to be. It is therefore a good introduction to 'the tone of the times', but focuses on painting and sculpture as the key media rather than video and film. The 'installation' debate which rolled through the journal *Art Monthly* in 1996–7, mainly by Ian Hunt and Catherine Elwes, is worth consulting (for example, no. 196, May 1996; no. 199, September 1996; no. 203, February 1997) as is Michael O'Pray's review of the artists' cinema (*Art Monthly*, no. 210, October 1997). During this period, a large number of art journals published special issues on film and video as art forms, but for the most part they featured the high-profile US artists Gary Hill and Bill Viola (who had major exhibitions in the UK during the 1990s) and on the 'art cinema' led by Greenaway and Jarman. The avant-gardes as understood in this book were largely missing, except of course where they merged with yBa film-makers such as Gordon, Wearing and Taylor-Wood (all of whom have had their film work catalogued). For an important grouping, see for example, *Scream and Scream Again: Film in Art* (Oxford: MOMA, 1996), exhibition (including Sadie Benning, Douglas Gordon, Isaac Julien, Tony Oursler and others), ed. with an extensive essay by Chrissie Isles (1996).

159 **some made . . . performance art**   Performance art in the UK has still to be tracked through the journals for its history, but the key US texts are Rose Lee Goldberg's *Performance Art: from Futurism to the Present* (London: Thames & Hudson, 1988), and Henry Sayre, *The Object of Performance* (London: University of Chicago Press, 1992).

160 **distant ancestors**   See *Diverse Practices* ed. Knight for further details.

161 **elusive self**   The examples here are liberally taken from Catherine Elwes's article in *Diverse Practices* although without her interpretation of their import for feminist art.

162 **Taylor-Wood**   See catalogue essay by Michael O'Pray in the catalogue *Sam Taylor-Wood* (London: Chisenhale Gallery/ White Cube, 1996).

163 **Wearing**   See TV programme on this artist and Gary Hume, March 1998. The *Sensation* catalogue has a bibliography, but also, see *Gillian Wearing*, with essays by Russell Ferguson and Donna di Salvo (London: Phaidon, 1999).

164 **Hirst**   See catalogues for *Spellbound* and *Sensation Young British Artists for the Saatchi Collection* (London: Thames Hudson/Royal Academy of Arts, 1997) for more details on Damien Hirst.

165 **Dean**   See the exhibition pamphlet *Foley Artist*, with text by Sean Rainbird (London: Tate Gallery, 1996), and the discussion 'Talking about Tacita Dean's *Foley Artist*' between Bartomeu Mari, curator, Simon Field, director of the International Film Festival Rotterdam, and art critic Michael Tarantino, in *Cahier*, no. 6, Witte de With Gallery, Centre for Contemporary Art (Düsseldorf: Rotterdam/Richter Verlag, 1996).

A later work shown at the Frith Street Gallery, 1997, took the form of a complex film-loop projection/installation.

'Where are we now?'

166 **Youngblood**   See his *Expanded Cinema*. The essays by Wright and others in *Diverse Practices* extend this area of study, as does *Electronic Culture* ed. Timothy Druckrey.

167 **Le Grice . . . computer-based**   For Le Grice's recent thoughts on digital art, see his essays 'Mapping in Multi-Space – Expanded Cinema to Virtuality' (1996) in *White Cube/Black Box – Skulpturensammlung* (Eng/Ger) (Vienna: E. A. Generali Foundation, 1996), foreword by Sabine Breitwieser; and 'A Non-Linear Tradition – Experimental Film and Digital Cinema' (1997) in *Katalog 43, Internationale Kurzfilmtage* (Eng/Ger), Oberhausen Festival, Germany. The second essay is an especially lucid analysis of narrative (and perspective) forms, with their social implications, and the alternative model which can be traced back through the history of underground, abstract and avant-garde film. Also, see *Millennium Film Journal*, no. 28, Spring 1995, for articles on non-linear interactivity and experimental film by Andrew Cameron, Grahame Weinbren, Richard Wright and Malcolm Le Grice. For other views on electronics, film and art, see essays by A. L. Rees ('Digital Daze'), Joan Key ('Painting and Cyberspace') and others in *ACT* (Art, Criticism and Theory), no. 4, ed. John Gange (London: Pluto/KIAD, 1998).

Points of resistance

The title is taken from Lauren Rabinovitz, *Points of Resistance: Women, Power and Politics in the New York Avant-garde Cinema 1943–71*, focused on Maya Deren, Shirley Clarke and Joyce Wieland. The content of this section acknowledges Michael Maziere's illuminating article in *Diverse Practices*.

168 **MTV**   A cultural and economic analysis of MTV, and the plagiarism of avant-garde film by the advertising industry (this includes imitations of Maya Deren) is in David James, 'Avant-Garde Film and Music Video: A View from Zurich', *Power Misses*, using American examples.

169 **active generations**   The current UK film-makers discussed here are included among over 100 UK artists whose work is described in *Directory of British Film and Video Artists*, ed. David Curtis (1996). This very useful directory contains biographical notes, critical assessments, film and videographies, bibliographies. The notes are designed to be used as programme support material for screenings. See for further details on Larcher, Maybury, Parker, Raban, Smith, and over 120 others.

170 **polemical Biennalle**   Catalogues with selectors' introductions and notes were published for each of the Biennales by the Institute of Contemporary Arts, London. Short catalogues of the first 'Pandaemonium' festivals were also published by the ICA and more recently by the Lux Centre which now hosts this event. The Exploding Cinema issues an impressive amount of ephemera to promote its informal and open screenings, and other information on this and related groups can be obtained from *Filmwaves* magazine. The Exploding Cinema is currently being archived and researched by Stefan Szczelkun at the Royal College of Art, School of Communications.

Bibliography

Abel, Richard *French Cinema: the First Wave,
1915–29* (Princeton, NJ: Princeton University
Press, 1984).

Abel, Richard (ed.) *French Film Theory and
Criticism* vol. I 1907–1929, vol. II 1929–1939
(Princeton, NJ: Princeton University Press,
1988).

AFA *A History of the American Avant-Garde
Cinema* (New York: American Federation of
Arts, 1976).

Alexander, William *Film on the Left: American
Documentary Film 1931–1942* (Princeton, NJ:
Princeton University Press, 1981).

Antliff, Mark *Inventing Bergson: Cultural Politics
and the Parisian Avant-Garde* (Princeton, NJ:
Princeton University Press, 1993).

Apollinaire, Guillaume *Apollinaire on Art: Essays
and Reviews 1902–1918* ed. L. C. Breunig
(New York: Viking Press, 1972); Da Capo
reprint 1988.

Apollonio, Umbro *Futurist Manifestos* (London:
Thames and Hudson, 1973).

Artaud, Antonin *Collected Works* vol. III (on cinema) (London: Calder & Boyars, 1972).

Aumont, Jacques *The Image* (London: BFI,
1997).

Aumont, Jacques *Montage Eisenstein* (London:
BFI, 1987).

Baines, Sally *Writing Dance in the Age of
Postmodernism* (Hanover, NH: Wesleyan
University Press, USA, 1994).

Ball, Hugo *Flight Out of Time: a Dada Diary*
(Berkeley: University of California Press,
1996).

Battcock, Gregory (ed.) *The New American
Cinema* (New York: Dutton, 1967).

Battcock, Gregory (ed.) *New Artists Video* (New
York: Dutton, 1978).

Berger, John *The Look of Things* (New York:
Viking, 1974).

Berger, John *Success and Failure of Picasso*
(Harmondsworth: Penguin, 1965).

Bois, Yves-Alain *Painting as Model* (London:
MIT Press, 1990).

Bordwell, David *Making Meaning: Inference and
Rhetoric in the Interpretation of Cinema*
(London: Harvard University Press, 1989).

Bordwell, David *The Cinema of Eisenstein*
(Cambridge, Mass.: Harvard University
Press, 1993).

Bordwell, David *French Impressionist Cinema:
Film Culture, Film Theory and Film Style*
(New York: Arno Press, 1980).

Bordwell, David and Thompson, Kristin *Film
Art* (4th edn) (New York: McGraw Hill,
1993).

Brakhage, Stan *The Brakhage Lectures* (Méliès,
Griffith, Dreyer, Eisenstein) (Chicago:
Chicago Art Institute, 1972).

Brakhage, Stan *Film at Wit's End* (Edinburgh:
Polygon, 1989).

Brakhage, Stan *Film Biographies* (Berkeley,
Turtle Island, 1977/1979).

Brakhage, Stan *Scrapbook: Collected Writings
1964–1980* ed. Robert A. Haller (New York:
Documentext, 1982).

Brougher, Kerry *Art and Film Since 1945: Hall of
Mirrors* (New York: Monacelli Press, 1996).

Brunette, Peter and Wills, David (eds)
*Deconstruction and the Visual Arts: Art,
Media, Architecture* (Cambridge University
Press, 1994).

Bryson, Norman, Moxon, Keith and Holly,
Michael Ann (eds) *Visual Theory* (Oxford:
Blackwell, 1991).

Burch, Noel *In and Out of Synch – The
Awakening of a Cine-Dreamer* (London:
Scolar Press, 1991).

Burch, Noel *Life to those Shadows* (London: BFI,
1990).

Bryson, Norman, Holly, Michael Ann and
Moxey, Keith (eds) *Visual Theory* (Blackwell
Oxford, 1991).

Bürger, Peter *Theory of the Avant-Garde*
(Manchester: Manchester University Press,
1984); originally in German, 1974.

Carroll, Noel *Theorizing the Moving Image* (New
York: Cambridge University Press, 1996).

Christie, Ian and Taylor, Richard *The Film
Factory: Russian and Soviet Cinema in
Documents 1896–1939* (London: Routledge,
1988).

Christie, Ian and Dodd, Philip (eds) *Spellbound:
Art and Film* (London: BFI, 1996).

Cornwell, Regina *Snow Seen – the Films and
Photographs of Michael Snow* (Toronto: Peter
Martin, 1980).

Crary, Jonathan *Techniques of the Observer: On
Vision and Modernity in the Nineteenth
Century* (Cambridge, Mass.: MIT Press, 1994).

Cubitt, Sean *Timeshift: on Video Culture*
(London: Routledge, 1991).

Cubitt, Sean *Videography: Video Media as Art and
Culture* (London: Macmillan, 1993).

Curtis, David *Experimental Cinema: a Fifty-year
Evolution* (London: Studio Vista, 1971).

Curtis, David *Norman McLaren* (Edinburgh: Scottish Arts Council Catalogue, 1977).

Curtis, David (ed.) *Directory of British Film and Video Artists* (Luton: John Libbey/Arts Council, 1996).

Debord, Guy *In Girum Imus Nocte et Consumimur Igni – a Film* (London: Pelagian, n.d. [1991]); translated from above.

Debord, Guy *Oeuvres Cinématographiques Complètes 1952–1978* (Paris: Editions Champ Libre, 1978).

Debord, Guy *Society of the Spectacle and Other Films* (London: Rebel Press, 1992); translated from *Oeuvres Cinématographiques Complètes*, above.

De Lauretis, Teresa and Heath, Stephen (eds) *The Cinematic Apparatus* (London: Macmillan, 1980).

Deleuze, Gilles *Cinema 1: the Movement-Image and Cinema 2: the Time-Image* (London: Athlone Press, 1986/1989).

Delmar, Rosalind *Joris Ivens: 50 Years of Film-Making* (London: BFI, 1979).

Deren, Maya *The Legend of Maya Deren* Parts 1 and 2, 1917–1947 (2 vols) (New York: Anthology Film Archives, 1984 and 1988).

Deren, Maya *Letters/Notebooks* in *October*, 14, Fall 1980.

Deren, Maya *Writings* in *Film Culture* 39, Winter 1965.

Dixon, W. Wheeler *The Exploding Eye: a Re-Visionary History of 1960s American Experimental Cinema* (Albany: State University of New York Press, 1997).

Druckrey, Timothy (ed.) *Electronic Culture: Technology and Visual Representation* (New York: Aperture, 1996).

Drummond, Phillip (ed.) *Un chien Andalou* (script with Vigo preface) (London: Faber, 1994).

Dusinberre, Deke and Rees, A. L. *Film as Film* (London: Arts Council/Hayward Gallery, 1979).

Dwoskin, Stephen *Film Is – The International Free Cinema* (London: Peter Owen, 1975).

Ehrenstein, David *Film: The Front Line 1984* (Denver: Arden,1984).

Elsaesser, Thomas (ed.) *Early Cinema – Space Frame Narrative* (London: BFI, 1990).

Fielding, Raymond (ed.) *A Technological History of Motion Pictures and Television* (London: University of California Press, 1983).

Film als Film 1910 bis heute eds Birgit Hein and Wulf Herzogenrath (Cologne: Kölnischer Kunstuerein, 1977).

Film und Foto Documents and exhibition of the 1929 exhibition (in German) ed. Jan-Christopher Horak (Stuttgart: Württembergischer Kunstuerein, 1979).

Flitterman-Lewis, Sandy *To Desire Differently – Feminism and the French Cinema* (Chicago: University of Illinois, 1990).

Foster, Hal *The Return of the Real* (Cambridge, Mass.: MIT Press, 1996).

Foster, Hal (ed.) *Vision and Visuality* (Washington: DIA/Bay Press, 1988).

Foster, Stephen C. (ed.) *Hans Richter: Activism, Modernism and the Avant-Garde* (Cambridge, Mass.: MIT Press, 1998).

Frampton, Hollis *Circles of Confusion: Film, Photography, Video Texts 1968–1980* (Rochester, NY: Visual Studies Workshop Press, 1983).

Frampton, Hollis Special Issue, *October,* **32**, Spring 1985.

Friedberg, Anne *Window Shopping: Cinema and the Postmodern* (Berkeley: University of California Press, 1993).

Frisby, David *Fragments of Modernity: Theories of Modernity in the Work of Simmel, Kracauer and Benjamin* (Oxford: Polity Press and Basil Blackwell, 1985).

Gidal, Peter *Andy Warhol* (Studio Vista, London: 1971; New York Da Capo, 1991).

Gidal, Peter *Materialist Film* (London: Routledge, 1989).

Gidal, Peter (ed.) *Structural Film Anthology* (London: BFI, 1976).

Graham, Dan *Rock My Religion – Writings and Art Projects 1965–1990* ed. B. Wallis (Cambridge, Mass.: MIT Press, 1993).

Hammond, Paul *L'Age d'or* (London: BFI, 1997).

Hammond, Paul (ed.) *The Shadow and its Shadow – Surrealist Writing on the Cinema* (London: BFI, 1978; Edinburgh: Polygon, 1991).

Hayward, Philip (ed.) *Culture, Technology and Creativity* (Luton: Arts Council/ John Libbey, 1991).

Hodgkinson, A. W. and Sheratsky, R. E. (eds) *Humphrey Jennings – More Than a Maker of Films* (Hanover: University of New England Press, 1982).

Hulton, Pontus *Marcel Duchamp* (London: Thames & Hudson, 1993).

Horak, Jean-Christopher *Lovers of Cinema: The First American Avant-Garde 1919–45* (London: University of Wisconsin Press, 1995).

Huyssen, Andreas *After the Great Divide: Modernism, Mass Culture and Postmodernism* (London: Macmillan, 1986).

James, David *Allegories of Cinema: American Cinema in the Sixties* (Princeton, NJ: Princeton University Press, 1989).

James, David *Power Misses* (New York: Verso, 1997).

James, David (ed.) *To Free the Cinema – Jonas Mekas and the New York Underground* (Princeton, NJ: Princeton University Press, 1992).

Jay, Martin *Downcast Eyes: the Denigration of Vision in Twentieth-century French Thought* (Berkeley: University of California Press, 1993).

Jenks, Chris (ed.) *Visual Culture* (London: Routledge, 1995).

Keller, Marjorie *The Untutored Eye – Childhood in the Films of Cocteau, Cornell and Brakhage* (Toronto: Farleigh Dickinson University Press, 1986).

Kern, Stephen *The Culture of Time and Space 1880–1918* (Cambridge, Mass.: Harvard University Press, 1983).

Kirby, Michael (ed.) *Futurist Performance* (New York: Dutton, 1971).

Knight, Julia (ed.) *Diverse Practices – A Critical Reader on British Video Art* (Luton: Arts Council/John Libbey, 1996).

Koch, Stephen *Stargazer: Andy Warhol's World and His Films* (London: Calder and Boyars, 1974).

Krauss, Rosalind *The Optical Unconscious* (Cambridge, Mass.: MIT, 1993).

Krauss, Rosalind *The Originality of the Avant-Garde and other Modernist Myths* (Cambridge, Mass.: MIT Press, 1985).

Krauss, Rosalind and Bois, Yves-Alain *Formless: A User's Guide* (New York: Zone Books, 1997).

Kuenzli, Rudolf (ed.) *Dada and Surrealist Film* (New York: Willis Locker and Owens, 1987).

Lawdor, Standish *The Cubist Cinema* (New York: New York University Press, 1975).

Le Grice, Malcolm *Abstract Film and Beyond* (London: Studio Vista, 1977).

Levin, Michael L. (ed.) *Modernity and the Hegemony of Vision* (Berkeley: University of California Press, 1993).

Leyda, Jay *Kino – A History of the Russian and Soviet Film* (London: George Allen and Unwin, 1973).

Lye, Len *Film Library Quarterly* vol. 14 nos 3/4, 1981: 'The Films of Len Lye', ed. William Sloan.

Lye, Len *Figures of Motion: Selected Writings* eds W. Curnow and R. Horrocks (Auckland: Oxford University Press, 1984).

Lye, Len *A Personal Mythology* (catalogue) (Auckland: Auckland City Art Gallery, 1980).

MacCabe, Colin *Theoretical Essays: Flm, Linguistics, Literature* (Manchester: Manchester University Press, 1985).

MacCabe Colin, Francis, Mark, and Wollen, Peter, (eds) *Who is Andy Warhol?* (London: BFI, 1997).

MacDonald, Scott *Avant-Garde Film: Motion Studies* (New York: Cambridge University Press, 1993).

MacDonald, Scott *A Critical Cinema – Interviews with Independent Filmmakers* (Berkeley: University of California Press, 1988/1992/1997).

MacDonald, Scott *Screen Writings – Scripts and Texts by Independent Filmmakers* (Berkeley: University of California Press, 1995).

Macpherson, Don (ed.) *Traditions of Independence – British Cinema in the Thirties* (London: BFI, 1980).

Manvell, Roger (ed.) *Experiment in the Film* (London: Grey Walls, 1949).

Marcus, Greil *Lipstick Traces: A Secret History of the Twentieth Century* (London: Secker & Warburg, 1989).

Mekas, Jonas *Movie Journal – The Rise of a New American Cinema 1959–1971* (New York: Collier, 1972).

Mellencamp, Patricia *Indiscretions: Avant-Garde Film, Video and Feminism* (Bloomington: Indiana University Press, 1990).

Mellor, David (ed.) *Germany: The new Photography 1927–33* (London: Arts Council of Great Britain, 1978).

Melville, Stephen and Readings, Bill (eds) *Vision and Textuality* (London: Macmillan, 1995).

Melzer, Annabelle *Dada and Surrealist Performance* (Baltimore, MD: Johns Hopkins University Press, 1994); original 1976.

Metzger, Gustav *damaged nature, auto-destructive art* (London, coracle/workfortheeyetodo, 1996).

Michelson, Annette (ed.) *New Forms in Film* (Montreux, 1974).

Morris, Robert *Continuous Project Altered Daily: The Writings of Robert Morris* (Cambridge, Mass.: MIT Press, 1990).

Motherwell, Robert (ed.) *The Dada Painters and Poets – an Anthology* (Cambridge, Mass.: Belknap Press, Harvard University Press, 1989); original, George Wittenborn, NY, 1951).

Mulvey, Laura *Fetishism and Curiosity* (London: BFI, 1996).

Munsterberg, Hugo *The Film – A Psychological Study* (1916) (New York: Dover, 1970).

Neale, Steve *Cinema and Technology: Image, Sound, Colour* (London: BFI, 1985).

Nowell-Smith, Geoffrey (ed.) *The Oxford History of World Cinema* (Oxford: Oxford University Press, 1996).

Nuttall, Jeff *Bomb Culture* (London: MacGibbon and Kee, 1968).

Nyman, Michael *Experimental Music* (London: Studio Vista, 1971).

O'Konor, Louise *Viking Eggeling 1880–1925* (Stockholm: Alkqvist and Wiksell, 1971).

O'Pray, Michael (ed.) *Andy Warhol – Film Factory* (London: BFI, 1989).

O'Pray, Michael (ed.) *The British Avant-Garde Film 1926–1995* (Luton: Arts Council/John Libbey, 1996).

Pedro, Patrice (ed.) *Fugitive Images: from Photography to Video* (Bloomington: Indiana University Press, 1995).

Penz, François and Thomas, Maureen (eds) *Cinema and Architecture: Méliès, Mallet-Stevens Multimedia* (London: BFI, 1997).

Peterson, James *Dreams of Chaos, Visions of Order: Understanding the American Avant-garde* (Detroit: Wayne State University Press, 1994).

148

Peterson, Sidney *The Dark Side of the Screen* (New York: Anthology Film Archives/ New York University Press, 1970).

Poggioli, Renato *The Theory of the Avant-Garde* (Cambridge, Mass.: Harvard University Press, 1968).

Polan, Dana *The Political Language of Film and the Avant-Garde* (Ann Arbor, Mich.: UMI Research Press, 1985).

Rabinowitz, Lauren *Points of Resistance: Women, Power and Politics in the New York Avant-garde Cinema 1943–71* (Chicago: University of Illinois Press, 1991).

Renan, Sheldon *The Underground Film* (London: Studio Vista, 1968).

Richter, Hans *Dada: Art and Anti-Art* (London: Thames & Hudson, 1965).

Richter, Hans *The Struggle for the Film* (London: Scolar, 1986).

Rose, Jacqueline *Sexuality in the Field of Vision* (London: Verso, 1986).

Rosen, Philip (ed.) *Narrative, Apparatus, Ideology: a Film Theory Reader* (New York: Columbia University Press, 1986).

Rosenbaum, Jonathan *Film: The Front Line 1983* (Denver: Arden, 1983).

Rubin, William (ed.) *Picasso and Braque: A Symposium* (New York: MOMA, 1992).

Salt, Barry *Film Style and Technology: History and Analysis* (London: Starword, 1983).

Sargeant, Jack *Naked Lens: Beat Cinema* (London: Creation Books, 1997).

Sayre, Henry *The Object of Performance: The American Avant-Garde since 1970* (Chicago: University of Chicago Press, 1989).

Sitney, P. Adams *The Essential Cinema – Essays on the Films in the Collection of Anthology Film Archives* (New York: New York University Press Anthology, 1975).

Sitney, P. Adams *Film Culture Reader* (London: Secker & Warburg, 1971).

Sitney, P. Adams *Modernist Montage: the Obscurity of Vision in Cinema and Literature* (New York: Columbia University Press, 1990).

Sitney, P. Adams *Visionary Film – the American Avant-Garde* (New York: Oxford University Press, 1974); 2nd edition 1979.

Sitney, P. Adams (ed.) *The Avant-Garde Film: A Reader of Theory and Criticism* (New York: New York University Press Anthology, 1978).

Snow, Michael *Cover to Cover* (Halifax: The Press of the Nova Scotia College of Art and Design, New York University Press, 1975).

Stott, William *Documentary Expression and Thirties America* (Chicago: University of Chicago Press, 1986); original, 1973.

Suleimen, Susan *Subversive Intent: Gender, Politics and the Avant-Garde* (Cambridge, Mass.: Harvard University Press, 1990).

Taylor, Richard (ed.) *Russian Poetics in Translation* vol. 9, *The Poetics of Cinema* (Somerset: RPT Publications, 1982).

Teitelbaum, Matthew (ed.) *Montage and Modern Life 1919–1942* (Cambridge, Mass.: MIT Press, 1992).

Themerson, Stefan *The Urge to Create Visions* (in English; Amsterdam: Gaberbocchus/Die Harmonie, 1983).

Tomkins, Calvin *The Scene: Reports on Post-Modern Art* (New York: Viking, 1976).

Turovskaya, Maya *Tarkovsky: Cinema as Poetry* (London: Faber, 1989).

Tyler, Parker *The Three Faces of the Film* (New York: Thomas Yoseleff, 1960).

Tyler, Parker *Underground Film* (1969) (London: Secker & Warburg, 1971).

Verkauf, Willy (ed.) *Dada: Monograph of a Movement* (London: Academy, 1975).

Virilio, Paul *The Aesthetics of Disappearance* (New York: Semiotext(e), 1991).

Virilio, Paul *The Vision Machine* (London: BFI, 1994).

Wallis, Brian *Art After Modernism* (New York: The New Museum of Contemporary Art, 1984).

Wees, William *Light Moving in Time: Studies in the Visual Aesthetics of Avant-Garde Film* (Berkeley: University of California Press, 1992).

Willemen, Paul *Looks and Frictions: Essays in Cultural Studies and Film Theory* (London: BFI, 1994).

Williams, Linda *Figures of Desire: A Theory and Analysis of Surrealist Film* (Berkeley: University of California, 1981).

Wollen, Peter *Raiding the Icebox: Reflections on Twentieth-Century Culture* (London: Verso, 1993).

Wollen, Peter *Readings and Writings* (London: Verso, 1982).

Wollen, Peter *Signs and Meaning in the Cinema*, expanded edition (London: BFI, 1998).

Wollen, Peter and Francis, Mark *On the Passage of a few People through a rather Brief Moment in Time: the Situationist International 1957–1972* (Cambridge, Mass: MIT Press, 1989).

Youngblood, Gene *Expanded Cinema* (New York: Dutton, 1970).

Index

150